HACKERS

GRAMMAR

해커스 어학연구소

H A C K E R S **T O E F L**

저자

David Cho

언어학박사

前 UCLA교수

1998년 7월 Hackers TOEFL Program을 만듦

2000년 6월 25일 1판 1쇄 발행

2001년 11월 27일 2판 7쇄 발행

2011년 3월 21일 3판 23쇄 발행

지은이 **David Cho** | 언어학 박사 前 UCLA 교수

펴낸곳 (주)해커스 어학연구소

펴낸이 해커스 어학연구소 출판팀

주소 서울시 서초구 서초동 1316-15 해커스 교육그룹

전화 02-566-0001 FAX 02-563-0622

홈페이지 www.goHackers.com

ISBN 978-89-951517-4-7 13740

정가 16,900 원

Serial Number: 03-23-01

이 책은 인생의 목표를 향해 나아가는 과정 중에 시험이라는 산을 효과적으로 넘을 수 있도록 인도하기 위한 책입니다. 더불어 이 책으로 시험을 준비하면서 익힌 지식이 영어에 필요한 지식이 되고자 했습니다.

토플이라는 시험을 준비하면서 종합문법서로 토플과는 관계없는 방대한 양의 영어 공부에 시간을 허비하는 안타까움과 시험에 출제되는 문제의 형식과 내용 중 그 일부분에만 국한된 지침서로 공부하는 것을 보는 안타까움, 그리고 토플 문법을 공부하는 방법에 대한 지침을 받지 못하는 이들에 대해 안타까움을 느끼던 중, 직장인과 지방에 계시는 분들의 요청으로 이 책의 발간을 서두르게 되었습니다. 책은 기존의 Hackers TOEFL에 사용하였던 유형별 정리를 뼈대로 하고 문법설명과 실제 문제에 가장 유사한 새롭게 만든 문제로 살을 입혔습니다. 그리고 기존의 교재들이 실전 문제집을 따로 출간하고 있는 것에 반하여 CD용 Actual Test를 5회분 실었습니다. 즉, 모든 문법공부를 마치고 실제 시험과 가장 유사한 문제로 스스로의 실력을 평가할 수 있도록 만든 것입니다.

Hackers TOEFL의 근간은 '원리와 공식을 통한 문제로의 접근'이라는 것입니다. 이러한 접근이 시간과 실수를 단축할 수 있는 길이고, 배출된 많은 Hackers들이 이 길을 함께 가면서 Hackers TOEFL을 증명해 왔습니다. 이렇게 함께해온 Hackers들이 오늘까지 Hackers TOEFL의 존재 이유입니다.

Hackers TOEFL이 Hackers들과 함께 가는 길이었듯 이 책 또한 저 혼자만의 작업은 아니었습니다. 크게는 Hackers가족이라 불리는 모든 이들과 함께 이루어온 것이며, 작게는 몇몇의 Hackers가족들과 함께 작업을 하였습니다. 저는 이들을 가족이라고 부릅니다. 서로의 가슴속에 지워지지 않는 기억과 추억을 간직하고 있기 때문입니다.

책이 나오기 1년 전부터 책표지를 만들어 주고 싶다고 하다가 결국에는 너무나도 예쁜 표지로 책을 감싸준 남희(5기), 책의 편집 혹은 교정을 도와준 'pigeon' 유신(11기), '차한' 동우(4.5기), '교수' 창호(4.5기), 혜진(10기), 은혜(2기), 민정(11.5기), 창현(5기), 성락(4기), 문선(11.5기), 은정(11.5기), 세신(11.5기), 승신(11.5기), 춘옥(12.5기), 영석(11기), 토플정보 편집을 도와 준 한경(10기), CD작업을 도와준 태수(13기), 그리고 이 책 출판을 위해 안팎으로 동분서주한 '해커스의 신사' 명원(4기)과 출판에 관한 폭넓은 도움을 주신 혜정님의 도움이 컸습니다. 또한, 책의 첫 글자를 시작할 때부터 책이 나오는 마지막까지 나를 괴롭혀 이 책이 나올 수 있게 산파역할을 했던 태영이(4.5기)의 도움은 지극히 컸습니다.

해커스 가족들의 아름다운 결집의 산물인 이 책이 진정으로 토플과 영어를 공부하는 이들에게 작은 빛과 길잡이가 되기를 기원합니다.

북한산 아래 | 해커스 어학연구소에서 | David 조 드림

HACKERS TOEFL

Contents

2부
Written Expressions

책의 특성 및 학습방법

| 특성 |

1 이 책은 토플공부를 시작하는 사람이나 토플 공부를 마지막으로 정리하려는 사람 모두를 위하여 작성된 책이다. 특히 토플 Section 2 (structure)에 대한 모든 패턴을 정리 하였으며 CBT 토플 실제 문제와 가장 유사한 CD용 Actual Test를 통하여 자신의 실력과 위치를 가늠하게 만든 토플 문법의 결정판이다. 굳이 부연한다면 시중에 나오는 문법 준비교재와 실전 문제집을 한 권에 통합하였다고 볼 수 있다.

2 이 책의 모든 문제는 ETS의 문제 패턴을 심도 있게 분석하여 자체 개발한 독창적인 문제로서 Hackers 토플의 공식과 원리를 통해 ETS와 기타 모든 문법시험의 패턴을 공략하기에 가장 적절한 문법들과 문제들을 수록한 것이다.

3 이 책은 크게 Structure와 Written으로 구성하였으며 각 패턴을 숙지하고 연습문제를 통해 내용을 확인한 후 실전문제를 통하여 실전문제 속에서 그 패턴을 확인하도록 하였다. 더하여 Mini Test를 통하여 학습한 내용을 재복습하도록 이중장치를 마련하였다.

| 학습방법 |

1 이 책을 학습하는 방법으로 크게 두 가지 방법을 권하고 싶다. 우선 토플을 처음 공부하는 이라면 진단고사를 본 후 자신이 틀린 부분부터 공부하는 방법이다. 자신이 약한 부분을 숙지한 후 책의 순서에 맞게 공부하는 것이다. 두번째, 이미 토플에 대한 상당한 준비를 한 후 마지막 정리를 위해 이 책을 공부하려는 이라면 바로 Actual Test 3회분을 풀고 자신이 약한 부분부터 공부해 나가면 된다. 책에 대한 모든 부분을 마친 후 나머지 2회분으로 자신의 최종 실력을 파악하면 된다.

2 이 책의 각 단원은 실제 기출 문제를 분석하여 만든 것으로서 단 하나도 그냥 지나치면 안될뿐더러 철저한 연습이 필요하다. 각 단원의 해설과 공식을 숙지한 후 철저한 연습을 통하여 실력을 다지고 실전문제를 통하여 실력을 자기 것으로 하여야 한다. 특히 이해가 안되는 것은 해답과 Hackers 문법의 반복 학습을 통해 철저히 소화하고 오답노트를 병행하여 모르는 문제와 문법에 대한 고리를 반드시 끊어야만 한다.

3 문장의 완벽한 공략을 위해서는 정확성을 기르는 훈련을 하여야 한다. 이는 구조의 유형을 분석하여 공식화한 해커스 문법에 의거하여 해결할 수 있다. 그러므로 진단고사, 실전문제와 CD Actual Test를 풀 때에는 이 책에서 소개된 구조와 공식에 입각한 문제 풀이 방식을 정확히 적용하며 기계적으로 답을 찾아내는 훈련을 하여야 한다.

4 문제를 풀고 난 다음 곧 정답을 확인하고, 틀린 문제는 그 문제에 대한 해답과 해설을 통해 이해하고 오답노트에 정리한다. 모르는 문제는 주위 동료나 www.goHackers.com을 이용하여서라도 반드시 자신의 것으로 만들도록 한다.

TOEFL이란?

TOEFL(Test of English as a Foreign Language)은 미국, 캐나다를 비롯한 영국, 호주, 뉴질랜드 등 영어권 국가에 유학을 가고자 하는 학생들을 대상으로 180여개국에서 ETS (Education Testing Service)의 주관 하에 실시되는 국제적인 영어 시험이다. 미국 대학의 대부분은 입학허가 조건의 하나로 토플의 일정수준 이상 공식 점수를 요구하고 있는데 만점은 300점이다. 요구 점수는 각 대학과 학과에 따라 다르나 일반적으로 학부는 213점, 대학원은 230점 이상이며 요구 점수는 지원하려는 학교의 해당학과에 확인하는 것이 필요하다.

Computer-Based TOEFL Test 란?

2000년 10월 시험부터는 한국에서도 기존의 Paper-Based TOEFL Test(PBT)가 사라지고 Computer-Based TOEFL Test(CBT)를 시행하고 있다. Computer-Based TOEFL Test는 이미 1998년 7월부터 세계각지에서 시행되고 있는 중이며, 2001년에 모든 TOEFL 시험이 CBT방식으로 대체되었다. CBT에서는 기존의 Paper-Based Test에서 볼 수 있었던 문제 형태와 함께 Computer상에서 구현될 수 있는 새로운 형식의 문제유형으로 구성되어 있다.

CBT TOEFL의 전체 구성

구성	항목	내용
· Tutorials 컴퓨터 사용에 관한 교육	실시 시간	• 약 40분동안 CBT에서는 시험 시작하기 전 시험에 필요한 기초적인 컴퓨터 사용에 관한 교육을 실시한다.
· Section 1 Listening Comprehension (청취 능력 측정)	응시 시간	• 40~60 분 (문제 청취 시간 제외) 응시 시간이 일정하지 않은 것은 문제의 정 · 오답 여부에 따라 변별적으로 다음 문항이 변경되고, 경우에 따라 문항 수 자체도 가변적으로 주어질 수 있기 때문이다.
	Part A	• Short Conversations 11~17 문항
	Part B	• Longer Conversations/Discussions/Lectures 19~32문항
· Section 2 Structure (문장 완성 및 오류 확인)	응시 시간	• 15~20 분
	문항 수	• 20~25 문항
· Section 3 Reading Comprehension (독해 능력 측정)	응시 시간	• 70~90 분
	문항 수	• 44~55 문항
· Section 4 Writing (주제에 따라 Essay 작성)	응시 시간	• 30 분
	문항 수	• 1 문항
	총 응시 시간	• 125~170 분
	총 문항 수	• 87~138 문항

Computer-Based TOEFL Test의 특징

• Computer-Adaptive Testing

TOEFL Computer-Based Test에서는 Listening과 Structure섹션이 adaptive형식을 취하고 있다. Paper-Based Test에서와 같이 응시자가 한꺼번에 일방적으로 제시된 문제들을 푸는 것이 아니라 본인의 수준에 따라 각각 난이도가 다르게 설정된 문제를 한 문제씩 풀게 된다. 예컨대, computer-adaptive섹션에서의 첫번째 문제는 중간 난이도의 문제로 출제되며, 이 문제에 대하여 응시자가 정답을 선택한다면 그 다음 문제는 좀더 높은 난이도의 문제가 출제되고, 반대로 첫 문제의 정답을 틀리게 선택하면 다음 문제는 난이도가 조금 더 낮은 문제 모음 중에서 하나가 선정되어 제시된다. 처음 몇 문제가 이런 식으로 출제되는 동안에 응시자의 수준에 맞는 전반적인 난이도가 정해지게 되며 나머지 문제들도 대체로 이 수준에서 크게 벗어나지 않는 범위 안에서 제시되게 된다.

• Writing이 필수로 채택

CBT에서는 writing 테스트가 필수로 채택되었다. 주어진 하나의 주제를 두고 적절한 근거가 뒷받침된 주장이 담긴 에세이를 30분내에 써야한다. 기존 TWE는 본인의 선택에 따라 시험여부를 결정했지만 CBT의 Writing은 Structure와 Writing을 합친 점수의 50%, 전체 총점의 약 1/6을 차지하게 되었다.

• Listening Test 시 문제사이의 시간 배분을 조정할 수 있다.

Listening Section의 전체시간은 정해져 있으나 문제와 문제 사이의 시간은 수험자가 조절할 수 있다.

• 이전 문제로 되돌아갈 수 없다.

한 문제씩 화면에 나타나므로 Confirm을 누르고 Next 버튼을 눌러 다음 문제로 넘어가 버리면 이전 문제의 답을 수정할 수 없게 된다. *단, RC문제는 뒤로 돌아갈 수 있다.

• 헤드폰의 사용

개인별로 헤드폰을 사용하게 되므로 Listening 시간에 주변 소음의 방해를 덜 받을 수 있고 음량조절도 가능하다.

• 시험 응시일의 선택이 용이하다.

모든 수험자는 날짜에 관계없이 1달에 1번씩 응시할 수 있다. 예를 들면 11월 30일 에 응시한 후 다음날인 12월 1일에 재응시가 가능하다는 것이다. 또한 본인의 희망에 따라 편리한 시간을 선택할 수 있게 되었다.

• 성적 즉시 확인가능 및 성적 발송일의 단축

기존에는 시험 후 약 5주 후에 전화나 우편으로 성적을 확인할 수 있었지만, CBT에서는 시험 후 즉시 Computer 화면을 통해 Writing을 제외한 성적확인이 가능하다. 이 때, Writing에서 최고점과 최저점을 가정한 후 점수변동을 고려하여 응시자 점수의 범위를 제시해준다. 공식 성적표는 약 2주 후 받아볼 수 있다.

CBT TOEFL 신청안내

· **등록안내**	안내 전화	• (02) 3211-1233, 3275-4027
	등록 fax	• (02) 3275-4029
	등록 시간	• 오전 9시-오후5시(월-금요일)
	시험 장소	• 서울(고합빌딩, 한미교육위원단)과 대구
	등록비	• US $130
· **시험 취소 및 변경**	가능기한	• 등록된 시험일 3일 전(Business day) 오전 12시까지
	시험 일자 변경비	• US $40
	시험 취소	• US $65 환불 : Bulletin에 있는 양식을 이용하여, 취소 후 60일 이내에 미국 ETS에 Refund를 요청하면 가능
· **유의 사항**	시험당일 신분 확인	• 본인의 서명이 들어있는 여권, 주민등록증, 운전면허증
	시험시간	• 4시간
	시험접수 준비	• 반드시 해당 시험의 Bulletin을 읽어 보기 : Fax나 우편등록시 International Test Scheduling Form을 다운 받는다.
	시험 시간 30분 전에 시험장에 도착한다.	
· **Fees for Testing**	$130	• Computer-Based TOEFL Test
	$40	• Rescheduling Fee
	$15	• one Additional Score Report Request
	$50	• Essay rescore
	$10	• Reinstatement of canceled scores
	$25	• Fee for Returned Check and declined credit cards

CBT와 PBT의 비교표

	Computer-Based Test	Paper-Based Test
Test구분	총 4 Section LC(CAT방식) SW(CAT방식) RC Writing(필수)	총 3 Section LC SW RC TWE(선택)
문항수 및 시간 배분	LC 30 ~ 49 (40 ~ 60분) SW 20 ~ 25 (15 ~ 25분) RC 44 ~ 55 (70 ~ 90분) Writing (30분)	LC 50 (35분) SW 40 (25분) RC 50 (55분)
소요 시간	약 4시간 ~ 4시간 반	약 3시간
취득가능 점수	LC 0 ~ 30 SW 0 ~ 30 (단, Writing포함) RC 0 ~ 30 TOTAL 0 ~ 300	LC 31 ~ 68 SW 31 ~ 68 RC 31 ~ 67 TOTAL 310 ~ 677
응시료 (환율에 따라 가변적)	130$	90$
응시 취소	가능	불가
시험 일정	매달 1회 시험, 월중 테스트 센터 가용일 중 예약 가능	매달 1회 시험으로 연 12회 실시
성적확인	시험 후 즉시 성적확인 가능 (단, Writing 제외) 약 2주 후 성적표 발송	약 5주 후 성적표 발송
난이도 조정	수험자의 정 · 오답 비율에 따라 즉시 문제의 난이도를 조정	난이도 조정 불가
유효기간	2년	2년

CBT와 PBT의 문제유형 구분

	Computer-Based TOEFL	Paper-Based TOEFL
Section 1	**Listening Comprehension** Part A : 두 사람의 짧은 대화 (11-17문항) Part B : 긴 대화 및 강의/토론 4~6개의 지문(지문 당 3~6 문항)	**Listening Comprehension** Part A : 두 사람의 짧은 대화(30문항) Part B : 긴 대화(7~8문항) Part C : 한 사람의 긴 이야기(12~13 문항)
Section 2	**Structure** 문장 완성하기 또는 틀린 부분 찾기 (20-25문항)	**Structure and Written Expression** Structure : 문장 완성하기(15문항) Written Expression : 틀린 부분 찾기 (25문항)
Section 3	**Reading** 장문을 읽고 답하기 4~5개의 지문으로 구성 (지문 당 11문항)	**Reading Comprehension** 장문을 읽고 답하기 5~6개의 지문으로 구성 (지문 당 9~10개의 문항)
Section 4	**Writing** 한 개의 주제를 30분동안 writing 해야 하며 필수. 답안지는 종이와 컴퓨터 중 선택 가능	(TWE는 선택)

CBT와 PBT의 점수비교

Score-to-Score							
CBT	**PBT**	**CBT**	**PBT**	**CBT**	**PBT**	**CBT**	**PBT**
300	677	230	573	163	490	100	407
297	673	230	570	163	487	97	403
293	670	227	567	160	483	97	400
290	667	223	563	157	480	93	397
287	663	220	560	153	477	90	393
287	660	220	557	150	473	90	390
283	657	217	553	150	470	87	387
280	653	**213**	**550**	147	467	83	383
280	**650**	210	547	143	463	83	380
277	647	207	543	140	460	80	377
273	643	207	540	137	457	77	373
273	640	203	537	133	453	77	370
270	637	200	533	**133**	**450**	73	367
267	633	197	530	130	447	73	363
267	630	197	527	127	443	70	360
263	627	193	523	123	440	70	357
263	623	190	520	123	437	67	353
260	620	187	517	120	433	63	350
260	617	183	513	117	430	63	347
257	613	180	510	113	427	60	343
253	610	180	507	113	423	60	340
253	607	177	503	110	420	57	337
250	603	**173**	**500**	107	417	57	333
250	**600**	170	497	103	413	53	330
247	597	167	493	103	410	50	327
243	593					50	323
243	590					47	320
240	587					47	317
237	583					43	313
237	580					40	310
233	577						

CBT와 PBT의 섹션별 점수비교

Listening Comprehension Range - to - Range		Structure Range - to - Range		Reading Comprehension Range - to - Range	
Computer	Paper	Computer	Paper	Computer	Paper
27~30	64~68	27~30	64~68	28~30	64~67
24~27	59~63	25~27	59~63	25~27	59~63
20~23	54~58	21~24	54~58	21~24	54~58
15~19	49~53	17~20	49~53	16~20	49~53
10~14	44~48	14~17	44~48	13~16	44~48
6~9	39~49	10~13	39~49	9~12	39~43
4~6	34~38	7~9	34~38	7~9	34~38
2~3	31~33	6~7	31~33	5~6	31~33

CBT 성적평가 및 확인

• 성적 평가

Listening과 Structure 점수는 CAT의 적용으로 정답률과 문제의 난이도, 문제를 푼 숫자에 따라 나온다. 따라서 어려운 문제를 많이 맞출수록 높은 점수를 받을 수 있다. 또한 Structure부분은 Writing과 합산한 점수로 나온다. Writing에서 본 Essay는 일정한 자격을 갖춘 두 명의 시험관이 채점하게 되는데 점수는 6.0, 5.5, 5.0, 4.5, 4.0, 3.5, 3.0, 2.5, 2.0, 1점으로 되어있다.

• 점수 환산법 : (전체점수의 합산)*10/3

시험이 끝난 직후 Writing을 제외한 나머지 Section의 점수를 확인할 수 있다. Writing은 별도 채점관에 의해 점수가 산출되므로 즉시 확인이 불가능하며 다음과 같이 Writing점수를 합산한 예상 범위가 제시된다.

 LC 22점, SW 3 - 23점, RC22점을 맞은 학생이 예상 점수는

(22 + 3 + 22)*10/3 = 157점에서 (22 + 23 + 22)*10/3 = 223점 사이이다.

- *Listening Comprehension 22*
- *Structure / Writing 3 - 23*
- *Reading Comprehension 22*

Total 157 - 223

이 응시자의 총점은 157점과 223점 사이에서 결정되며 총점은 Writing점수의 영향을 받게 된다.

• Canceling Scores

점수를 취소하고자 한다면 컴퓨터로 점수를 보기 전에 해야만 한다. 일단 점수를 본 이후에는 취소가 불가능하다. 당연히 점수를 취소한 경우에는 자신의 점수를 볼 수 없다.

• Score Report

만약 Essay를 Handwriting으로 작성했다면 약 5주 후에 점수가 발송된다. 만약 컴퓨터로 Essay 작성을 한 경우에는 시험일로부터 2주 후면 성적이 발송될 수 있다.

CBT에서 Computer 사용방법은?

● CBT 화면 미리 보기

• Direction 화면

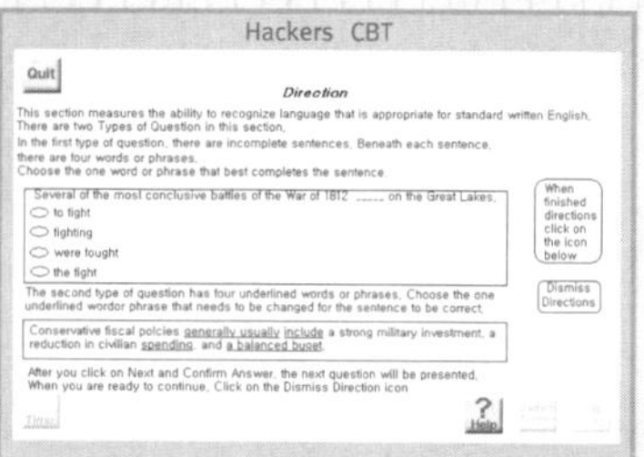

Directions

각 파트의 문제 시작 전에 출제 형식이나 정답 요령 등을 설명해 준다. 만일 바로 문제 풀이로 들어가고 싶은 경우에는 Dismiss Directions을 클릭한다.

• 문제 Tool

문제에 답을 표시한 후 새로운 문제로 넘어가기 위해서 Next를 클릭한다.

Next후 답을 Confirm함으로써 새로운 문제로 넘어갈 수 있다. CBT에서는 일단 풀고 Confirm한 문제는 다시 되돌아갈 수 없다.

바로 이전 문제나 화면으로 돌아가는 기능을 갖고 있다. 다만 Reading Section에서만 가능하다.

사용방법 등을 보여준다.

Time을 클릭하면 남은 시험시간 표시가 나타나며, 시험종료 5분전부터는 자동적으로 나타난다.

Writing Section에서 삭제하기 원하는 텍스트를 잘라낼 때 사용한다.

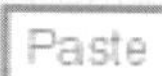

Writing Section에서 텍스트를 삽입하기 원할 때 사용한다. 붙여넣기를 원하는 텍스트를 잘라낸 후, 원하는 지점을 클릭한 뒤 Paste를 클릭한다.

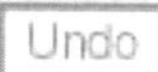

바로 이전 행동을 취소하기 위해서 사용한다. 예컨대, 바로 이전에 텍스트를 잘라냈거나 붙여넣기 했다면 각각의 자료가 그 이전으로 복원된다.

Structure Section

• 출제형식

• 소요시간 : 15~20분

• 문제수 : 20~25문제

  • **Structure 문제** : 빈 공간에 선택지 중 맞는 부분을 찾아 완전한 문장을 만드는 문제

  • **Written 문제** : 밑줄 친 보기 중 틀린 부분을 찾아내는 문제

• 사용방법

• 불완전한 문장 채우기는 다른 문제와 마찬가지로 보기의 원 안을 클릭하면 된다.

• 틀린 부분 고치기의 경우는 자신이 정답이라 생각되는 부분의 단어만큼을 마우스로 검게 선택한다.

• LC와 마찬가지로 각 문항마다 답을 선택하고 Confirm을 click해야만 다음 문제로의 진행이 가능하다.

• CBT 화면 보기

1

Structure 문제

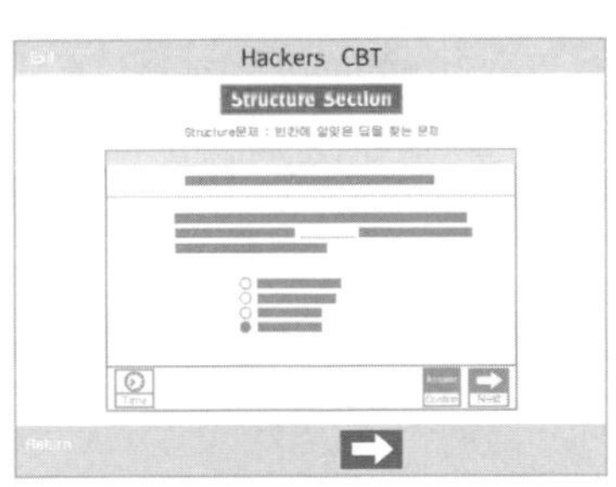

2

Written 문제

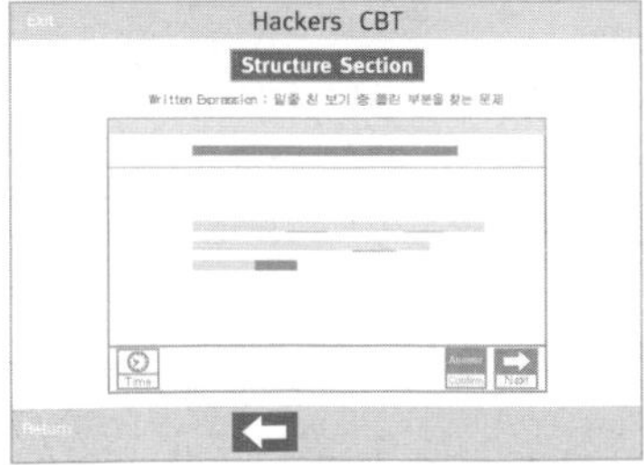

- **출제형식**

• 소요시간 : 30분

• 문제수 : 1문제

• 주어진 topic에 대해 자신의 주장을 구체적으로 뒷받침할만한 근거를 들어 논지를 정당화하는 에세이를 작성

- **사용방법**

• 주제가 명시되기 전 에세이를 컴퓨터로 타이핑할 것인지 종이에 쓸 것인지 결정해야 한다.

• 컴퓨터의 경우 화면의 Essay Box에, 종이를 사용하는 응시자는 일괄 지급된 Essay용 Answer Sheet만이 허용된다.

• Cut은 삭제하기 원하는 텍스트를 잘라낼 때, Paste는 텍스트를 삽입하기 원할 때, Undo는 바로 이전 행동을 취소하기 위해서 사용한다.

• 시간이 지나면 화면은 자동으로 닫힌다.

• Essay를 마친 다음 [Next → Answer Confirm]을 하면 다음 화면으로 이동한다.

• CBT 화면 보기

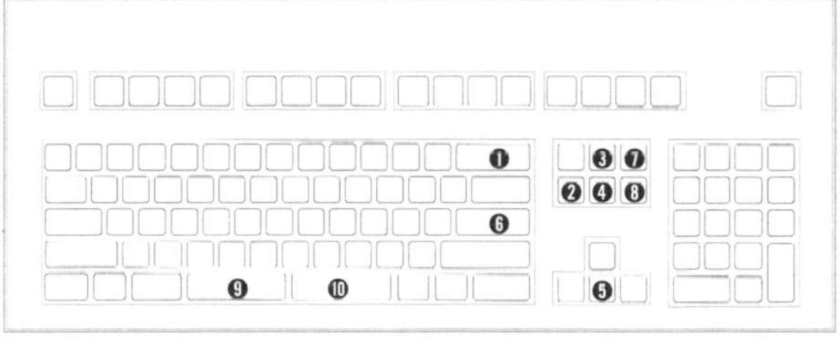

• Topic에 따라 essay를 작성한다.

① Backspace : 뒤쪽으로 글자를 삭제해 간다.

② Delete : 우측에 선택되어 있는 글자를 삭제한다

③ Home : 문장의 맨 처음으로 간다.

④ End : 문장의 맨 끝으로 이동한다.

⑤ Arrows : 화살표로 문장의 상하, 좌우로 이동한다.

⑥ Enter : 한 문장을 완성하고 다음 줄에서 새로운 문장을 작성할 때 사용한다

⑦ Page up : 해당 페이지의 위로 이동한다

⑧ Page down : 해당 페이지의 아래로 이동할 때 사용한다.

⑨ Space bar : 커서가 좌측으로 이동한다.

⑩ Space bar : 커서가 오른쪽으로 이동한다.

Writing Scoring Guide

6점 이 점수 수준의 에세이는

- 주어진 작문 주제를 효과적으로 서술하고 있으며
- 글의 구성이 짜임새 있고 그 전개가 잘 되어 있을 뿐만아니라
- 주장이나 설명하고자 하는 바를 뒷받침하는 적절한 사례나 근거를 명확히 사용하고 있고
- 언어의 사용에 있어서 그 유려함이 일관성 있게 나타나며
- 다양한 구문과 적절한 어휘 선택을 보여주는 글이다.

5점 이 점수 수준의 에세이는

- 작문 주제에 대한 내용 중 일부가 다른 부분에 비해 잘 설명되어 있을 경우이며
- 대체로 글의 전개가 짜임새있게 되어있고
- 주장이나 설명하고자 하는 바를 뒷받침해주는 사례나 근거를 제시하고 있으며
- 언어 사용에 있어 그 유려함이 나타나며
- 어느 정도의 구문표현과 어휘수준을 보여주고 있다.

4점 이 점수 수준의 에세이는

- 작문 주제를 적절히 다루고 있지만 주제와 관련된 핵심 사항을 설명하지 못하는 경우가 있으며
- 글의 짜임새와 전개가 적절하고
- 주장이나 설명하고자 하는 바를 뒷받침하는 사례나 근거를 일부 사용하고 있으며
- 구문과 어법의 정확한 사용이 간혹 결여되어 있으며
- 때때로 발견되는 실수들이 글의 의미를 불분명하게 할 때도 있다.

3점

이 점수 수준의 에세이는
아래에 있는 항목들 중 하나 혹은 그 이상의 결함을 보여준다.

- 부적절한 글의 구성과 전개
- 주장과 일반화를 뒷받침해주거나 설명해주는 사례와 근거가 타당치 못하거나 불충분한 경우
- 상당히 부적절한 어휘와 어휘형태의 선택
- 문장구조나 그 용법에서 발견되는 많은 실수들

2점

이 점수 수준의 에세이는 아래에 나와 있는 하나 또는 그 이상의 항목들로 인해
심각한 결함이 보여지는 작문이다.

- 글의 구성과 전개가 제대로 되어 있지 않은 글
- 사례나 근거가 빈약하거나 없고, 또는 내용과 관계없는 사항들을 제시하는 경우
- 문장 구조와 어법에서의 심각하고 빈번한 실수들
- 주제의 초점을 벗어난 심각한 문제일 경우

1점

이 수준의 에세이는,

- 일관성이 없고 앞뒤가 맞지 않으며
- 글의 전개가 되어 있지 않고
- 심각한 작문상의 실수들을 포함하고 있는 경우가 많다.

0점

작문 점수가 0점이 나올 수 있는 경우는

- 작문을 하지 않았을 경우
- 작문의 주제만 그대로 적어 놓았을 경우
- 주제와 완전히 벗어난 글이거나 영어가 아닌 외국어로 작성된 경우,
또는 단어 몇 자만 적어 놓았을 경우이다.

|진|단|고|사|

1 The hookworm lives in (A) the intestines of humans (B) and other animals, stealing (C) necessary food and nutrients from it (D) host.

2 Plants have traditionally provided (A) the basis for nearly (B) all drugs, and wood has served (C) the most common (D) building material.

3 The physical ________ have to do with providing energy for muscle actions.

Ⓐ causes of fatigue
Ⓑ as causes
Ⓒ the causes of fatigue
Ⓓ because the causes

4 Other landscape artists (A) followed the lead of the Hudson River school in depict (B) the spectacular (C) West and its (D) plains, prairies, wildlife, settlers, and Native Americans.

5 Shield volcanoes are not ________ composite volcanoes, but they include some of the largest volcanoes in the world.

Ⓐ tall as
Ⓑ so tall nearly as
Ⓒ as taller as
Ⓓ nearly as tall as

6 Plants have been (A) important aesthetically (B), used to beautify (C) the environment in who (D) we live and work.

7 Volcanic gas <u>usually carries</u> a great deal of <u>volcanic ashes</u> which
A B

makes <u>it</u> look <u>like</u> black smoke.
C D

8 All birds have feathers, which is, rather than the ability to fly, what _______ from other animals.

Ⓐ to make them different
Ⓑ makes them different
Ⓒ it makes different
Ⓓ as it makes them different

9 A planet's year, or sidereal period, <u>is</u> the time <u>requiring</u> for it to
A B

complete <u>one full</u> circuit <u>around</u> the sun.
C D

10 _________ his ambition to be an artist, Carver earned his master's degree in horticulture in 1896.

Ⓐ In spite
Ⓑ Although
Ⓒ Because
Ⓓ Despite

11 Life-style is considered more of a health determinant <u>than</u> it was <u>in</u>
A B

1900, <u>when</u> the leading cause of death was infectious disease, <u>alike</u>
C D

pneumonia and influenza.

12 _______ established in the colonial period was the system of public education first founded in New England.

Ⓐ Most significant institution
Ⓑ That most significant institution
Ⓒ For the most significant institution to be
Ⓓ The most significant institution

13 Although he never <u>held</u> elective office, Frederick Douglass was indisputably one of the most famousest public figures and orators of the 19th century.

A: held; B: indisputably; C: most famousest; D: the

14 Material that gathers outside the conduits large the size of the volcano, sometimes to heights measuring several thousands of feet.

A: gathers; B: large; C: measuring; D: of feet

15 American physicians, _______ have observed Chinese surgery, have verified that acupuncture is effective for some patients.

Ⓐ who
Ⓑ which
Ⓒ are when
Ⓓ whose

16 During photosynthesis, light absorbed by a green-colored substance called chlorophyll.

A: During; B: light; C: absorbed; D: green-colored

17 _______, Frank Norris was even more naturalistic than Crane, which is to say more "realistic."

Ⓐ A novelist, who was
Ⓑ Was a novelist
Ⓒ A novelist be
Ⓓ A novelist

18 The immediately occasion for Lincoln' s speech was the dedication of a national cemetery near Gettysburg, Pennsylvania.

A: immediately; B: was; C: a; D: near

19 Sinus infections do demand treatment not only because they are painful _______ they can spread.

Ⓐ and with because
Ⓑ as with
Ⓒ but because
Ⓓ because of

20 Symbiosis is the biological (A) term using (B) to describe two species (C) which live together in a close, interdependent relationship (D).

21 Cow skulls and other bare bone (A) found (B) in the desert were (C) frequent motifs in (D) O' Keefe's paintings.

22 The topic of early human evolution at first seems difficult because of the many names ______ early humans and their predecessors.

Ⓐ to give
Ⓑ be given to
Ⓒ giving
Ⓓ given to

23 Almost 30% of surgical patients receive (A) adequate analgesia from acupuncture, which (B) is now done by sending an electrical current through (C) the needles rather than with twirling (D) them.

24 The huge forces of a (A) hurricane can led (B) to immense (C) amounts of erosion along hundreds (D) of miles of coastline.

25 Along the eastern seaboard, extending north and west to the Great Lakes, ______.

Ⓐ when the Algonquian-speaking people were
Ⓑ were the Algonquian-speaking people
Ⓒ the Algonquian-speaking people
Ⓓ that the Algonquian-speaking people

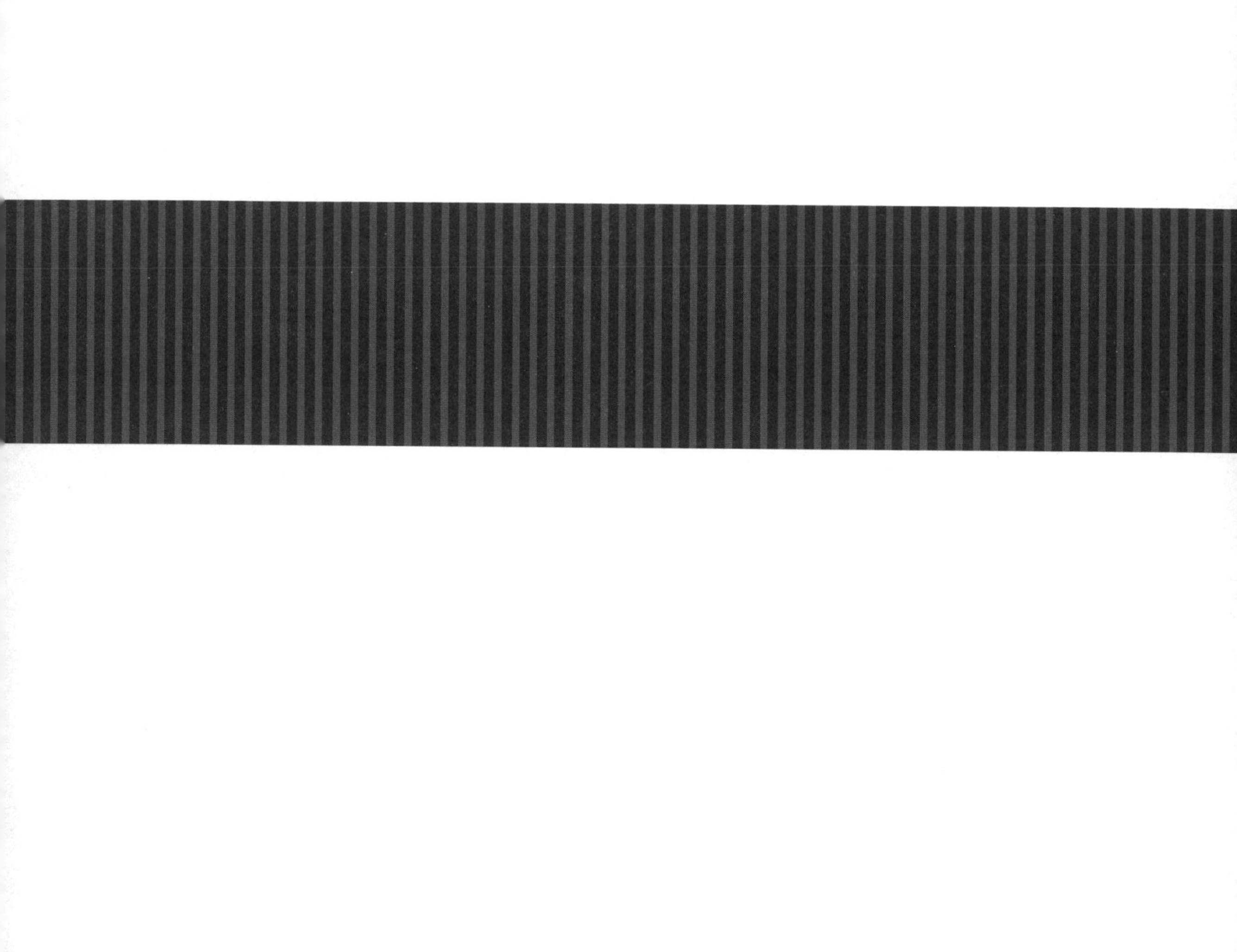

1부

HACKERS TOEFL

Structure

chapter 1.

Rule & Pattern

chapter 2.

Clause & Phrase

chapter 3.

Construction

1

chapter

HACKERS TOEFL

Structure

Rule & Pattern

TOEFL에서 실제로 출제되는 문장들을 기본으로 하여, 문장내의 구조, 문장간의 구조를 문장의 기본규칙과 공식들로 파악하는 것이 chapter의 목적이다.

1 S+V Rule

Outline

문장은 주어와 동사를 기본으로 동사에 이끌리는 술어로 구성되어 있으며,
모든 문장은 적어도 하나의 주어와 하나의 동사가 있어야 완전한 문장이 된다.

'주어 · 동사 찾기' 문제를 공략하기 위해서는 다음과 같은 훈련이 필요하다.

- **주어가 될 수 있는 요소를 외우기!**
- **문장의 실제 동사를 찾아내기!**
- **문장의 거품인 수식어구를 제거하고 문장의 골격(주어 동사) 남기기!**

Hackers Rule

Sentence(문장) = **S**(Subject:주어) + **V**(Verb:동사)

Hackers Grammar

Structure 문제에서 빈 자리에 주어 혹은 동사를 채워넣는 다음의 공식을 사용하는 문제가 출제된다.

S+V Rule 1	● + 동사	● : 명사구, 동명사구, **to** 부정사구, 명사절
S+V Rule 2	주어 + ●	● : 동사
S+V Rule 3	(수식어구) + ● + (수식어구)	● : 주어 + 동사

❶.1 주어 찾기

Structure 문제 중 주어 자리에 빈 칸이 있을 때, 들어갈 수 있는 것은 명사구, 동명사구, to 부정사구, 명사절 중에서 하나가 된다.

주어	예문
1. 명사구 / 대명사	*The sky* is blue. *The airport of San Francisco* is very clean. *He* is my friend.
2. 동명사구	*Running in the early morning* is very difficult for me.
3. to 부정사구	*To specialize* is to focus efforts on a certain task.
4. 명사절	*That the invention of the railroad helps development of industry* is very clear.

With the advance of genetics and the development of techniques for identifying the elements of an individual's chromosomes, _______ of human origins has generated unusually high levels of scientific interest.

Ⓐ as enigma
Ⓑ because the enigma
Ⓒ the enigma
Ⓓ for the enigma

Tip
· 문장의 기본 골격과 관계없는 전치사구 거품 'With~chromosomes' 를 걷어내면 하나의 문장이 남는다. 동사가 'has generated' 이므로 보기에서 주어가 될 수 있는 것을 고르면 답은 Ⓒ이다.

Structure

www.goHackers.com

❶.2 동사 찾기

'주어의 동작이나 상태를 기술하는 문장의 실제 동사'를 정동사라고 하며 이러한 정동사는 다음의 특성을 갖는다.

- 주어와 '수일치'가 이뤄질 것!
- 문장 내용이나 시간부사와 '시제일치'가 이루어 질 것!
- 타동사는 목적어를 가질 것!

ex The state ***produces*** a third of the nation's corn.

Half of the children ***went*** to public schools.

Hackers Skill **준동사가 아닌 정동사를 찾는다.**

1. 준동사인 동명사를 제외한다.

Tom ***avoided*** ~~*mentioning*~~ the incident to his mother.
정동사 준동사(동명사)

2. 준동사인 분사를 제외한다.

Tom ***gestured*** toward the three cards ~~*lying*~~ on the table.
정동사 준동사(분사)

The students ~~*questioned*~~ ***gave*** very different opinions.
준동사(분사) 정동사

3. 준동사인 부정사를 제외한다.

John ***locked*** the door ~~*to stop*~~ us from getting in.
정동사 준동사(부정사)

FOOTNOTE

· 준동사 : 동명사(V+-ing), 현재분사(V+-ing), 과거분사(V+-ed), 부정사(to+V)를 통틀어 준동사라고 한다. 이들은 동사에서 나왔지만 다른 품사 −명사, 형용사, 부사 −로 기능하기 때문에 문장에서 실제 동사로 기능하지 못한다.

The Neanderthal face, dominated by a projecting and full nose, __________ the faces of other hominids.

Ⓐ have differed clearly from
Ⓑ differed clearly from
Ⓒ differing clearly from
Ⓓ differed clearly

Tip · 'dominated~nose'는 분사구문 거품이므로 걷어 내면 동사가 없는 문장이다. 여기서 dominated는 과거형 동사(정동사)가 아닌 과거분사이므로 동사가 될 수 없다. 보기에서 적당한 동사를 찾으면 답은 Ⓑ이다.

❶.3 주어 · 동사 찾기

- 만약 문장의 골격을 이루는 주어와 동사 없이 수식어구로만 이루어져 있다면, 주어와 동사를 선택지에서 찾아낸다.
- 문장의 거품인 부가구문을 걷어 내면 문장의 주요 구조인 주어, 동사, 목적어, 보어가 남아 아무리 긴 문장의 문제라도 쉽게 골격을 이해할 수 있다.

Hackers Skill 문제와 관계 있는 구조만 남긴다.

거품 걷어내기	**1. 문제와 관계없는 부가구문은 거품이니 걷어내라.** 부가구문 : 부사구, 부사절, 전치사구, 분사구문, 동격, 관계절 등 **2. 문제와 관계없는 주절은 걷어내라.** 종속절을 가진 주절이 문제와 무관하면 주절을 걷어낸다.

The traveler ~~***who crosses the U.S. by car***~~ will find the food as worthy of attention as the scenery. (관계절 거품)

Tip · 거품인 관계절을 걷어내면, 주어는 'The traveler' 이고 동사는 'will find' 가 된다.

~~***Based on the premise that light was composed of color***~~, the impressionists came to the conclusion that shadows were not really black. (분사구문 거품)

Tip · Based 이하는 the impressionists를 수식하는 분사구문이므로 거품에 해당한다.
주어는 the impressionists이고 동사는 came이 된다.

~~***In the mid-ninth century***~~ both Canterbury and London were pillaged and burned. (전치사구 거품)

Tip · In the mid-ninth century는 전치사구이므로 거품에 해당한다.
주어는 both~London이고 동사구는 were 이하이다.

~~***It became clear that***~~ resolving the dilemmas surrounding the public domain might prove necessary to preserve the union itself. (문제와 관계없는 주절의 경우)

Tip · that 이하 명사절에 주어 · 동사가 있고 주절에도 주어 · 동사가 있다.
하지만 문제의 초점이 종속절에 맞춰져 있다면, 앞에 주절의 주어 · 동사를 걷어낸다.

Hackers **Practice** | 연습문제 |

다음 문장에서 거품을 구별하여 주어와 동사를 찾으시오.

1 As the air shot through the furnace, the bubbling metal would erupt in showers of sparks.

2 The universe consists of billions of galaxies flying apart as if from an explosion that set them in motion.

3 Democratic candidate, General George B. McClellan, promised peace at any price.

4 One scientist has estimated that the sea's plankton generates more than twice as much.

5 Growing to two or three inches long, krill provide the major food for the giant blue whale.

6 Mercury, closest to the Sun, receives the most solar energy.

7 To describe her research, she has written or edited seven books.

8 Despite such an impressive research background, she also enjoys her work in helping guide young scientists.

9 Like its relatives, the ancient tapir and rhinoceros, eohippus had four toes on its front feet, three on the rear, and teeth adapted to a forest diet of soft leaves.

10 Owning a phone in some countries is a well-known status symbol.

■ 정답 p319

Hackers TEST | 실전문제 |

1 Cape Cod, a summer resort on the Atlantic Ocean, __________ for its clambakes.

Ⓐ they are famous
Ⓑ famous
Ⓒ is famous
Ⓓ been famous

2 In contrast to classical music, which follows formal European traditions, __________ spontaneous and freeform.

Ⓐ is
Ⓑ the
Ⓒ jazz being
Ⓓ jazz is

3 __________, people would desert the small states for the large.

Ⓐ They are drawn by fresh lands and low taxes
Ⓑ Drawn by fresh lands and low taxes
Ⓒ Drawing by fresh lands and low taxes
Ⓓ Fresh lands and low taxes drawn

4 The third and final reforming document for the Ottomans __________, which was issued over the signature of Sultan Abdul Hamid II.

Ⓐ the Constitution of 1876
Ⓑ was the Constitution of 1876
Ⓒ what the Constitution of 1876 was
Ⓓ that the Constitution of 1876

5 New Orleans, having belonged first to France, then to Spain, then to France again, __________ very cosmopolitan and sophisticated about entertainment.

Ⓐ was
Ⓑ to be
Ⓒ has
Ⓓ have

6 In 1885 the association' s territories, renamed the Congo Free State after the Berlin conference, ________, at the expense of the natives.

Ⓐ which was one of the world' s major sources of rubber
Ⓑ it was one of the world' s major sources of rubber
Ⓒ one of the world' s major sources of rubber became
Ⓓ became one of the world' s major sources of rubber

---

7 With the Spanish army driven from France, ________ strong enough to issue the Edict of Nantes in April 1598.

Ⓐ feeling
Ⓑ and Henry felt
Ⓒ which Henry felt
Ⓓ Henry felt

---

8 His scientific work with electricity ________ Franklin world fame.

Ⓐ earning
Ⓑ earned
Ⓒ was earned
Ⓓ be earned

---

9 In frontier regions, of course, ________ was the standard type of house.

Ⓐ the log cabin which
Ⓑ that the log cabin
Ⓒ the log cabin has
Ⓓ the log cabin

---

10 The military conquest of the vast land of India with its hundreds of millions of people ________.

Ⓐ were completed by the beginning of the nineteenth century
Ⓑ the beginning of the nineteenth century was completed
Ⓒ being completed by the beginning of the nineteenth century
Ⓓ was completed by the beginning of the nineteenth century

11 __________ decorated with fish and bone motifs are found in grave sites, especially of women.

Ⓐ That stone tools and pottery are
Ⓑ Stone tools and pottery be
Ⓒ Although stone tools and pottery are
Ⓓ Stone tools and pottery

12 At every major temple site there was a court __________ like a capital I where ball games took place.

Ⓐ was shaped
Ⓑ shaped
Ⓒ whose shaping
Ⓓ shaped which

13 During his stay in Egypt, __________ built on the western edge of the Nile delta.

Ⓐ Alexander picked a site for a harbor to be
Ⓑ a site for a harbor was picked by Alexander
Ⓒ picking a site for a harbor, and Alexander
Ⓓ Alexander be picked a site for a harbor

14 A revolt __________ meant the revival of a small Jewish state.

Ⓐ by the Maccabees in Palestine
Ⓑ is the Maccabees in Palestine
Ⓒ which the Maccabees in Palestine
Ⓓ has been the Maccabees in Palestine

15 __________ because of the forms that the universal substance took.

Ⓐ To be appeared
Ⓑ Diversity which
Ⓒ Appeared by diversity
Ⓓ Diversity appeared

16 __________ money on future prospects was so popular that no politician felt any need to think through how these debts would be repaid.

Ⓐ Borrowing
Ⓑ That borrowing
Ⓒ Once been borrowed
Ⓓ What borrowing

■ 정답 p320

Structure Patterns

Outline

Structure의 기본이 되고 자주 출제되는 문장의 유형을 공식화하여 도표로 정리하였다.

Structure 문제를 공략하기 위해서는 다음과 같은 훈련이 필요하다.

- 예문을 이용하여 공식화된 pattern을 완전히 습득하기!
- comma와 동사를 이용하여 문제에 맞는 pattern을 잡아내기!
- 선택지의 보기들에 공식화된 가능구문을 적용하기!

＊ 이 도표는 이 과의 설명을 먼저 익힌 후 보시길 바랍니다. ● =문제에서 밑줄부분

Structure Patterns	Key Point	● 의 동사형태	→	● 의 구조
Pattern 1 ● + V	주어 없이 동사만 있을 때 주어 찾기	정동사 준동사 No verb	→ → →	Pattern A/B/C 동명사구 / to 부정사구 명사구
Pattern 2 ● + S + V	뒤에 완전한 주어동사가 있을 때	No verb	→	부사구 / 전치사구
Pattern 3 ● + , + S + V	comma 뒤에 완전한 주어동사가 있을 때	정동사 준동사 No verb	→ → →	부사절 분사구문 / to 부정사구 주어동격 / 부사구 / 전치사구
Pattern 4 S + V + ●	앞에 완전한 주어동사가 있을 때	정동사 준동사 No verb	→ → →	부사절 / 관계절 분사구문 / to 부정사구 부사구 / 전치사구
Pattern 5 S + V + , ●	comma 앞에 완전한 주어동사가 있을 때	정동사 준동사 No verb	→ → →	대등절 / 관계절/ (부사절) 분사구문 동격 / 부사구 / 전치사구
Pattern 6 S + ● + V	주어동사 사이에 comma 없을 때	정동사 준동사 No verb	→ → →	관계절 분사구문 / to 부정사구 부사구 / 전치사구
Pattern 7 S, + ● + , V	주어동사 사이에 comma를 끼고 있을 때	정동사 준동사 No verb	→ → →	부사절 / 관계절 분사구문 주어동격 / 부사구 / 전치사구

❷.1 Hackers Patterns

Pattern 1 : ● + V

- 동사 앞에 빈 칸이 있다면, 그것은 주어 자리이므로 주어가 될 수 있는 문장구성성분인 명사구, 동명사구, to 부정사구, 혹은 명사절을 넣으면 된다.

Hackers Skill ● 에 주어가 될 수 있는 요소를 찾아 삽입하라.

Pattern	● 자리에 올 수 있는 성분	● 에 포함된 동사형태
● + V	**명사구** : (관사) + (형용사) + 명사 + (전치사구)	No Verb
	동명사구 : V + ing **to 부정사구** : to V	**준동사**
	명사절 : NC + (S) + V	**정동사**

FOOTNOTE

· NC (Nominal Connector)는 명사절 접속사로 that, what, whether, 의문사절이 올 수 있다.

The flowers of the tea plant are small and white. **[명사구]**

Solving algebra is very difficult. **[동명사구]**

To get up early every morning is not always possible. **[to 부정사구]**

What he really needs is a cup of coffee. **[명사절]**

In terms of style, ____________ are short and exact, made mainly of nouns and verbs.

Ⓐ which is sentenced by
Ⓑ as Hemingway's sentences
Ⓒ made Hemingway's sentences
Ⓓ Hemingway's sentences

Tip · comma 앞의 전치사구 거품을 걷어 내고, 동사를 찾는다. 동사 앞에 주어 없이 빈칸이 있으므로 주어가 될 수 있는 구문을 선택지에서 고르면 된다. 선택지 중에서 정동사를 포함하고 있는 Ⓐ와 Ⓒ는 명사절이 아니므로 정답이 될 수 없다. No Verb이지만 명사구가 아닌 Ⓑ역시 정답이 아니며 명사구인 Ⓓ가 정답이다.

* Pattern A, B, C : ● + V1

- 비어 있는 주어 자리를 채우는 Pattern 1중에서 ● 에 정동사가 포함된 경우를 Pattern A, B, C로 세분화 하였다. 절에서 두개의 정동사가 있고 첫번째 동사 앞에 빈 칸이 있다면, 뒤의 동사는 전체문장의 정동사이므로, 빈 칸이 그 문장에서 주어 역할을 할 수 있도록 명사절 혹은, 관계절이나 전치사구의 수식을 받는 명사구로 만들어 줘야 한다.

Hackers Skill

Blank절이 절로 시작 : 명사절로 만들어라.(Pattern A)
Blank절이 명사구로 시작 : 관계절로 연결하라.(Pattern B)

Pattern	● 자리에 올 수 있는 성분	
● + V1	**명사절 주어** : NC + (S) + V2	Pattern A
	관계절의 수식을 받는 명사구 주어 : 명사구 + 관계대명사 + (S) + V2	Pattern B
	전치사구의 수식을 받는 명사구 주어 : (수량대)명사 + of + 명사절	Pattern C

FOOTNOTE

- 수량대명사 : all, some, most, much, many, both, either, neither, none, etc.

What made John happy made Mary happy, too. [Pattern A]
V2 V1

The picnic that we had planned for weeks was canceled. [Pattern B]
V2 V1

Each of what they called 'monsters' appeared in the mid-night. [Pattern C]
V2 V1

The role ________ has played in shaping the local society cannot be denied.

Ⓐ the valley was unique that
Ⓑ that the unique topography of the valley
Ⓒ although the unique topography is the valley
Ⓓ is the unique topography of the valley

Tip · 문장에서 'has played', 'cannot be denied' 두 개의 동사를 찾을 수 있는데, 그 중에서 'cannot be denied'가 전체 문장의 정동사이다. 빈 칸 앞에 명사 'the role'이 명사 주어이므로 Pattern B나 Pattern C가 적용될 수 있다. 선택지에 Pattern B를 만족시키는 Ⓑ가 있으므로 정답은 Ⓑ이다.

Pattern 2 : ● + No Comma + 독립절(S+V)

- 빈칸 뒤에 comma가 없이 주어+동사를 완벽하게 갖춘 문장이 나오면, 완전한 문장을 수식하는 부가어구를 찾는다.

Hackers Skill 기존의 주어 · 동사 문형을 파괴하지 않는 부가어구를 찾아라.

Pattern	● 자리에 올 수 있는 성분	● 에 포함된 동사 형태
● + S + V	전치사구/부사(구)	No Verb

In science class we are learning how to analyze our experiments. **[전치사구]**

Recently I have been feeling good. **[부사(구)]**

_______ Mr. Manna observed that sales are growing rapidly, but profits have been lower than expected during the past year.

Ⓐ In his annual budget review
Ⓑ His annual budget reviewed
Ⓒ He reviewed his annual budget review
Ⓓ When his annually reviewed budget

Tip · 빈 칸 뒤에 comma 없이 완벽한 구조를 갖는 문장이 오므로 Pattern 2를 적용할 수 있다. 기존의 문법성을 깨지 않는 부가어구를 보기에서 찾으면, 전치사구인 Ⓐ가 답이 된다.

Structure www.goHackers.com

Pattern 3 : ● + Comma + 독립절(S+V)

• 빈칸 다음에 comma가 있고, 뒤의 문장이 주어+동사 구조로 완벽한 독립절이 오면, 기존의 문형을 파괴하지 않는 부가구문을 찾는다.

Hackers Skill 기존의 주어 · 동사 문형을 파괴하지 않는 부가구문을 찾아라.

Pattern	● 자리에 올 수 있는 성분	● 에 포함된 동사 형태
● + , + S + V	부사절	정동사
	분사구문 to 부정사구	준동사
	부사구(전치사구) 주어의 동격	No Verb

When the sculpture was unveiled, everyone cheered. [부사절]

Pointing to the sentence in the book, the teacher explained its meaning. [분사구문]

To become in the majority, immigrants tended to congregate in neighborhoods. [to 부정사구]

From about 1910-1930, most physicists believed that atomic energy would be of no practical value. [부사구(전치사구)]

Once ***the most subservient of Soviet allies,*** Bulgaria threw out its communist rulers and turned toward democracy. [주어의 동격]

__________ in his own right, his primary instrumental expression was his orchestra.

Ⓐ An impressive pianist, Ellington was
Ⓑ Ellington was an impressive pianist
Ⓒ As an impressive pianist Ellington
Ⓓ Although Ellington was an impressive pianist

Tip · comma 뒤에 완벽한 문장이 있으므로, comma 앞에는 기존 주절에 영향을 주지 않는 부가구문을 넣어야 한다. 정동사가 포함되어 있는 Ⓐ와 Ⓑ는 부사절의 형태가 아니므로 답이 될 수 없다. 따라서 부사절인 Ⓓ가 정답이다. Ⓒ는 As를 접속사로 볼 경우, 절이 완전하지 않아 틀리며 전치사로 본다 하더라도 의미상 어색하다.

Pattern 4 : 독립절 (S+V) + No Comma + ●

- 완전한 문장 뒤에 comma없이 빈칸이 있으면, 앞의 문장을 파괴하지 않는 부가구문을 찾는다.

Hackers Skill 기존의 주어 · 동사 문형을 파괴하지 않는 부가구문을 찾아라.

Pattern	● 자리에 올 수 있는 성분	● 에 포함된 동사 형태
S + V + ●	부사절 관계절	정동사
	분사구문 to 부정사구	준동사
	부사구(전치사구)	No Verb

FOOTNOTE
부사절 앞에 간혹 comma가 삽입될 수도 있음에 주의하라.

John ordered more to eat *even though he was not hungry.* [부사절]

An ideal is a standard *by which people judge real phenomena.* [관계절]

A deep-tissue massage is a type of massage therapy *concentrating on one part of the body.* [분사구문]

They made a separate sleeping floor *to conserve space in houses.* [to 부정사구]

John arrived at the airport *in a hurry.* [부사구(전치사구)]

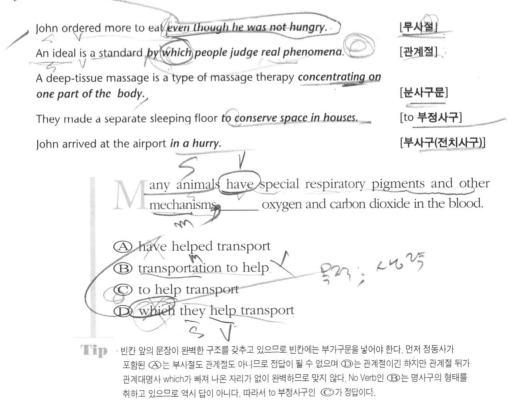

Many animals have special respiratory pigments and other mechanisms ______ oxygen and carbon dioxide in the blood.

Ⓐ have helped transport
Ⓑ transportation to help
Ⓒ to help transport
Ⓓ which they help transport

Tip 빈칸 앞의 문장이 완벽한 구조를 갖추고 있으므로 빈칸에는 부가구문을 넣어야 한다. 먼저 정동사가 포함된 Ⓐ는 부사절도 관계절도 아니므로 정답이 될 수 없으며 Ⓓ는 관계절이긴 하지만 관계절 뒤가 관계대명사 which가 빠져 나온 자리가 없이 완벽하므로 맞지 않다. No Verb인 Ⓑ는 명사구의 형태를 취하고 있으므로 역시 답이 아니다. 따라서 to 부정사구인 Ⓒ가 정답이다.

Pattern 5 : 독립절(S+V) + Comma + ●

• 완벽한 독립절 다음에 comma가 있고 빈칸이 있다. comma 앞의 독립절을 파괴하지 않는 부가구문을 찾는다.

Hackers Skill 기존의 주어 · 동사 문형을 파괴하지 않는 부가구문이나 대등절을 찾아라.

Pattern	● 자리에 올 수 있는 성분	● 에 포함된 동사 형태
S + V + , + ●	관계절 대등절	정동사
	분사구문	준동사
	동격 부사구(전치사구)	No Verb

FOOTNOTE
1. 대등절 : 등위접속사 and, but, or, yet, for 등으로 연결된 절 (Structure 2-1 참조)
2. 대등절 앞에 comma가 오지 않는 경우도 간혹있다.
3. comma뒤에 부사절이 올 수도 있다.

They planted fertilized oyster eggs, ***which hatched into larvae within two or three weeks.*** **[관계절]**

The president of the U.S. appoints the cabinet members, ***but their appointments are subject to Senate approval.*** **[대등절]**

Jazz bubbles with energy, ***expressing the moods, interests, and emotions of the people.*** **[분사구문]**

Alchemists searched for the elixir of life, ***a substance that could cure disease and prolong life.*** **[동격]**

There was a wide variety of flowers in the show, ***from simple carnations to the most exquisite roses.*** **[부사구(전치사구)]**

Wheat was probably first cultivated in the Euphrates nearly 9,000 years ago, _______ it is now grown from the Arctic Circle to the tropics in the New World.

Ⓐ which Ⓑ with
Ⓒ but Ⓓ in addition

Tip · comma 앞이 완전한 독립절이므로, 빈칸 뒤에는 부가구문이나 대등절이 올 수 있다. 빈칸 뒤에 정동사가 포함되어 있으므로 두번째 절은 관계절과 대등절 중 하나가 될 수 있다. 그런데 두번째 절이 관계대명사 which가 빠져 나온 자리가 없이 완벽하므로 Ⓐ의 관계대명사 which는 사용이 불가능하다. Ⓓ의 in addition은 접속사가 아니므로 답이 될 수 없다. 따라서 대등접속사인 Ⓒ가 정답이다.

Pattern 6 : S + No Comma + ● + No Comma + V

- 주어 S1에 이끌리는 동사가 V1이고 V1이 문장전체의 정동사일 때, 이 둘 사이에 빈 칸이 있으면 기존의 완전한 문장구조를 해치지 않는 부가구문을 찾는다.

Hackers Skill 기존의 주어 · 동사 문형을 파괴하지 않는 부가구문을 삽입하라.

Pattern	● 자리에 올 수 있는 성분	● 에 포함된 동사 형태
S + ● + V	관계절	정동사
	분사구문 to 부정사구	준동사
	전치사구 부사구	No Verb

FOOTNOTE
S + to 부정사구 + V에서 'to 부정사구'는 앞의 주어와 동격일 때만 가능하다. (Structure 2-7 참조)

The work ***which people in the Leisure Center do*** can be included as leisure. [관계절]

The Democratic candidate ***running for president*** criticized the current administration. [분사구문]

The ability ***to assume the social roles*** appears in many different contexts. [to 부정사구]

Men and women ***under about 30*** have a different outlook toward each other and toward marriage. [전치사구]

Neutrinos ***very rarely*** interact with other matter and so are difficult to observe. [부사구]

The most Australian thing ________ is to lie on a clean, wide, beautiful beach.

Ⓐ who can do
Ⓑ you can do
Ⓒ which can do it
Ⓓ done it by you

Tip · 'is'가 문장의 동사(V1)이므로 'is' 앞의 빈 칸은 'the most Australian thing' (S1)을 수식하는 부가구문을 넣어야 한다. 선택지에서 정동사를 포함하고 있는 보기는 Ⓐ, Ⓑ, Ⓒ. 먼저 Ⓐ는 선행사가 사물이므로 관계대명사 who를 쓸 수 없으므로 틀리다. Ⓒ는 'can do it'의 주체가 'the most australian thing'이 되어 의미상 어색하다. 그러므로 목적격 관계대명사가 생략된 관계절 Ⓑ가 정답이다. 준동사를 포함하고 있는 Ⓓ는 과거분사가 목적어를 취하고 있어 맞지 않다.

Pattern 7 : S + Comma + ● + Comma + V

• 주어와 동사 사이에 comma가 있으면, 문장구조에는 전혀 영향을 주지 않는 부가구문들을 찾는다.

Hackers Skill 완벽한 주어와 동사 사이에 부가구문을 넣어라.

Pattern	● 자리에 올 수 있는 성분	● 에 포함된 동사 형태
S + , + ● + , + V	부사절 관계절	정동사
	분사구문	준동사
	부사구(전치사구) 동격	No Verb

Young women in the 1930's, ***when I grew up,*** had real heroines. [부사절]

The bell, ***which hangs in the museum,*** is over two hundred years old. [관계절]

The bell, ***hanging in the museum,*** is over two hundred years old. [분사구문]

South Australia, ***except for the charming town of Alice Springs,*** is virtually a void. [부사구(전치사구)]

The managing director, ***one of Thai owners,*** merged two old companies. [동격]

The laser beam, ____________, is the latest in an array of new energy sources, and scientists are identifying an amazing number of possibilities for it.

Ⓐ which a special form of light
Ⓑ a special form of light
Ⓒ forms a special light
Ⓓ a special form is light

Tip · comma 뒤에 동사가 있고, comma 앞에 주어가 있으므로, comma를 사이에 두고 완전한 주어 · 동사 구조를 이루는 Pattern7이 적용되는 문제이다. 따라서 보기에서 기존의 문형을 파괴하지 않는 구문을 고르면 된다. 정동사가 포함되어 있는 보기 Ⓒ와 Ⓓ는 부사절도 관계절도 아니므로 답이 될 수 없다. 그리고 Ⓐ는 정동사가 포함되어 있지 않은 관계절의 형태를 취하고 있으므로 틀리다. 따라서 No Verb 구조인 동격어구 Ⓑ가 답이다.

Hackers Practice | 연습문제 |

다음 각 문장의 밑줄 친 부분을 blank(●)로 간주하고, 해당되는 Pattern을 쓰시오.

1 A distinctive feature of the Brahman religion was an emphasis on human differences.

2 What gave the people living in the Fertile Crescent an advantage was the potential for irrigation in the valleys and an adequate supply of rainfall.

3 In the first century A.D. the condition of the peasants was once again approaching disaster.

4 To lessen the strain on heating and air-conditioning equipment, builders of skyscrapers have begun to use double-glazed panels of glass.

5 Settlement houses modeled on Hull House were founded in many poor neighborhoods to help children and adults to make their lives more meaningful.

6 By 1765 a few hundred had settled in Louisiana, while 2,500 impoverished Acadians congregated in French maritime ports.

7 Vinegar, which is a dilute solution of acetic acid, is an example of a weak acid.

8 Most aristocracies, in historical perspective, are noted for their shortsightedness and greed.

9 All of Earth's communities are collectively called the biosphere.

10 Although the carnivorous adaptation is most widespread and conspicuous among green plants, some microscopic species of fungi also catch and digest animal prey.

■ 정답 p321

Hackers TEST | 실전문제 |

1 ____________ New England towns had a special democratic system of government.

Ⓐ Their beginnings
Ⓑ From their beginnings
Ⓒ When their beginnings were
Ⓓ In beginning

2 In November 1620, the Pilgrims ____________ Cape Cod Bay in Massachusetts to start their new life.

Ⓐ sailing into
Ⓑ been sailed into
Ⓒ sailed into
Ⓓ to be sailed into

3 Much of ____________ scientists know about dinosaurs has been recently discovered.

Ⓐ are
Ⓑ what
Ⓒ which
Ⓓ whose

4 The phenomenon of ________ are known as corporate networks has also attracted attention.

Ⓐ those
Ⓑ what
Ⓒ which
Ⓓ their

5 In the past, oysters were raised in much the same way as dirt farmers raised tomatoes ____________.

Ⓐ and transplanting them
Ⓑ though transplanted them
Ⓒ as transplant them
Ⓓ by transplanting them

6 __________, our capacity to behave would be seriously impaired.

(A) Regular supplies of some hormones
(B) Regular supplies of some hormones work
(C) That without regular supplies of some hormones
(D) Without regular supplies of some hormones

---

7 After his release from the home, __________ playing in a jazz band.

(A) then Louis got a job
(B) Louis got a job
(C) getting a job
(D) to get a job

---

8 Cloisonne has an enameled surface decorated with elaborate designs; _____ are formed by small bands of metal.

(A) the outlines of them
(B) the outlines of which
(C) which the outlines
(D) because that the outlines

---

9 The emergence __________ as a separate discipline can probably be traced to the experiments of Bayliss and Starling on hormone secretion.

(A) is
(B) of endocrinology
(C) that to be endocrinology
(D) which endocrinology

---

10 While working as a firefighter at the University of Mississippi, __________ submitted 37 stories to magazines.

(A) to be William Faulker
(B) William Faulker' s work
(C) William Faulker who
(D) William Faulker

Structure

www.goHackers.com

11 Franklin had to demonstrate inexhaustible wealth and generosity ________.

Ⓐ food and goods distributed
Ⓑ which distributing food and goods
Ⓒ by distributing food and goods
Ⓓ from food and goods

12 The name ________ is Homo erectus, for one of their characteristics was erect posture.

Ⓐ gave individuals of the first people
Ⓑ has given individuals of the first people
Ⓒ the first people gave individuals
Ⓓ given to individuals of the first people

13 In 800 B.C. La Venta was the largest town in North America, ________ for the next 200 years.

Ⓐ this position was held
Ⓑ holding this position
Ⓒ to hold this position
Ⓓ that this position held

14 ________ was considered a basic part of an education for the young.

Ⓐ Training is in poetry and music
Ⓑ Poetry and music was trained
Ⓒ Poetry and music trained
Ⓓ Training in poetry and music

15 The other impetus came from popular English writers, ________ should be shared with the Indian elite.

Ⓐ believed that the superiority of British culture
Ⓑ have believed that the superiority of British culture
Ⓒ who believed that the superiority of British culture
Ⓓ the superiority of British culture was believed

16 Each city sponsored its favorite athletes, __________.

Ⓐ much of them professionals
Ⓑ which were professionals
Ⓒ they were professionals
Ⓓ many of whom were professionals

17 The cortex, __________ was much larger than that in any other primate.

Ⓐ the outer layer of the brain had been
Ⓑ was the outer layer of the brain
Ⓒ the outer layer of the brain
Ⓓ to the outer layer of the brain

18 __________, Athens escaped for unknown reasons.

Ⓐ When the Dorian invasion struck the other poleis of Greece
Ⓑ The Dorian invasion struck the other poleis of Greece
Ⓒ However the Dorian invasion struck the other poleis of Greece
Ⓓ That the Dorian invasion struck the other poleis of Greece

■ 정답 p321

ch1 Mini TEST | 실전문제 |

1 _______________ helps people become more conscious of their spending habits.

Ⓐ That keeping a budget generally
Ⓑ Being kept a budget generally
Ⓒ Keeping a budget generally
Ⓓ What keeping a budget generally

2 _______ the hardy pioneers who built up the American West.

Ⓐ To become
Ⓑ There is
Ⓒ Being
Ⓓ It was

3 Together with his team Edison brought out a stream of inventions, _________.

Ⓐ is over one thousand patents
Ⓑ to be accumulated by over one thousand patents
Ⓒ by accumulating over one thousand patents
Ⓓ accumulates over one thousand patents

4 The art of ___________ is practiced throughout the world.

Ⓐ having made more productive
Ⓑ to make land more productive
Ⓒ that making land more productive
Ⓓ making land more productive

5 Many of today's descendants of immigrants respect the cultures _______.

Ⓐ they once rejected
Ⓑ who they once rejected
Ⓒ having once rejected
Ⓓ as they are rejected

6 ________, Hooper produces a graceful groundeating glide.

Ⓐ Rapidly alternating skis
Ⓑ To skis were rapidly alternated
Ⓒ Being alternated rapidly
Ⓓ What was alternated by skis

---

7 __________, congratulators would all join in a merry party.

Ⓐ That celebrate completion of the work
Ⓑ Celebrated completion is the work
Ⓒ To celebrate completion of the work
Ⓓ Being celebrated completion of the work

---

8 Basically _______, liberalism held that the lower classes were a danger to good government.

Ⓐ is a middle class phenomenon
Ⓑ a middle class phenomenon was
Ⓒ a middle class phenomenon
Ⓓ that a middle class phenomenon was

---

9 ___________ his artistic accomplishments, Morse is well known for his work developing the telegraph and what is known as Morse Code.

Ⓐ And
Ⓑ That
Ⓒ In addition to
Ⓓ Which is

---

10 ____________ is that the process of creating Mount Rushmore was not exactly an uneventful one.

Ⓐ Known is not so well
Ⓑ That is not so well known
Ⓒ So well known is that
Ⓓ What is not so well known

11 In 1927 Borglum was granted a commission by the federal government ___________ on Mount Rushmore.

Ⓐ the sculpture was created
Ⓑ to create the sculpture
Ⓒ that the sculpture was created
Ⓓ and to create the sculpture

---

12 The medium _________ is a reflection not only of the artist's perception of aesthetic beauty but of resources that society has to supply.

Ⓐ for being chosen the artist
Ⓑ the artist was chosen
Ⓒ what chosen by the artist
Ⓓ chosen by the artist

---

13 When the body lacks a sufficient amount of carbohydrates, it must then use its protein supplies for energy, __________.

Ⓐ what a process is called gluconeogenesis
Ⓑ a process is called gluconeogenesis
Ⓒ it is a process called gluconeogenesis
Ⓓ a process called gluconeogenesis

■ 정답 p322

chapter 2

HACKERS TOEFL

Structure

Clause & Phrase

절과 절은 접속사로 연결된다. 연결되는 절의 구조적 성격과 절의 내용에 따라 접속사의 종류가 선택된다. 이 chapter에서는 TOEFL에서 출제되는 이러한 접속사 선택문제를 다룬다.

TOEFL에 많이 출제되고 오답 선택 비율이 높은 축약 관계대명사, 축약 부사절, 동격의 축약 과정과 본래의 문장으로 원상복귀 과정을 이해하고 훈련함으로써 분사구문과 동격에 관한 구문 선택의 정밀도를 높일 수 있도록 한다.

접속사

Outline

접속사는 절과 절을 연결해 주는 역할을 하며, 그 역할에 따라 등위접속사, 부사절 접속사, 형용사절 접속사(관계절), 명사절 접속사로 나뉜다. 이번 과에서는 등위접속사와 부사절 접속사에 대해 파악한다.

접속사가 들어가 있는 문장의 구조를 파악하기 위해서 다음의 훈련이 필요하다.

- **접속사에 따라 절의 의미와 문법성이 달라지는 것을 파악하기!**
- **문장의 구조를 파악하기 위해서 접속사가 이끄는 절만 따로 묶기!**

TOEFL에서 접속사와 관련된 문제는 문법뿐 아니라 의미상으로도 적절한 접속사 선택하기, 주절 및 종속절의 문장구조 잡기, 그리고 접속사와 비접속사 또는 접속사와 전치사 구별하기 등이 있다.

Hackers Grammar

접속사의 분류

절과 절은 접속사로 연결한다. 절을 이끄는 접속사에 따라 그 절의 문장 내 위치가 달라짐을 주목하라.

접속사	기능	위치
등위접속사	주절과 주절을 연결	S1 + V1, 등위접속사 + S2 + V2
부사절 접속사	주절을 수식하는 종속절	S1 + V1 + 부사절 접속사 + S2 + V2 부사절 접속사 + S2 + V2, S1 + V1
형용사절 접속사	명사를 수식하는 관계절	명사 +(,) 관계사 + (S2) + V2(,)+ V1 S1 + V1, 관계사 + S2 + V2
명사절 접속사	명사의 역할	동사/전치사 + 명사절 접속사 + (S) + V 명사절 접속사 +(S2) + V2 + V1

❶.1 등위접속사

등위접속사는 주절 뒤에서 대등절을 이끈다. 두 개의 주절과 그에 따른 두 개의 정동사가 있다.

등위접속사	뜻	절 + 접속사 + 절
and	그리고	Mary is studying, and John is working.
but	그러나	Mary is studying, but John is playing.
or	혹은	Mary must study, or she will not pass the exam.
so	그래서	John was sick, so he couldn' t hand in his paper.
yet	그러나	Mary missed her class, yet she got the note from her friend.
for	왜냐하면	Mary should check every answer, for she usually misses some.

❶.2 부사절 접속사

부사절 접속사는 주절의 앞이나 뒤에서 부사절을 이끌어 '부사절 + 주절' 혹은 '주절 + 부사절' 구조를 갖는다.

시간	after, before, at/by the time, every time, as, as long as, as soon as, once, since, until, when, whenever, while
장소	where, wherever
목적	so that, in order that
이유	now that, since, because, as, in that
조건	if, in case, provided (that), providing (that), unless, whether
양태	however (no matter how), as
대조	though, although, whereas, while

FOOTNOTE
주절+부사절경우, 부사절 앞에 comma가 없는 것이 일반적이나 comma가 오는 경우도 있다.

I decided to stop and have lunch, ________ I was feeling hungry.

Ⓐ despite
Ⓑ but
Ⓒ for
Ⓓ therefore

Tip · 주절 뒤 comma가 나오고도 다른 절이 나왔으므로 보기에서 의미가 적절한 대등 접속사인 Ⓒ가 답이다.

Hackers Skill 절과 절은 접속사로 연결한다. (다음은 접속사가 아니므로 주의한다)

접속사가 아닌 부사	therefore, then, thus, consequently, however, nevertheless, furthermore, moreover, besides, in fact, otherwise, for instance, later, afterwards 등
접속사가 아닌 전치사	despite, in spite of, because of, during, according to, in case of, irrespective of, regardless of, concerning, like 등

FOOTNOTE

However는 but의 의미가 아닌 no matter how의 뜻일 때에는 접속사로 사용 될 수 있다.

However reluctant he may be, Scott has to study abroad. (however은 접속사이므로 맞음)

Many explanations have been mentioned, however three reasons are most often cited.
(however ⇒ but. '그러나'의 뜻일 때 however은 접속사가 아니므로 등위접속사 but으로 정정)

Hackers Skill 〈부사절 + 주절〉의 경우 주절은 문장 부사나 접속사 없이 주어 · 동사로 시작한다. 단, 접속사가 if인 경우 주절에 then이 올 수도 있다.

Although many colonial scholars consider Jonathan Edwards an important writer, *but* his works are not widely read anymore. ⇒ but 삭제

Because commodities are subject to external price fluctuations, *therefore* underdeveloped economies are exposed to inflationary pressures.
⇒ therefore를 삭제하고 직접 주어 · 동사로 시작한다.

If the pollsters reduce their sample below 1,200, *then* their sampling error will rise rapidly. ⇒ if로 시작했기 때문에 then 사용가능

Hackers **Practice** | 연습문제 |

알맞은 접속사를 아래의 박스에서 골라 빈 칸에 넣으시오.

[보기] while, when, since, until, however, because, although

1 The larvae drifted ________ they attached themselves to the clean shells on the bottom.

2 Because of their pink color, they often appear as a solid reddish mass ________ viewed from a ship or from the air.

3 ________ observing comet Bowell, astronomers were able to measure the amount of light.

4 ________ jazz lacks any academic formulas, its performers develop their natural musical instinct.

5 ________ the nobility accepted Philip, he was never able to gain the loyalty of a majority of the Portuguese people.

6 A small group in society lived very well, ________ the mass of people worked to support them.

7 In 1951 a Conservative government returned to power ________ British citizens were tired of social change.

8 ________ the bird is about four months old, the second phase of training is started.

9 ________ the general public denounced Epstein's work, many artists and critics praised it.

■ 정답 p323

Hackers **TEST** | 실전문제 |

1 Fish rubbings and nature printing have been developing as art forms in North America over the past 40 years, ________ the techniques may date as far back as the time of early cave dwellers.

Ⓐ but when　　Ⓑ until then
Ⓒ in spite of　　Ⓓ although

2 The lowest strata of the caste system are referred to as 'untouchables' ________ excluded from the performance of rituals which confer religious purity.

Ⓐ since　　Ⓑ because they are
Ⓒ because of their　　Ⓓ which because they are

3 ________ blight disease came from America into Ireland, it caused a national disaster.

Ⓐ Late　　Ⓑ When the late
Ⓒ It was the late　　Ⓓ The late

4 Determining the values of parameters for functions is the primary goal of regression analysis, ________.

Ⓐ which others are　　Ⓑ but there are others
Ⓒ there are others　　Ⓓ others there

5 The difference between class and elite rests largely on the fact that classes are defined in terms of economic position and power, ________ elites may have a non-economic basis.

Ⓐ how　　Ⓑ whether
Ⓒ by　　Ⓓ whereas

6 When questionnaires are completed by the respondents, ________ to use the closed-end format as much as possible.

Ⓐ it is common
Ⓑ common is
Ⓒ so the common
Ⓓ is the common

7 Exocrine glands are called duct glands, ________ endocrine glands are called ductless.

Ⓐ despite
Ⓑ after
Ⓒ the fact that
Ⓓ while

8 ________ but they also engage in fine craftwork.

Ⓐ The farmers of the Pueblo Indians,
Ⓑ Because the Pueblo Indians are farmers,
Ⓒ The Pueblo Indians are farmers,
Ⓓ To be farmers of the Pueblo Indians,

9 ____________, pioneers went on to areas still farther west, toward the Mississippi River.

Ⓐ On account of the years passed
Ⓑ The years passed
Ⓒ As the years passed
Ⓓ For the years passed

10 When the bloodshed ended, ________ an energetic person.

Ⓐ their new exhausted ruler finding in China
Ⓑ finding the exhausted Chinese were their new ruler of
Ⓒ the exhausted Chinese found their new ruler
Ⓓ and the exhausted Chinese finding their new ruler

■ 정답 p323

2 관계대명사

Outline

관계대명사는 동일인물이나 사물이 동시에 두 개의 문장에서 쓰였을 때 이용된다.
두 절 중에서 뒤에 있는 절의 공통 명사 부분을 관계대명사로 바꾼다.
이 때 관계대명사가 두 절을 연결시켜 준다.

TOEFL에서 출제되는 형식은 알맞은 관계대명사 선택문제, 관계대명사절의 주어 · 동사 구성문제들이다. 따라서 이러한 문제들을 풀기 위해서는 다음과 같은 훈련이 필요하다.

- **관계대명사의 종류와 사용법을 외우기!**
- **관계절의 어순에 대해 숙지하기!**

She has two sons. + Her sons are doctors. → She has two sons who are doctors.
Two sons와 her sons는 동일 인물이므로 관계사 who를 사용하여 한 문장으로 만든다. 이 때, two sons는 who의 선행사이다.

Hackers Grammar

❷.1 관계대명사의 종류

격	관계대명사의 종류	예문
주격	Who (사람) Which (사물) That (사람/사물)	The person ***who*** lived there was a painter. He gave the cynical smile ***which*** was usual with him. He ascended the few steps ***that*** led to the verandah.
목적격	Whom (사람) Which (사물) That (사람/사물)	Jane liked the man ***whom*** she met at the party. I found the keys ***which*** I lost. The music ***that*** Jane listened to this evening was good.
소유격	Whose + noun (사람/사물)	I know a girl ***whose*** sister is a singer.

FOOTNOTE
목적격 관계대명사는 생략이 가능하고, 주격 관계대명사 + be동사는 축약이 가능하다.

ex. What sets the real artist apart is mysterious ability ***we call talent.***

Tip · 예문 중 'ability which we call talent' 에서 which(목적격 관계대명사)가 생략되었다.

Hackers Skill

관계대명사 that을 comma 다음에 계속적 용법으로 사용하지 못한다.	They were able to penetrate the contradiction, ***that*** was concealed from traditional workers. (that → which)
관계대명사 that은 전치사의 목적격으로 사용하지 못한다.	What is far from simple is the leap of the imagination by ***that*** Picasso recognized a bull's head (that → which)

FOOTNOTE
계속적 용법은 comma 뒤에 관계절이 오는 형태로 부가적인 (non-essential) 정보를 제공하고자 할 때 쓰인다.

ex. Mary has three brothers, ***who are in Hawaii.***

❷.2 관계대명사의 선택

어순	격	예문
관계대명사 + 동사	주격	I like the girl ***who lives*** next door.
관계대명사 + 주어 + 동사	목적격	The people ***whom we visited*** yeserday were very kind.
관계대명사+명사+동사 **관계대명사+명사+주어+동사**	소유격	I met the girl ***whose car was stolen.*** Jane has a sister ***whose song I hate.***

Hackers Skill **목적격 관계대명사와 소유격 관계대명사 구분법**

'관계대명사 + 명사 + 동사'의 경우 관계대명사가 목적격이 올 것인지 소유격이 올 것인지의 판단은 타동사 뒤에 목적격 자리가 비어 있으면 목적격 관계대명사라고 판단하면 된다.

Some chemicals have been shown to disperse oil spills into droplets, ______ microbes can then destroy.

Ⓐ which Ⓑ whom
Ⓒ whose Ⓓ with which

Tip 절과 절을 연결하기 위해 접속사가 필요하고 관계대명사가 접속사 역할을 한다. 빈 칸 뒤에 명사와 동사가 왔으므로 소유격이나 목적격이 올 수 있다. 만약 소유격 관계대명사가 사용된다면 타동사인 destroy의 목적어가 없다. 따라서 destroy의 목적격 관계대명사가 와야한다. 선행사인 droplets가 사물이므로 whom은 사용 불가능하고 which인 Ⓐ가 정답이다.

❷.3 수량 표현 관계대명사

관계대명사로 받은 선행사의 일부 또는 전부를 표현하고자 할 때는 『선행사 + 수량표현 + of + 관계대명사』 표현을 사용한다. 여기서 사용될 수 있는 관계대명사는 which와 whom 이다.

선행사 + **수량 표현** + of + **관계대명사**

The building blocks of the proteins necessary for life are amino acids.
+ ***Many of them*** cannot be synthesized by the body.

⇒ The building blocks of the proteins necessary for life are amino acids, ***many of which*** cannot be synthesized by the body.

Tip · 첫번째 문장의 many of them의 them이 amino acids를 선행사로 가지므로 many of them ⇒ many of which로 바꾸어 관계절을 만든다.

❷.4 전치사 + 관계대명사

관계대명사와 함께 쓰이는 전치사는 동사에 의해 선택되는 경우가 있다.

Several generalizations are made.
+ several conclusions are ***drawn from*** them. (***from***은 ***drawn***과 연관되어 사용되었음)

⇒ Several generalizations are made ***from which*** several conclusions are ***drawn***.
(전치사가 관계대명사와 함께 절 앞으로 이동한 경우)

Hackers Skill **전치사 + 관계대명사 문제는 원상복구한 후 풀어라.**

Noise causes effect ________ the body never becomes accustomed.

Ⓐ which　　Ⓑ to which
Ⓒ from which　　Ⓓ whose

Tip · 두 절이 연결되었으므로 접속사가 필요하다. 전치사 to와 함께 사용되는 accustomed가 사용되었으므로, 원상복귀시키면 the body never becomes accustomed to effect가 되어 Ⓑ가 정답이다.

Hackers **Practice** | 연습문제 |

괄호 안에 알맞은 관계대명사를 넣으시오.

1 The person ______ has acquired knowledge of a language has internalized a system of rules.

2 A child ______ knows a language has mastered a system of rules that assigns sound and meaning in a definite way for an infinite class of sentences.

3 There would be no reason not to expect to find some language ______ grammar contained a syntactic rule.

4 We have a syntactic rule ______ application depends on pragmatic information.

5 An unmarked phenomenon is one ______ accords with universal principles in language.

6 The traveler ______ would like to sample the real flavor of American cooking must explore the country as a whole.

7 There is the Northeast, stretching from Maine to Maryland, ______ is famous for its seafood.

8 The blacks ______ were brought to America already possessed a rich musical tradition.

9 As the people were converted to Christianity, they composed lovely spirituals, ______ have become a permanent part of American music.

10 People all around the country ______ were unable to see him in person could enjoy his music on records.

■ 정답 p324

Hackers TEST | 실전문제 |

1 Arid regions in the southwestern United States have become increasingly inviting playgrounds for thc growing number of recreation seekers ________ such as motorcycles.

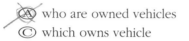

Ⓐ who are owned vehicles Ⓑ whose are vehicles
Ⓒ which owns vehicle Ⓓ who own vehicles

2 A black sculptor was one of a small number of women artists ________ .

Ⓐ who work was on view Ⓑ whose work was on view
Ⓒ that have been working Ⓓ whose is working

3 The classic Neanderthals, __________ between about 70,000 and 30,000 years ago, shared a number of special characteristics.

Ⓐ who lived Ⓑ which lived
Ⓒ who are living Ⓓ whose lived

4 Most lichens are crusted lichens, _________ that they cannot be removed intact.

Ⓐ the rock so tightly grips
Ⓑ which grip the rock so tightly
Ⓒ who is gripping the rock so tightly
Ⓓ then so tightly the rock is gripped

5 There are over 74 varieties of scorpions, ________ .

Ⓐ which is harmless to humans
Ⓑ much of which is harmless to humans
Ⓒ humans are harmless
Ⓓ most of which are harmless to humans

6 Late nineteenth century sociology was dominated by various theories of social evolution, __________ was Social Darwinism having nothing to do with C. Darwin himself.

Ⓐ in that Ⓑ which one
Ⓒ which Ⓓ one of which

7 Parsons shows that social systems differentiate into sub-systems, __________ has distinct functions with respect to various environments which include other subsystems.

Ⓐ which Ⓑ what
Ⓒ each Ⓓ each of which

8 The spat grew larger by drawing in seawater __________ derived microscopic particles of food.

Ⓐ which from they
Ⓑ from which they
Ⓒ through which
Ⓓ from who they

9 The Academy of Dog Training supplies law enforcement agencies with German shepherds __________ trained to recognize the smell of marijuana.

Ⓐ of them
Ⓑ who are
Ⓒ of which
Ⓓ which are

10 Franklin's many practical inventions included the Franklin stove, __________ a very efficient heater.

Ⓐ it was
Ⓑ whose
Ⓒ what was
Ⓓ which was

11 The world ________ is known as the Paleolithic Age or Old Stone Age.

Ⓐ lived in which Homo erectus men and women
Ⓑ Homo erectus men women lived in
Ⓒ each of which Homo erectus men and women lived in
Ⓓ in which Homo erectus men and women lived

---

12 Others see Jim as an ambitious man ________ was dedicated to his own aggrandizement no matter what it cost in blood and suffering for others.

Ⓐ who life
Ⓑ what life
Ⓒ whose life
Ⓓ life

■ 정답 p324

3 명사절

Outline

명사절은 '명사절 접속사 + 주어 + 동사'의 형식으로 이루어 진다. 명사절은 명사의 역할(주어, 목적어, 보어)을 할 수 있다. 적절한 명사절 접속사를 선택하는 문제가 출제된다.

- 명사절에 따라서 각각 어떤 명사절 접속사가 오는지 파악하기!
- 명사절 문장 성격을 파악하기!

Hackers Grammar

❸.1 명사절 접속사 이후가 완벽하지 않은 경우

명사절이 아래의 접속사로 시작되고, 명사절이 그 문장에서 주어와 목적어 역할을 한다.

명사절 접속사의 역할 및 구조

주어	who(ever), what(ever) + [___ + V + (목적어)] : 주어 자리 비어있음
목적어	whom(ever), what(ever) + [S + Vt + ___] : 목적어 자리 비어있음

* Vt : 타동사

명사절은 접속사가 주격인지 목적격인지에 따라 다음과 같은 생성과정을 거친다.

■ 주 격

I know [someone did it]

⇒ I know [who did it] (someone을 모를 경우 ⇒ who로 바뀐다)

⇒ I know who [__ did it] (who가 종속절의 앞으로 나간다.)

who가 빠져나간 종속절의 주어 자리가 비어 who 이후의 절이 불완전하다.

■ 목적격

I know [you did something]

⇒ I know [you did what] (something을 모를 경우 ⇒ what으로 바뀐다)

⇒ I know what [you did ___] (what이 종속절의 앞으로 나간다.)

what이 빠져나간 종속절의 목적어 자리가 비어 what 이후의 절이 불완전하다.

❸.2 명사절 접속사 이후가 완벽한 문장

다음의 명사절 접속사가 쓰일 때는 명사절 접속사 이후의 문장이 완벽하다.

what / who,

관계부사	when, where, why, how + [S + V + (O)]
그 외	that, whether, if + [S + V + (O)]

· **관계부사는 문중의 부사가 변하여 절의 앞으로 옮겨간 것으로, 접속사 역할을 한다.**

Hellen asked me when ***I started studying English*** _______.

when **이하가 완벽한 문장**

Tip · when은 yesterday 등 문장에 부가적인 시간부사가 변한 것으로 문장의 문법성에 영향을 주지 않는다.

· that, whether, if **는 이동된 것이 아니므로 빠져나간 자리가 없다.**

I don't know whether ***you like coffee or tea.***

whether **이하가 완벽한 문장**

❸.3 명사절의 위치

명사가 주어, 목적어, 보어의 위치에 올 수 있듯이 명사절도 주어, 목적어, 보어의 위치에 올 수 있다.

What Scott could not do was go to Jane's party. **[주어]**

They describe ***what people actually say.*** **[동사의 목적어]**

It doesn't tell us anything about ***what the student is studying.*** **[전치사의 목적어]**

Seward's Folly is ***what people called Alaska.*** **[보어]**

Hackers Practice | 연습문제 |

주어진 문장의 주어에 원을 그리고 동사에는 밑줄을 그으시오.

1 That rent control laws inhibit landlords from repairing properties is unfortunate, but true.

2 Sophia realized that the experience caused her to see her world differently.

3 How glass is blown in a cylinder was demonstrated at the Stuart Crystal factory.

4 A top architect lamented that culture uniqueness had been replaced by international sameness.

5 Why consumers hesitated to buy the controversial digital audiotape players is a subject the article ignored.

6 Whom the late Dr. Bishopstone left his fortune to will be revealed this afternoon.

7 Richards claimed that the documents were taken from archives in Portugal.

8 Recent scientific studies show that off-road vehicles can cause damage to desert landscapes.

9 What they found when they got there was very disappointing.

10 He knew that the Federal forces held more than a modest advantage in terms of men and supplies.

11 Whatever came out has been beautiful to me.

12 Several pieces of musical notation are extant, but no one today knows exactly how they sounded.

■ 정답 p325

Hackers **TEST** | 실전문제 |

1 Luther showed __________ in a public demonstration of defiance.

Ⓐ how little he cared by burning the excommunication
Ⓑ what little he cared by burning the excommunication
Ⓒ how he cared by burning the excommunication little
Ⓓ which little he cared by burning the excommunication

2 Since Muhammad died rather suddenly, his community had no clear instrument on __________ his successor should be chosen.

Ⓐ whom
Ⓑ what
Ⓒ who
Ⓓ how

3 American architecture began as imitation of __________ the early settlers were familiar with in their home countries.

Ⓐ when
Ⓑ which
Ⓒ what
Ⓓ where

4 Kulha can picture ______________ can keep a woman friend and me occupied for three hours over a single pot of coffee.

Ⓐ that
Ⓑ what
Ⓒ which
Ⓓ this

5 Adams was also afraid __________ modern machines would become the masters rather than the servants of people.

Ⓐ that
Ⓑ what
Ⓒ which
Ⓓ whose

6 Jullie wrote about the principle of peacefully resisting __________ to be immoral acts of government.

Ⓐ which a person judges
Ⓑ what a person judges
Ⓒ where a person judges
Ⓓ a person judges

7 We form an idea of __________ others want and expect and how they react to us.

Ⓐ the
Ⓑ what
Ⓒ which
Ⓓ that

8 No one seemed exactly sure __________ the boundaries of the new states should be drawn.

Ⓐ what
Ⓑ which
Ⓒ whom
Ⓓ how

9 As we grow, we learn to know __________ we are like by seeing ourselves in others.

Ⓐ that
Ⓑ what
Ⓒ which
Ⓓ this

10 The New England colonists found __________ a new construction technique was needed to keep out the cold winter winds.

Ⓐ what
Ⓑ whose
Ⓒ whether
Ⓓ that

11 Domestication means __________ can be brought under human control to provide a dependable source of food.

Ⓐ what plants with wild ancestry
Ⓑ whether plants with wild ancestry are
Ⓒ that plants with wild ancestry
Ⓓ how plants with wild ancestry

■ 정답 p325

4 What/That

Outline

이번 장에서는 전 장에서 공부한 명사절 중 what과 that에 관하여 집중적으로 공부한다. what과 that의 문법적 차이는 what 이후에는 불완전한 문장이 오는데 반하여 that 이후에는 완전한 문장이 온다는 것이다.
즉 what 이후에는 주어, 목적어, 보어 등이 실종된 불완전한 문장이 따라오지만 , that 이후에는 완전한 문장이 온다.

- what과 that 이하의 절의 구조 파악하기!
- what과 that이 이끄는 명사절의 특징을 구별하기!

Hackers Grammar

❹.1 What

명사절을 이끄는 what은 명사절 내의 주어, 목적어, 보어가 절 앞으로 빠져 나왔으므로 what 이후는 주어, 목적어, 보어 중의 한 자리가 비어 있다.

I knew what [___ killed the elephant][what**이후에 주어가 비어서 불완전하므로 정문**]
I knew what [John killed _____][what**이후에 목적어가 비어서 불완전하므로 정문**]

Tip · 형용사 what : what은 명사 앞에 위치하여 '무슨~' 뜻으로 형용사 역할을 하기도 한다.

❹.2 That

명사절을 이끄는 that이후는 완벽한 문장이 온다.

I knew that [the mouse killed the elephant]. **[that이후의 절이 완전하므로 정문]**

That은 명사절을 이끄는 명사절 접속사이고, 관계대명사와 동격 역할을 하기도 한다. 관계대명사와 동격의 역할에 대한 설명은 다른 chapter에서 하기로 한다.

Nutritionists have found _______ not in favor of using vitamin C to prevent the common cold.

Ⓐ what medical authorities are
Ⓑ of which medical authorities
Ⓒ that medical authorities are
Ⓓ whose medical authorities

Tip · found의 목적이가 있어야 한다. 목지절 중 Ⓐ는 what 이후의 절이 완전하여 정답이 아니다. Ⓒ의 that이후는 완전하여 Ⓒ가 답이다.

Hackers Skill

명사절접속사 **what**과 **that**의 선택은 **what/that**이후가 완전하면 **that**이다.

Hackers **Practice** | 연습문제 |

다음 문장에 틀린 부분이 있으면 올바르게 고치시오.

1 That John killed was an elephant.

2 Everyone was surprised at what he brought for the picnic.

3 The General Court named the college after the minister in appreciation for what he had done.

4 Carver's first step was to analyze plant parts to find out that they were made of.

5 Hemingway believed that the strength of a story was in that lay beneath its surface.

6 Books or scrolls became cheap enough that they spread all over China.

7 When he recognized what he would not recover, he requested to review his soldiers a last time.

8 The need to keep occupation forces in place all over East Asia meant what Japanese armies were spread very thin.

9 Government officials, alarmed at what the Soviet Union might do, declared martial law.

10 In the United States and Great Britain there was an expectation what the governments of East Europe would be freely elected.

11 That once was a stream of refugees became a river and threatened the East German economy.

■ 정답 p326

Hackers TEST | 실전문제 |

1 Even at the early stage, many believed ________ king Oliver, the star of the band.

Ⓐ that he could outperform
Ⓑ what he could outperform
Ⓒ that could outperform
Ⓓ which could outperform

2 Harriet Tubman knew ________ given to children to keep them from crying.

Ⓐ that drugs could be
Ⓑ whom drugs could be
Ⓒ that what the drugs could be
Ⓓ that could be

3 Williams met a Forty-niner who said that ________ was tough trousers to replace the badly torn ones that he was wearing.

Ⓐ he needed
Ⓑ to need what
Ⓒ what he needed
Ⓓ so he needed

4 Sociologists claim that given our options and our preferences, we choose to do ________ will be most rewarding.

Ⓐ that we expect
Ⓑ we expect
Ⓒ what we expect
Ⓓ expecting

5 Architects would buy sculptures already done or show sketches of ________.

Ⓐ what they wanted carved
Ⓑ that they wanted carved
Ⓒ what did they want carved
Ⓓ which they wanted carved

6 Some disapproved of __________ Clinton's meddling in other people's affairs.

Ⓐ that they considered
Ⓑ so that they considered
Ⓒ which they considered
Ⓓ what they considered

---

7 It claims ________ society as a whole would benefit if every person were allowed to develop his or her abilities fully.

Ⓐ what
Ⓑ if
Ⓒ so that
Ⓓ that

---

8 Anthony was amazed in the first place _______ Greg was attracted to me.

Ⓐ whether
Ⓑ if
Ⓒ that
Ⓓ what

---

9 The monetary overinvestment theory seemingly argues __________ must lead first to over investment and then to breakdown.

Ⓐ which expand every credit
Ⓑ what every credit expansion
Ⓒ every credit was expanded
Ⓓ that every credit expansion

---

10 The fact _______ a bookworm and always got good marks didn't help.

Ⓐ which was
Ⓑ what Harriet was
Ⓒ was
Ⓓ that Harriet was

■ 정답 p326

부사절 축약

Outline

부사절 축약이란 부사절 접속사와 주어를 생략하고 동사를 축약시켜
시간 · 양보 · 조건 · 이유 · 연속동작 등을 표현한다.
단, 접속사를 복원할 수 있을 때는 접속사 생략이 가능하다.

문제의 유형은 접속사가 생략된 후 부사절의 주어와 주절의 주어를 일치시키기, 축약된 동사 찾기, 축약절을 보고 알맞은 주어의 선택 등이 출제된다.

- 도표와 예를 통해 축약 과정을 익히기!
- 축약절을 원상복귀 시키는 훈련을 통하여 생략된 주어 복원하기!

Hackers Grammar

⑤.1 부사절의 축약과정

	일반동사		일반동사 + ~ing
	be 동사 + p.p.		p.p.
접속사 + 주어 +	be 동사 + ~ing	⇒ (접속사) + (주어)	~ing
	be 동사 + 형용사		(being) 형용사
	be 동사 + 전치사구		전치사구

· 접속사 생략 가능 : 생략해도 의미가 명확할 때
· 주절의 주어와 동일할 때 부사절 주어 생략
· 부사절의 시제가 주절보다 시제가 선행할 때는 완료분사 「having + p.p.」 사용
· 'while(접속사) + 주어 + be동사 + 명사(보어)' 는 'while +명사' 로 축약이 가능하다.

When Joan was released from captivity, he went into exile in Great Britain.

① 접속사(when) 생략(접속사를 복원할 수 있을 때는 접속사 생략이 가능하다.)

② 주절과 동일 주어(he = Joan) 생략

③ be동사(was) 생략

⇒ ***Released from captivity,*** Joan went into exile in Great Britain.

After Jonas Salk developed the polio vaccine, he retired.

① 접속사 생략시, 그 접속사를 복원할 수 없을 때는 접속사를 생략하지 않는다.

② 동일주어(he = Jonas Salk) 생략

③ 일반동사 → 일반동사 + ~ing (developing)

⇒ ***After developing the polio vaccine,*** Jonas Salk retired.

Hackers Skill

축약 부사절 문제는 원상복귀 시켜서 풀어라.

Hackers **Practice** | 연습문제 |

밑줄 친 부분을 축약 하세요.

1 When he was only in elementary school, James displayed artistic talent.

→

2 While he was an extraordinary pitcher, Babe was also developing a reputation as a powerful left-handed hitter.

→

3 A frame made of limbs or large animal bones provided a structure when it was covered with hides.

→

4 After he finished campaigning in France, Henry landed at Waterford in A.D. 1171 to prevent Strongbow from establishing an independent position on the island.

→

5 Religious enthusiasm, when it is out of control, can become a dangerous thing.

→

6 The Jains, although they are not numerous, are still a part of the religious mosaic of modern India.

→

7 One story has it that Babe pointed to a spot in center field before he hit his powerful homer.

→

8 Janet was promoted to anchor, the most important position on the news team, while she was still a senior.

→

9 When she was still in high school, Oprah got a part-time job reading news on the radio.

→

10 After he recognized the value of the Museum, Ptolemy ordered construction of a great library.

→

■ 정답 p326

Hackers **TEST** | 실전문제 |

1 _________ of failure, some children become truants and get into trouble.

Ⓐ To be afraid
Ⓑ Been afraid
Ⓒ Being afraid
Ⓓ They are afraid

2 According to a myth, _________, the Aztecs received a message from their god.

Ⓐ searched for a place to settle
Ⓑ while searching for a place to settle
Ⓒ as though being searched for a place to settle
Ⓓ settled a place for searching

3 Isolated by two oceans from the rest of humanity, _________ of America developed their own unique cultures for thousands of years.

Ⓐ with the Indian populations
Ⓑ and the Indian populations
Ⓒ the Indian populations
Ⓓ have been uncovered by the Indian populations

4 _________, Indians did not receive communion or enter the priesthood.

Ⓐ They were baptized
Ⓑ Where they were baptized
Ⓒ Because of baptizing
Ⓓ Although baptized

5 For decades the Soviet Union poured money into Cuba _________ its sugar in partial payment.

Ⓐ when received
Ⓑ received
Ⓒ to be receiving
Ⓓ while receiving

6 After reading about the Iditarod race in a magazine, ________ to Alaska.

Ⓐ which Susan moved
Ⓑ Susan moved
Ⓒ moving with Susan
Ⓓ Susan's biography made people move

7 In 1984, ______, Susan Butcher continued the race and came in second.

Ⓐ when have fallen into freezing cold water
Ⓑ fell into freezing cold water
Ⓒ even after falling into freezing cold water
Ⓓ she fell into freezing cold water

8 __________, Oprah was offered a job as a news broadcaster at a local television station.

Ⓐ Because been still in college Ⓑ She was still in college
Ⓒ Been still in college Ⓓ While still in college

9 ________ no longer worked, the US government sold the right to collect state revenues to Genoese bankers.

Ⓐ It was debasing the coinage
Ⓑ When debased the coinage
Ⓒ Although was debasing the coinage
Ⓓ When debasing the coinage

10 Although once the leading country, __________ powerless to resist becoming a center of foreign intrigue.

Ⓐ then Ⓑ Spanish were
Ⓒ which were Spanish Ⓓ Spain was

11 __________, the chiefs of Medina's tribes delegated their ambassadors to invite him to their city.

Ⓐ Because have learned of Muhammad
Ⓑ Learned of Muhammad
Ⓒ Having learned of Muhammad
Ⓓ After learned of Muhammad

■ 정답 p327

형용사절(관계대명사)축약

Outline

관계대명사 축약절은 주격 관계대명사를 생략하고 관계절의 동사를 축약시켜 선행사를 수식하는 형용사구를 만드는 것이다.

주어와 일치시켜 축약된 동사 형태를 고르는 문제와 축약된 동사형태를 보고 알맞은 주어를 찾는 문제가 출제된다.

- 도표와 예를 통해 축약 과정 익히기!
- 축약된 절을 다시 원상복구 시키는 훈련하기!

Hackers Grammar

형용사절의 축약과정

주격 관계대명사	+	일반동사	⇒ 관계대명사 생략	동사의 ~ing
		be 동사 + ~ing		~ing
		be 동사 + p.p.		p.p.
		be 동사 + 전치사구		전치사구

ex The homework ***which is given*** to freshmen is difficult.

① 관계대명사 which 생략

② be동사 생략

③ 과거분사 그대로 사용

⇒ The homework ***given*** to freshmen is difficult.

ex There were researchers ***who studied*** many flowers.

① 관계대명사 who 생략

② 일반동사 (study)에 ing 붙임

⇒ There were researchers ***studying*** many flowers.

ex Christmas Island, ***which was discovered by James Cook,*** was once populated by many bird species.

① 관계대명사 which 생략

② be동사 생략

③ 과거분사 그대로 사용

⇒ Christmas Island, ***discovered by James Cook,*** was once populated by many bird species.

④ 축약절의 강조를 위해 축약후 문두로 이동 가능

⇒ ***Discovered by James Cook,*** Christmas Island was once populated many bird species.

ex Scree, which abounds in the Rocky Mountains, has its origins in the ice ages.

① 주격관계대명사 which 생략

② 일반동사에 ~ing붙임

⇒ Scree, ***abounding in the Rocky Mountains,*** has its origins in the ice ages.

③ 축약절의 강조를 위해 축약 후 문두로 이동 가능

⇒ ***Abounding in the Rocky Mountains,*** Scree has its origins in the ice ages.

Hackers **Practice** | 연습문제 |

다음 밑줄 부분의 축약된 문장을 Who, Which, or That을 사용하여 원상복귀 시키시오.

1 Wooden shelves <u>along the wall</u> were used as beds.

→

2 Robert Stroud was stupid, including his cell mate <u>taking some correspondence courses</u>.

→

3 A peddler <u>named Adam Gimbel</u> set up a store <u>called Gimbel Brothers</u>.

→

4 Some of the farmers, <u>having no cash</u>, would bring produce to barter for their purchases.

→

5 Many immigrants <u>from northern and western Europe</u> settled on farms in the Middle West.

→

6 In 1848 a settler <u>in remote, undeveloped California</u> discovered gold near Sacramento.

→

7 A reward is something <u>given to honor merit, service, or achievement</u>.

→

8 A remarkable leader <u>in this operation</u> was Harriet Tubman, herself a runaway slave.

→

9 In the middle years of this century Jonathan became the inspiration of many people <u>dissatisfied with the machine age and with modern ways of life</u>.

→

10 Millions of sweat glands in the human skin provide an excellent cooling system for people <u>doing hard work in hot climates.</u>

→

■ 정답 p327

Hackers TEST | 실전문제 |

1 The Spanish soldiers, ________, no longer frightened the rest of Europe.

Ⓐ who poorly paid and seldom on time
Ⓑ had poorly paid and seldom on time
Ⓒ they were poorly paid and seldom on time
Ⓓ poorly paid and seldom on time

2 Troubled by problems in his native France, ________ in the Netherlands.

Ⓐ Descartes' leaving the country was to make his home
Ⓑ the country was left by Descartes to make his home
Ⓒ Descartes left the country to make his home
Ⓓ and to make his home Descartes left the country

3 The ancient Greeks, __________, left the world magnificent works of art and architecture.

Ⓐ to have a great sense of beauty
Ⓑ had a great sense of beauty
Ⓒ being had a great sense of beauty
Ⓓ having had a great sense of beauty

4 ______, Belgrade was the key to any further advance into central Europe.

Ⓐ Although locating where the Danube and Sava Rivers meet
Ⓑ To be located where the Danube and Sava Rivers meet
Ⓒ Located where the Danube and Sava Rivers meet
Ⓓ The Danube and Sava Rivers are located where

5 ___________, Francis retracted his promises and sought allies among the Italian city states and the pope.

Ⓐ To be releasing from prison and safely back in Paris
Ⓑ Releasing from prison and safely back in Paris
Ⓒ They were released from prison and safely back in Paris
Ⓓ Released from prison and safely back in Paris

6 The huge building, _______ almost a thousand years, is partially hollowed out of the cliff and structured of adobe, a sun-baked clay.

Ⓐ dated back
Ⓑ being dating
Ⓒ to date back
Ⓓ dating back

---

7 Groundwater, ___________ under the earth's surface, is a major source of mankind's usable water.

Ⓐ finding everywhere
Ⓑ which found everywhere
Ⓒ found everywhere
Ⓓ for finding everywhere

---

8 The horse, __________ in the early 16th century, was quickly adopted by the Indians.

Ⓐ importing the Spanish
Ⓑ the Spanish
Ⓒ imported by the Spanish
Ⓓ which imported by the Spanish

---

9 An ancient legend, ____________ by archeological findings, says that the Chinese people settled along the Yellow River many centuries ago.

Ⓐ because confirmed Ⓑ confirming
Ⓒ to confirm Ⓓ confirmed

■ 정답 p327

7 동격

Outline

· 명사구 동격은 선행사를 수식하는 관계절이 축약된 후 명사가 남아 선행사와 동격이 된 것이다.
· 동격명사는 문두, 문중, 문미에서 주어, 목적어, 보어 등의 동격이 된다.
· 동격에는 명사구 동격, to 부정사 동격, that절 동격이 있다.
이 과에서는 명사의 동격만을 다룬다. to 부정사 동격과 that절 동격은 관련 과에서 다루기로 한다.

Hackers Grammar

Europa, ***which is one of Jupiter's moons,*** is the place where enormous quantities of water are known to exist.

■ 문중 동격 → Europa, ***one of Jupiter's moons,*** is the place where enormous quantities of water are known to exist.

[관계대명사 축약 (관계대명사 + be 동사 생략)]

■ 문두 동격 → ***One of Jupiter's moons,*** Europa is the place where enormous quantities of water are known to exist.

[관계절이 축약된 동격이 문두로 이동]

A weak attractive force organizes oxygen and hydrogen atoms into a frozen molecular crystal, ***which is a perfectly organized lattice of molecules.***

■ 문미 동격 → A weak attractive force organizes oxygen and hydrogen atoms into a frozen molecular crystal, ***a perfectly organized lattice of molecules.*** [관계절 축약]

Hackers **Practice** | 연습문제 |

다음 문장에서 밑줄 친 부분을 관계절은 동격으로 축약시키고, 동격은 관계절로 원상복귀 시키시오.

1 The French physicist, Joseph Nicephore Niepce, made the first negative on paper in 1816 and the first known photograph on metal in 1827.

2 Bats produce sounds with the larynx, which is an organ in the throat that has undergone certain adaptations that make it unusually effective in producing high-frequency sounds.

3 Vinegar, a dilute solution of acetic acid, is an example of a weak acid.

4 Women such as the German-born Anne Heinel, the first female dancer to do double pirouettes, were also gaining in technical proficiency.

5 Two properties of water, which are cohesion and adhesion, are particularly important in the transport of water and dissolved minerals in plants.

6 Nelson Mandela, South Africa's First black president, remains a staunch advocate for human rights.

7 The best remaining work, which is especially the intricate sculptures over the doors of a church, is found at Vezelay.

8 In July 1187 Salahal-Din crushed a party of knights at Hittin, capturing Guy, who was the king of Jerusalem.

9 Feldspar, which is a common family of minerals in granite, is changed into clays.

10 Below the crust is the mantle, which is a dense, hot layer of semi-solid rock approximately 2,900 km thick.

■ 정답 p328

Hackers **TEST** | 실전문제 |

1 They believe that the United States, ________, would benefit by retaining aspects of its many cultural backgrounds.

Ⓐ because a land of immigrants
Ⓑ a land of immigrants
Ⓒ which a land of immigrants
Ⓓ it was a land of immigrants

2 After Louis's death the Habsburg Ferdinand of Austria became king of Royal Hungary, ________.

Ⓐ which a narrow corridor of lands bordering Austria
Ⓑ a narrow corridor of lands was bordered by Austria
Ⓒ it bordered a narrow corridor of lands Austria
Ⓓ a narrow corridor of lands bordering Austria

3 Today well over a thousand Christian churches exist, ________, its founder.

Ⓐ each had claimed to speak in the name of Jesus of Nazareth
Ⓑ because each claimed for speaking in the name of Jesus of Nazareth
Ⓒ each claiming to speak in the name of Jesus of Nazareth
Ⓓ of each claiming to speak in the name of Jesus of Nazareth

4 In 1521 Francis first invaded northern Spain and then sent an army into Italy against the duchy of Milan, ________.

Ⓐ Charles claimed a territory as Habsburg land
Ⓑ for a territory Charles claiming Habsburg land
Ⓒ while claimed a territory as Habsburg land
Ⓓ a territory Charles claimed as Habsburg land

5 In 1500 Aztec Indians' empire covered a distance that extended from the Atlantic to the Pacific and held up to 20,000,000 people, ________.

Ⓐ for one of the world's densest populations
Ⓑ because of one of the world's densest populations
Ⓒ the world's densest populated
Ⓓ one of the world's densest populations

---

6 In England, William Laud, ________ and later archbishop of Canterbury, was recognized as the leading Anglican churchman of the age.

Ⓐ was bishop of London
Ⓑ bishop of London
Ⓒ who bishop of London
Ⓓ when was bishop of London

---

7 Robert Bellarmine, ________, and the church historian Cesare Baronio represented Catholic scholarship.

Ⓐ who a Jesuit cardinal theologian
Ⓑ to a Jesuit cardinal theologian
Ⓒ which to be a Jesuit cardinal theologian
Ⓓ a Jesuit cardinal theologian

---

8 Francesco Morosini, ________, landed an army in the Peloponnesus and soon brought the whole peninsula under his control.

Ⓐ is an able Venetian general
Ⓑ an able Venetian general
Ⓒ who an able Venetian general
Ⓓ because an able Venetian general

---

9 In 1713 the Asiento, ________in the treaty ending the War of Spanish Succession, gave the British the right to sell slaves in the Spanish colonies of the Americas.

Ⓐ which a provision　　Ⓑ which being a provision
Ⓒ a provision　　Ⓓ is a provision

■ 정답 p328

8 명사 + to부정사/that절

Outline

다음과 같은 경우, 명사 뒤에 to 부정사나 that절을 수반할 수 있다.

- 동격관계를 나타내는 to 부정사나 that절!
- 서수, 최상급 등을 포함한 선행사 뒤에 to 부정사나 that절!

문제의 유형은 to 부정사와 that절을 수반하는 명사 뒤의 빈 칸에서 to 부정사나 that절을 고르는 문제가 출제된다.

- to 부정사와 that절이 쓰이는 경우를 익히기!
- to 부정사와 that절을 취하는 명사 익히기!

Hackers Grammar

8.1 명사 + to 부정사

· '명사 +to 부정사'에서 to 부정사는 목적, 의무, 필요, 무연 설명(농 부)을 나타내는 역할을 한다.

– We arranged a meeting ***to discuss*** the proposed recreation center.(목적)

– I have packages ***to send.***(의무)

(1) 동격 to부정사의 수식을 받는 명사 (이 명사들의 동사형 혹은 형용사형이 to 부정사를 취함)

ability (←be able to)	attempt (←attempt to)	desire (←desire to)
failure (←fail to)	need (←need to)	willingness (←be willing to)

Chimpanzees gained the ***ability to communicate*** with people.(동격)

(2) 기타 to 부정사의 수식을 받는 명사

inability	unwillingness	chance	opportunity	capacity	effort

Lincoln didn't think he had a ***chance to be reelected.***

(3) 서수, 최상급, 그리고 'next', 'last', 'only'를 포함한 명사

He was ***the first*** man ***to be elected*** to the student council.

Mrs. Holmes was ***the oldest*** person ***to attend.***

The only person ***to listen*** to me was James.

Tip · to~ 이하는 that절로 바꿀 수도 있다.
ex. He was the first man ***that was elected to the student council.***

❽.2 명사 + 동격 that절

· '명사 + that절'에서 that절의 수식을 받는 명사들은 충고, 희망을 나타낸다.

(1) 동사형이 목적어를 that절로 받는 명사

advice (←advise that)	agreement (←agree that)	belief (←believe that)
claim (←claim that)	conclusion (←conclude that)	decision (←decide that)
feeling (←feel that)	hope (←hope that)	promise (←promise that)
threat (←threat that)	warning (←warn that)	doubt (←doubt that)

It is my firm ***belief that*** mental disorders have supernatural engines.

I had a ***feeling that*** he worked on a canvas with all the force of his violent personality.

(2) 기타 that절을 받을 수 있는 명사

advantage	confidence	concept	effect	evidence	idea	fact
opinion	news	possibility	rumor	impression	view	

I had an ***idea*** that he seldom brought anything to completion.

There is ***evidence*** that market segmentation is fairly universal.

Hackers **Practice** | 연습문제 |

다음 각 문장의 괄호에서 옳은 것을 고르시오.

1 It is often impossible to identify a single characteristic common to all members of a society who claim (to/that/which) belong to a common nation.

2 The teacher had the feeling (to/that/on which) he worked on a canvas with all the force of his violent personality.

3 There is no doubt (to/which/that) he looked upon himself as the victim of injustice.

4 Black holes of course cannot be seen because of the inability of light (that/which/to) escape the star's powerful gravity.

5 The Ottoman Empire was on a similar course, governed by those who lacked the will (that/to/which) strengthen the state.

6 Giddens has been criticized in a number of respects, chiefly for a failure (to/that/which) provide empirical illustration.

7 It also contains the idea (to/which/that) certain freedoms and rights are necessary for the continued well-being of capitalist society.

8 We need (that/to/which) show we can pass good legislation.

9 A talent is a natural aptitude or ability (to/which/that) do something.

10 As a result, there have been attempts (which/to/that) alert the public to these dangers.

■ 정답 p328

Hackers **TEST** | 실전문제 |

1 Mary's tragic life has given authors and playwrights ample opportunity ________ ever since.

Ⓐ expanding on her misfortunes
Ⓑ has expanded on her misfortunes
Ⓒ to expand on her misfortunes
Ⓓ which expands on her misfortunes

2 She realized that there were few chances for independent artists __________ their works.

Ⓐ which exhibit or sell
Ⓑ to exhibit or sell
Ⓒ exhibit or sell
Ⓓ exhibited or sold

3 Carbon has a great ability __________ in chains of varying lengths and configurations.

Ⓐ bonds with other carbon atoms
Ⓑ other carbon atoms bond and
Ⓒ that bonding with other carbon atoms
Ⓓ to bond with other carbon atoms

4 The idea __________ may be destroyed by nuclear weapons has raised questions about the justification of their development and use.

Ⓐ which the world
Ⓑ that the world
Ⓒ is the world
Ⓓ being the world

5 There is no doubt ___________ of road rage exists.

Ⓐ by the phenomenon
Ⓑ to the phenomenon
Ⓒ in which the phenomenon
Ⓓ that the phenomenon

6 The first people ________ the unknown lands west of the Appalachian Mountains were the trappers and traders.

Ⓐ which penetrating
Ⓑ has penetrated
Ⓒ penetrated
Ⓓ to penetrate

---

7 Many colleges and universities have been making special effort ________ more minority students.

Ⓐ to enroll
Ⓑ enrolling
Ⓒ which enrolls
Ⓓ enrolled

---

8 As one process was speeded up, there arose a need ________.

Ⓐ which performs the others faster
Ⓑ performing the others faster
Ⓒ to perform the others faster
Ⓓ performed the others faster

---

9 The fact ________ Kennedy did not have a father added to his lonely feelings.

Ⓐ what
Ⓑ which
Ⓒ whether
Ⓓ that

---

10 The first men and women's capacity ________ was somewhat more restricted.

Ⓐ that speak
Ⓑ speaking
Ⓒ to be spoken
Ⓓ to speak

11 Corinthian-style temples were the latest ________ and had taller columns with capitals that resembled acanthus leaves.

Ⓐ for building
Ⓑ what built
Ⓒ to build
Ⓓ to be built

---

12 The 50-million-year old fossils of an ancient whale found in the Himalayan foothills of Pakistan give strong evidence ____________ descended from a four-legged, land-dwelling animal.

Ⓐ to modern whales are
Ⓑ which was to be modern whales
Ⓒ what the modern whales are
Ⓓ that modern whales are

■ 정답 p328

ch2 Mini TEST | 실전문제 |

1 Two open markets existed for the exchange of goods through barter, _______________.

Ⓐ while the Aztecs had no coinage
Ⓑ having no coinage
Ⓒ for the Aztecs had no coinage
Ⓓ the Aztecs had no coinage

2 In the eighteenth century tensions increased and violent uprisings broke out, joined by Indians _____________.

Ⓐ who grievances were in fact much more serious
Ⓑ which were in fact much more serious
Ⓒ whose were grievances in fact much more serious
Ⓓ whose grievances were in fact much more serious

3 One Buddhist group, ____________, claimed that a savior would appear to drive out their hated rulers.

Ⓐ is the White Lotus Society
Ⓑ which the White Lotus Society
Ⓒ the White Lotus Society
Ⓓ the White Lotus Society was

4 Elizabeth, _______________ of Catholicism, at heart remained an Anglican throughout her half-sister's reign.

Ⓐ outwardly conformed to the restoration
Ⓑ the restoration of conforming outwardly
Ⓒ of being conformed the restoration
Ⓓ while outwardly conforming to the restoration

5 Much of the land is high plateau, such as Bolivia's altiplane or the grassland in Patagonia, ___________.

Ⓐ a region shared between Chile and Argentina
Ⓑ a region sharing between Chile and Argentina
Ⓒ a region was shared between Chile and Argentina
Ⓓ which a region shared between Chile and Argentina

---

6 For most people, _________, yet it is one of the most important decisions.

Ⓐ choosing a career isn't easy
Ⓑ choosing a career which isn't easy
Ⓒ who choose a career which isn't easy
Ⓓ that choosing a career isn't easy

---

7 Although Henry VII discovered little to interest the Tudor monarch, ________ in the Americas.

Ⓐ then Cabot's voyage established an English claim
Ⓑ Cabot's voyage establishing an English claim
Ⓒ Cabot's voyage established an English claim
Ⓓ for Cabot established an English claim

---

8 The buffalo, or American bison, is a large bovine ______________ in huge herds.

Ⓐ which it once roamed the western plains
Ⓑ which once roamed the western plains
Ⓒ whom it once roamed the western plains
Ⓓ to which once roamed the western plains

---

9 Navarre and Catalonia were poor and isolated in the beginning, hardly a match for Muslim Spain, __________ of western Europe in the ninth and tenth centuries.

Ⓐ that the most prosperous region
Ⓑ to be the more prosperous region
Ⓒ what was the most prosperous region
Ⓓ which was the most prosperous region

10 According to Aztec belief, Huitzilopochtli told them to look for a place where an eagle, ___________, would be perched on a cactus.

Ⓐ held a snake on its back
Ⓑ holding a snake on its back
Ⓒ being held a snake on its back
Ⓓ being a snake on its back

---

11 Lord Byron, ___________ of the English poets, went to Greece to join the rebellion and died there.

Ⓐ who is romantic
Ⓑ more romantic
Ⓒ be the most romantic
Ⓓ the most romantic

---

12 In September 1774 at Philadelphia the First Continental Congress gathered to seek ways to redress ______________ .

Ⓐ that the delegates considered the wrongs
Ⓑ the delegates be considered the wrongs
Ⓒ the delegates were considered the wrongs
Ⓓ what the delegates considered the wrongs

---

13 ___________ was its use of granite to build a palace complex and a solid stone tower.

Ⓐ That made Hyde town so distinctive
Ⓑ What made Hyde town so distinctive
Ⓒ What it made Hyde town so distinctive
Ⓓ Which made Hyde town so distinctive

---

14 Many families, as the Robbinsons learned, find the new method an excellent way ______________ from year to year.

Ⓐ to grow in net worth
Ⓑ to be grown in net worth
Ⓒ which to grow in net worth
Ⓓ what grow in net worth

15 The last people __________ were the Magyars or Hungarians, who made their homes deep inside the steppe land of Ukraine.

Ⓐ that the European community entered
Ⓑ enter the European community
Ⓒ which to enter the European community
Ⓓ to enter the European community

---

16 When the French were gone, Egypt was thrown into chaos, for the local Mamluk nobility had no desire __________ into their country.

Ⓐ that allows Ottoman governors back
Ⓑ allowing Ottoman governors back
Ⓒ to allow Ottoman governors back
Ⓓ allowed Ottoman governors back

---

17 Unfortunately many men who sat on the council had no experience with Spanish America and based their legislation on ______________.

Ⓐ which they knew of European government
Ⓑ what they knew of European government
Ⓒ that knew of European government
Ⓓ European government knew

■ 정답 p329

HACKERS TOEFL

Structure

Construction

TOEFL에서 난이도가 높은 문제로 자주 출제되는 도치, 비교급 어순 문제와 make possible, it vs. there 구문 등에 대해 분석적, 유형별 접근을 통하여 근본적으로 해결하는 것이 이 chapter의 목표이다.

1 도치

Outline

주어·동사 도치는 주어 뒤에 있는 조동사 혹은 동사구가 주어 앞으로 옮겨가는 것을 말한다. 주로 동사의 보어나 혹은 부사구를 강조하기 위해 문두로 옮길 때 도치가 일어난다.

- **도치가 일어날 수 있는 특정 어구를 익히기!**
- **동사구 전체 도치인지 조동사/ be동사를 이용한 도치인지에 따라 바뀌는 문형의 구조 이해하기!**

Hackers Grammar

도치의 종류

동사구 도치	장소/방향/출처 부사구 도치 순서 도치 분사 도치
조동사 /be동사 도치	If 생략시 도치 부정어구 도치 Only 부사구 도치 / Only 부사절 도치 So / Neither / Nor 도치 So + 형용사 도치 As / Than의 선택적 도치

❶.1 동사구 도치

동사구 전체가 주어 앞으로 이동한다.

부사구 도치	동사 뒤의 장소/방향/출처 부사구가 문두로 이동 할 경우 주어와 동사구 도치 → 장소/방향/출처 부사구+동사구+주어 ***Out of John Kenneth Galbraith's The Affluent Society*** came the argument for an increase in public goods. (출처 부사구) ***Here*** is the book that you lent me. (장소 부사구)
순서 도치	순서 부사가 동일 문장 내에서 나열될 경우 주어와 동사구 도치 → Order expression + V + S ***First*** had come the Persians and ***then*** the Muslim Arabs.
보어 도치 **(분사 도치)**	동사의 보어인 형용사 또는 현재분사나 과거분사가 문두로 이동할 경우 주어와 동사구 도치 → 현재분사/과거분사/형용사 + be 동사 + 주어
	The issue of women's suffrage was untouched. → ***Untouched*** was the issue of women's suffrage.
	The novelist Charles Dickens was writing in English. ⇒ ***Writing in English*** was the novelist Charles Dickens.
	The country's impressive population growth is basic to any understanding of China ⇒ ***Basic to any understanding of China*** is the country's impressive population growth.

❶.2 조동사/ be 동사가 도치 될 경우

조동사 도치는 조동사나 be동사가 주어 앞으로 이동한다.

1. 가정법 도치 : 조동사/ be동사만 if 절에서 도치되는 경우

[If + S + were/had/should]에서 if 탈락시 → were/had/should + S

If it had not been for Russian help, the sultan could well have lost his throne.

⇒ ***Had it not been*** for Russian help, the sultan could well have lost his throne.

They risked becoming ritually unclean if people should associate with anyone of a lower one.

⇒ They risked becoming ritually unclean ***should people*** associate with anyone of a lower one.

Structure www.goHackers.com

2. 부정어구 도치 : 동사 뒤의 부정어구가 문두로 이동했을 때 주어 · 동사 도치

부정어 + 조동사/ be동사 + S + V

We have never seen her sing a song.

⇒ ***Never*** have we seen her sing a song.

부정어 + do 조동사 + S + V

I rarely see such polite children.

⇒ ***Rarely*** do I see such polite children.

FOOTNOTE

· 동사구 도치에서 장소 부사구가 문두에 올 때 동사구 전체가 도치되는 것과 달리 조동사 도치에서 부정어가 문두에 나올 때에는 조동사만 도치됨을 주의하라.

· 동사가 be동사 하나이고 부정어가 문두에 나올 경우, S + be동사 ⇒부정어 + be동사 + S이며, 이때 be동사는 조동사로 간주되나, become은 조동사로 간주되지 않는다.

· 원래부터 주어를 수식하는 부정어가 문두에 올 경우는 도치시키지 않는다.

ex. *No* one seems to have an idea.

no, not, never, no sooner, not only, not until, not once, nowhere, barely, hardly, only, rarely, scarcely, seldom, by no means, under no circumstances, etc.

ex. ***Under no circumstances*** should you wait any longer.

ex. ***No sooner*** had we arrived than it began to rain.

3. Not until-부사구 도치 : Not until-부사구가 문두에 오면 not until을 포함한 절에서 주어와 조동사를 도치

Not until 구 + 조동사/ be동사/ do동사 + S + V

Until the 19th century the construction of higher buildings did not become possible.
⇒ ***Not until the 19th century*** did the construction of higher buildings become possible.

Tip · until은 전치사, not이 전치사구인 until the 19th century를 수식

4. Not until-부사절 도치 : Not until-부사절이 문두에 오면 주절의 주어와 조동사를 도치

Not until 부사절 + 조동사/ be동사/ do동사 + S + V

Until he received her letter he did not fully understand the depth of her feelings.
⇒ ***Not until he received her letter*** did he fully understand the depth of her feelings.

Tip · not until-부사절의 경우 until부사절 내에서 도치가 일어나지 않고 주절에서 도치가 일어남에 주의한다.

5. Only-부사구 도치 : Only로 강조되는 부사구가 문두에 왔을 때

Only 부사구 + 조동사/ be동사 + S + V

Only **부사구**	You can learn only by asking questions. ⇒ ***Only by asking questions*** can you learn. The law made Labor Day a legal holiday only in Washington. ⇒ ***Only in Washington*** did the Law make Labor day a legal holiday.

6. Only-부사절 도치 : Only로 강조되는 부사절이 문두에 왔을 때

Only 부사절 + 조동사/ be동사/ do동사 + S + V

Only **부사절**	You should call Mr. Franklin at home only if you have a serious problem. ⇒ ***Only if you have a serious problem*** should you call Mr. Franklin at home. You go on a picnic only if it stops raining. ⇒ ***Only if it stops raining*** do you go on a picnic.

FOOTNOTE
Only+접속사(if, when, because, after, until)로 이끌리는 부사절 뒤에 comma가 없음을 주의하라.

7. So 관련 어구의 도치

So, Neither, Nor + 대동사(do, be) + S

Susan studies at the library, and John studies at the library.
⇒ Susan studies at the library, and ***so*** does John.

Susan isn't studying on Saturday, and John isn't studying on Saturday.
⇒ Susan isn't studying on Saturday, and ***neither*** is John.

8. So + 형용사 도치

So + 형용사 + 조동사/be 동사 + 주어 + 동사 (+ that절)

She looked so ridiculous that everybody burst out laughing.
⇒ ***So ridiculous*** did she look that everybody burst out laughing.

Hair styling in Assyria was so important.
⇒ ***So important*** was hair styling in Assyria.

9. As, Than 절에서의 선택적 도치

My brother spends more time in the library ***than John does.***
⇒ My brother spends more time in the library ***than does John.***

She was very religious, ***as most of her friends were.***
⇒ She was very religious, ***as were most of her friends.***

FOOTNOTE
as와 than 뒤의 동사는 주절의 동사가 일반동사일 경우 do를, be동사일 경우는 be동사를 사용하고, 조동사를 사용했을 경우에는 그 조동사를 사용한다.

❶.3 도치가 필요하지 않은 구문

부사구, 주절 (S + V)

Only at the Wild Park, people can see emus. (can people은 틀림)

Tip · 장소부사가 문두에 이동해도 장소 부사 뒤에 comma가 있으므로 주어 · 동사를 도치시키지 않는다.

Hackers **Practice** | 연습문제 |

다음 도치구문이 맞으면 (C)를, 틀리면 (I)를 쓰고 틀린부분을 고치시오.

1 _____ Only if is the law changed will proper labeling be essential.

2 _______ Not only do the hippo's eating habits keep the water clear, but they prevent the river from overflowing..

3 _____ Not until 1865 when did Joseph Lister try the first antiseptic treatment on a compound fracture.

4 ______ Built into one corner of the Ka'bah was a large black stone considered especially sacred.

5 ______ West of Robina stands the stately Jill home, one of the many mansions surrounded by acres of parks.

6 ______ No longer these protohorses could slip away through thick forest when danger threatened.

7 _____ So isolated was Santa Fe from the U.S. that mail reached the city only once a month from Missouri.

8 _____ Floating on the oceans every year are 9,659 trillion metric tons of ice.

9 _____ Never during the war did the government suffer from inadequate funds or credit.

10 _____ Only at 20 years do the brain achieve full maturity.

11 _____ No longer did people have to worry about letting their fire go out.

12 _____ Adjacent to the gymnasium were bathes and massage rooms.

13 _____ There were housed collections of all previous Mesopotamian literature.

■ 정답 p331

Hackers **TEST** | 실전문제 |

1 No longer ________ he wants to take advantage of her.

Ⓐ she thinks that
Ⓑ does she thinks
Ⓒ to think
Ⓓ does she think

2 Not until the potato was introduced into Ireland ________ for its great food value.

Ⓐ it recognized
Ⓑ recognizing it
Ⓒ was it recognized
Ⓓ to recognize

3 Until recently, only by a complicated test ________ .

Ⓐ chlamydial infections be detected
Ⓑ chlamydial infections could be detected
Ⓒ could chlamydial infections be detected
Ⓓ be chlamydial infections detected

4 By the time the dinosaurs roamed the earth some 180 million years ago, seed-bearing trees had evolved that shed their leaves in winter; ________ the angiosperms and our present deciduous forests.

Ⓐ from these have sprung
Ⓑ have sprung these
Ⓒ to have sprung
Ⓓ these have been sprung

5 Jefferson's reference to the voluntary allegiance of colonists to the crown was struck; also ________ that censured the monarchy for imposing slavery upon America.

Ⓐ was deleted a clause
Ⓑ a clause deleted was
Ⓒ was a clause deleted
Ⓓ deleted was a clause

6 Living on land __________ properly called tortoises, of which there are approximately forty different kinds.

Ⓐ are the land turtles
Ⓑ the land turtles
Ⓒ is the land turtles
Ⓓ it was the land turtles

---

7 "William" is not only a popular name today ______ many famous people in the past.

Ⓐ and also the name of
Ⓑ but also the name of was
Ⓒ also the name of
Ⓓ but also the name of

---

8 Only in households that could afford a seamstress ________.

Ⓐ wives escaped this drudgery
Ⓑ did wives escape this drudgery
Ⓒ were wives escape this drudgery
Ⓓ which escaped this drudgery

---

9 Originally, only in science fiction movies and books _________.

Ⓐ being found as robots
Ⓑ robots were found
Ⓒ were robots found
Ⓓ to be robots

---

10 So successful _________ supervised the work that over 100 temples were built.

Ⓐ the priests
Ⓑ which the priests to be
Ⓒ were the priests who
Ⓓ being the priests

11 Only in the twentieth century __________, for his tomb was found nearly intact.

Ⓐ did he reach fame
Ⓑ he reached fame
Ⓒ to be reached fame
Ⓓ for reaching fame

12 Surrounding a courtyard __________ to meet with friends, cook, eat and store their belongings.

Ⓐ rooms were for the family
Ⓑ which was for the family
Ⓒ they were rooms for the family
Ⓓ were rooms for the family

13 Close by the citadel buildings __________, resembling a swimming pool.

Ⓐ which were large baths
Ⓑ to be large baths
Ⓒ large baths were
Ⓓ were large baths

14 At the center of Kaifeng's life __________.

Ⓐ were the imperial palace
Ⓑ was the imperial palace
Ⓒ that was the imperial palace
Ⓓ being the imperial palace

15 The Germans settled in East Europe followed Luther into the Reformation, __________.

Ⓐ as the Teutonic knights of the Baltic was
Ⓑ the Teutonic knights of the Baltic did
Ⓒ as did the Teutonic knights of the Baltic
Ⓓ as being the Teutonic knights of the Baltic did

■ 정답 p331

2 비교급

Outline

비교급은 두 개의 사람이나 사물의 형용사 · 부사적 성질을 비교하기 위해서 형용사(부사)의 비교급 +than」의 형태를 이용하여 두 개 중 한 쪽이 「··보다 ··한(–하게)」의 뜻을 나타내는 문법이다.

비교급 표현에는 「비교급 + than」이외에 명사비교, 원급비교, 명사동급비교, 이중비교가 있다. 어순문제, 비교급 형태문제, 비교 대상문제, 비교급 강조문제가 출제된다.

- 비교급 각각의 기본형태를 외우기!
- 형용사 · 부사의 비교급 변화형에 대해 연습하기!
- 비교 대상이 무엇인지 파악할 수 있도록 할것!

Hackers Grammar

비교급 구문 · 형태 ·

S + V +(배수부사)+ 형용사·부사의 비교급 **+ than +** 명사/대명사/절

· Jane is ***taller than*** Mary.
· Steel is ten times ***stronger than*** iron rails.

2음절 이하의 단어 ⇒ 형용사· 부사 + er
3음절 이상의 단어 ⇒ more + 형용사· 부사
cf) 열등비교 ⇒ less + 형용사· 부사

FOOTNOTE
단, 2음절 단어 중 –able, –ful, –re, –le, –less, –ous, –ing, –ive로 끝나는 단어는 more를 붙인다.

(1)명사비교(비교하려는 명사의 단수, 복수를 확인한다.)

more + **가산/불가산명사** + than	Mary has ***more free time than*** I do.
fewer + **가산명사** + than	There were ***fewer chairs*** in that room ***than*** there were people.
less + **불가산명사** + than	There is ***less chocolate*** in this cookie ***than*** I like.

(2)원급비교

(배수부사)+ as + **형용사/부사 원급** + as	The girls are (half) ***as old as*** the boys. He did ***as well as*** I had expected.
not + as + **형용사/부사 원급** + as	Cocaine is not ***as effective as*** morphine for stopping pain.

* 원급 비교의 강조

as~as 비교급은 almost/nearly/just/quite가 수식할 수 있다.
이와 관련하여 어순 문제가 출제됨에 유의하라.
「almost/nearly/just/quite + as~as」
「not + almost/nearly/just/quite + as~as」

Pope Julius II prized artists ***almost as*** much ***as*** military victories.

(3) 동급비교의 표현

S + V + the same + (명사) + as + 명사/대명사/절

The mountain has almost ***the same*** height ***as*** the Everest.

동급 비교의 유사 표현—the same as, similar to, different from

Brazil has about ***the same*** amount of coal ***as*** Norway.
Synthesizing a molecular crystal is ***similar to*** designing a building.
Scientists have discovered a spider which is remarkably ***different from*** any other known spider.

More about "the same as" the same은 **보어처럼 쓰일 수 있다.**

the same as + **명사 상당어구, 형용사절**

the same (as) **앞에** almost/just/nearly/much/quite**가 올 수 있다.**

(4) 명사 동급 비교

S + V + **(배수부사)** + as + many/few + **가산명사** + as + **명사/대명사/절**

We read (three times) ***as many*** books ***as*** we did when we were children.

S + V + **(배수부사)** + as + much/little + **불가산명사** + as + **명사/대명사/절**

The shoes cost ***as much*** money ***as*** pants.

(5) 이중 비교(비교급 짝짓기)

The 비교급 **+** 구문**1, the** 비교급 **+** 구문**2 (**구문**1**과 구문**2**는 동일구문**)**

- ***The more*** knowledge we acquire, ***the less*** wisdom we seem to have.
- ***The more*** worldly pleasure we enjoy, ***the less*** satisfied and contented we are with life.

Tip · 구문 1과 구문 2에서 be동사는 종종 생략되기도 한다.

(6) 비교급 강조– much/far + 비교급 [어순주의]

- My girl friend is ***much/far older than*** I.
- Chinese is ***much/far more difficult than*** Japanese.
- There are ***much/far more beautiful parks*** in the town center.

Hackers Skill 1

as ~ as 사이에 형용사인지 부사인지를 선택하기 위해서는 양쪽에 as를 모두 걷어내고 구조를 파악하라.

Hackers Skill 2

배수부사나 비교급 강조어는 비교급의 앞에 위치하는 어순임에 주의하라.

Hackers **Practice** | 연습문제 |

다음 문장에서 틀린 부분이 있으면 (I) 를, 옳은 문장이면 (C)를 쓰시오.

1 _____ The origins of this music are as interesting as the music itself.

2 _____ It is more a mansion to a house.

3 _____ Judy owes me more than any other person.

4 _____ Scott puts a little more life into it than you usually do.

5 _____ That' s twenty-five hundred least than you're offering.

6 _____ The footage is very similar than Vietnam footage.

7 _____ We have more people down here which wc can handle.

8 _______ It is far less complicated than the Earth, one of the Sun's most trivial members.

9 _____ The more thoroughly scientists investigate the universe, the more clearly its simplicity shines through.

10 _______ The pursuit of wisdom was as more important as physical fitness and social prestige.

11 ______ Scenes of farming, more than any other subjects, are pictured on tomb walls.

■ 정답 p332

Hackers TEST | 실전문제 |

1 The U.S. Department of the Interior has put ________ on the endangered species list.

Ⓐ no fewer 109 species
Ⓑ 109 species no fewer than
Ⓒ than no fewer 109 species
Ⓓ no fewer than 109 species

2 The greater the experience, __________.

Ⓐ there is the salary
Ⓑ the salary is the higher
Ⓒ the salary it is
Ⓓ the higher the salary

3 There has never been an adult scientist who has been _______ any child between the ages of four months and four years.

Ⓐ as half curious as
Ⓑ half as curious as
Ⓒ as half as curious
Ⓓ curious as half as

4 The peoples of North Africa found themselves in _______ south of the Sahara.

Ⓐ much same position as those
Ⓑ the much same position as
Ⓒ much the same position as those
Ⓓ the same position much as those

5 The women had ________ in the community as the men, and there was no radical discrimination.

Ⓐ more power and respect
Ⓑ less power and respect
Ⓒ much more power and respect
Ⓓ as much power and respect

---

6 The object is to knock ________.

Ⓐ many as marbles out of the circle as possible
Ⓑ as many as marbles out of the circle possible
Ⓒ as many marbles out of the circle as possible
Ⓓ many marbles as out of the circle as possible

---

7 Changes in housing prices have ________ a drought that raises the cost of vegetables.

Ⓐ a far great impact than on the CPI
Ⓑ far great impact on the CPI than
Ⓒ a far greater impact on the CPI than
Ⓓ far greater impact on the CPI as

---

8 On the whole, galaxies are scarcely ________ than the stars that compose them.

Ⓐ more complicated
Ⓑ complicated
Ⓒ to be complicated
Ⓓ complicateder

---

9 It is now shown that the human papilloma virus responsible for the common venereal warts is ________ than are herpes viruses.

Ⓐ more close tied to cervical cancer
Ⓑ closely tied to cervical cancer
Ⓒ more closely tied to cervical cancer
Ⓓ as closely tied to cervical cancer

10 Between 1900 and 1950 college enrollment multiplied tenfold, and it has grown __________.

Ⓐ very greater since then
Ⓑ the most great since then
Ⓒ the greatest since then
Ⓓ much greater since then

---

11 Once the mighty Nile, a river 4,100 miles long, carried __________ it does today.

Ⓐ a much more great volume of water than
Ⓑ a volume of water much greater
Ⓒ a greater much than volume of water
Ⓓ a much greater volume of water than

---

12 The Songs never had as much territory __________.

Ⓐ as under their command
Ⓑ under their command than the Tangs
Ⓒ more under their command as the Tangs
Ⓓ under their command as the Tangs

---

13 The government deserves to be recalled in such a way because Xuanzong brought __________.

Ⓐ great wealth to the country than ever before
Ⓑ greater wealth to the country as ever before
Ⓒ to be great wealth to the country as ever before
Ⓓ greater wealth to the country than ever before

■ 정답 p332

3 최상급

Outline

최상급은 세 개 이상을 비교해서 「가장 –한(–하게)」을 나타내는 형용사(부사)의 형태이다. 최상급의 형태, 최상급 신호에 따라 최상급 선택, 최상급을 강조하기 위해 사용되는 부사, 그리고 최상급과 관련된 어순 문제들이 출제된다.

- 최상급 신호에 따라 최상급 선택하기!
- 최상급의 한정사 및 강조어의 어순 파악하기!

Hackers Grammar

❸.1 최상급 구문 · 형태 ·

S + **V** + **the** + 최상급 + **of** 복수 or 집합단수 / **in** 집합 or 장소표현 / **that**절

- Mary is ***the prettiest*** of the four sisters.
- Last night's play was ***the most exciting*** in the series.
- The tree is ***the tallest*** that I have ever seen.

2음절 이하의 단어 ⇒ 형용사 · 부사 + est
3음절 이상의 단어 ⇒ most + 형용사 · 부사

FOOTNOTE
단, 2음절 단어 중 –able, –ful, –re, –le, –less, –ous, –ing, –ive로 끝나는 단어는 most를 붙인다.

❸.2 최상급 어순

the + 최상급
소유격

Jonathan is ***the fattest*** kid in the whole third grade.
It was ***his worst*** decision that he would get married to her.

최상급 강조 부사(much/by far) + the + **최상급**
He is ***much the most*** imaginative of them all.

FOOTNOTE

소유격과 the는 함께 나올 수 없다.
ex. ***the Tom's*** youngest child. (X)
the his best friend (X)

단, **'특정명사(the+명사)의 소유격 + 최상급'**의 경우, the는 최상급 구문에 붙는 the 가 아니라 명사(world, planet,man etc)에 붙는 정관사 the 임을 유의해야 한다.
ex. ***the world's*** largest island (O)
the planet's most distinctive feature (O)
the man's oldest car (O)

❸.3 비교급을 이용한 최상급 표현

S + V + **비교급** + than + any other + **단수명사**
California is ***larger than any other state.***

S + V + the **비교급** + of the two : **비교대상 둘 중 우위이므로 최상의 의미**
This painting is ***the more interesting of the two.***

Tip · any other에서 other를 빼면 자신도 포함하여 비교하게 되므로 모순이다.

By the middle of the sixteenth century, the Spanish __________ in Europe.

Ⓐ the most powerful
Ⓑ were the most powerful
Ⓒ to be the most powerful
Ⓓ were more powerful

Tip '부사구 + comma + 주절' 구문이므로 the Spanish이하는 주어와 동사 모두를 갖춘 완벽한 문장이 되어야 한다. 그러므로 Ⓐ, Ⓒ는 동사가 없으므로 제외된다. 뒤에 최상급 신호인 in + 장소명사가 나오므로, 앞에 형용사 최상급이 있는 Ⓑ가 정답이다.

Hackers Skill

of/in/that**이 오면 앞에 최상급이 오게됨을 의심하라.**

Hackers **Practice** | 연습문제 |

다음 문장 중에서 틀린 문장에는 (I) 를, 바른 문장에는 (C)를 쓰시오.

1 ________ A stradivarius violin responds more quickly and easily to the touch than any other violins.

2 _______ She gets the oldest and most valuable one.

3 _______ Winter is the worse season for fires.

4 __________ Philip was probably the more hated man in late sixteenth-century Europe.

5 _______ Thebes, the most important Egyptian city of Upper Egypt, was in ruins after the Assyrians passed through.

6 ________ From kindergarten through college, I was always taller and homelier in any group.

7 _______ Pittsburgh was the greatest steel city of all.

8 ________ The Wishram, Kwakiutl, and Haida, like most Northwest tribes, thrived equally well by gathering catch less challenging than whales or seals.

9 _______ Rogers has also found that dump-fed bears are the stronger and larger in the population.

10 ________ The more interesting architectural phenomenon of the 1970's was the enthusiasm for refurbishing older buildings.

■ 정답 p332

Hackers **TEST** | 실전문제 |

1 Marine life in many other forms - small mammals, shellfish, giant halibut, and sturgeon - was plentiful and ________ all was salmon.

Ⓐ more abundant than
Ⓑ most abundant
Ⓒ most abundant of
Ⓓ the most abundant of

2 The popular work probably was ________ that had yet been made by a Black American artist about the beauty of an African people.

Ⓐ the most forthright statement
Ⓑ the more forthright statement
Ⓒ most forthright statement
Ⓓ the forthrightest statement

3 The battle on March 9, 1862, between the USS Monitor and the CSS Merrimack, officially the CSS Virginia, is one of ________ in world history.

Ⓐ the more revolutionary naval battles
Ⓑ the most revolutionary naval battle
Ⓒ most revolutionary battles naval
Ⓓ the most revolutionary naval battles

4 The term community is ____________ in sociology and is by now largely without specific meaning.

Ⓐ most elusive one
Ⓑ of the most elusive
Ⓒ one of the most elusive
Ⓓ the one of most elusive

5 The great cat had __________ in the Western Hemisphere.

Ⓐ wider distribution of any mammal
Ⓑ the most distribution of any mammal to be
Ⓒ the widest distribution of any mammal
Ⓓ the wide distribution of any mammal was

---

6 __________ was as chief author of the Declaration of Independence, a great statement of human rights and liberties.

Ⓐ Jefferson was outstanding
Ⓑ Jefferson's more outstanding achievement
Ⓒ Jefferson's the most outstanding achievement
Ⓓ Jefferson's most outstanding achievement

---

7 __________ in Rome was the Pantheon, which still stands as a church in the modern city.

Ⓐ Most impressive construction
Ⓑ The more impressive construction
Ⓒ It was the most impressive construction
Ⓓ The most impressive construction

---

8 Among __________ in establishing free public education was the labor union.

Ⓐ most active one
Ⓑ the most active
Ⓒ more active one
Ⓓ the activest

---

9 Andrew Carneige, an exceptionally energetic man, became one of __________ by pioneering in the steel industry.

Ⓐ the world's most rich men
Ⓑ more rich men in the world
Ⓒ the richer men in the world
Ⓓ the world's richest men

10 Later pharaohs ordered the construction of ______________ ever to be constructed, the pyramids of the Giza plateau.

Ⓐ larger stone monuments
Ⓑ it was the largest stone monuments
Ⓒ to be the largest monuments
Ⓓ the largest stone monuments

---

11 The rise of Assyria was ___________ in Mesopotamia.

Ⓐ the more striking evens
Ⓑ the most striking event
Ⓒ being the most striking event
Ⓓ the strikingest event

---

12 He welcomed new ideas and inventions and made Qungan ___________ in eastern Asia.

Ⓐ the beautifulest city
Ⓑ the more beautiful city
Ⓒ it the most beautiful city
Ⓓ the most beautiful city

■ 정답 p332

4 It/There

Outline

It과 There은 주어역할을 하므로 주어동사문제로 출제되는데, 둘다 가주어로 사용되어 서로 혼동을 일으킬 수 있으므로, It과 There를 구분할 수 있는가를 묻는 문제가 출제된다.

가주어 It은 뒤에 있는 to 부정사나 that절을 받는데 사용된다.
반면에 가주어 There은 뒤에 있는 의미상 주어이자 문법상 보어인 명사를 받는데 사용된다.

- It과 There가 각각 쓰이는 곳 파악하기!
- There의 보어로서의 자격!

Hackers Grammar

4.1 It 관련 구문

1. It…to 부정사	It…형용사/부사구/명사구…to 부정사 It was important to be free. It is my plan to book in advance.
2.가주어It… that/wh-절	It…형용사/부사구/명사구…명사절 It doesn't interest me what you think. It is surprising how many unhappy marriages there are. It is clear that she is smart.
3. It…that 강조	It…부사구/명사구 + that/who It was in New Mexico that Georgia O' Keeffe produced her greatest works of art. (부사구 강조) It was John who killed his cat. (주어 강조)
4. take…time…to	It + takes + time phrase + to 부정사 It took her a few years to learn English. It took me months to get to know her.

❹.2 There 관련 구문

there + be동사 + 부정명사구 (Indefinite Noun Phrase)

1. There + be + 부정관사 a/an + 명사
   There was ***a car accident*** yesterday.

2. There + be + (형용사) + 복수명사
   There were ***two students*** in the classroom.

3. There + be + 부정형용사 some/many/no + 명사
   There was ***no student*** in the classroom.
   There were ***many students*** in the theater.

4. There + be + some이나 no등이 포함된 명사 (somebody, something, nothing, nobody, etc.)
   There is ***nothing*** worrying them.

5. There + be + some, many, none 등 명사구를 대신하는 부정대명사
   There were ***some*** in the library.

Tip There 구문에서의 동사 수 일치
- There is(was) + 단수명사 : There was a student in the classroom.
- There are(were) + 복수명사 : There are many books on the shelves.

FOOTNOTE
정명사구(Definite Noun Phrase)는 그 명사구가 지칭하는 것을 문맥상에서 밝혀낼 수 있는 명사구로서, 부정명사구(Indefinite Noun Phrase)와는 달리 there구문이 불가능하다.
- 정명사구의 형태 : the + 명사, 소유격 + 명사, 고유명사, 대명사 등

ex. There is ***the book*** on the desk. (x) (the book-> a book)
There was ***John's book*** under the piano. (x)
There was ***my book*** in the classroom. (x)
There was ***John*** under the chair. (x)
There was ***he*** in the seminar. (x)

Within the smaller areas ________ difficult to maintain many of their customs.

Ⓐ there have
Ⓑ they are
Ⓒ it was
Ⓓ there are

Tip 형용사 difficult와 to maintain이 있으므로 It … to 부정사 구문임을 알 수 있다. 따라서 답은 Ⓒ가 된다.

Hackers **Practice** | 연습문제 |

It 구문이나 There 구문 중 적당한 것을 넣으시오.

1 _______ not difficult to find in these a trace of the influence of African art.

2 _______ easy to see how the specialization of labor increases efficiency.

3 _______ clusters of galaxies.

4 _______ such a thing as "men's talk" or "women's talk".

5 _______ not surprising that each one devours more than one ton of krill daily.

6 _______ no modern edition of her works.

7 _______ 26 million autos and trucks on United States roads.

8 _______ also a great joy to see students developing.

9 _______ at least a grain of truth in this.

10 _______ no positions available.

11 _______ noteworthy that Plato allowed women into the guardian class.

12 _______ no completely adequate explanation for the migration of the Dorians into Greece.

13 _______ the Egyptians who developed the solar calendar, assigning 30 days to 12 months.

■ 정답 p333

Hackers **TEST** | 실전문제 |

1 ________ two strains of the bacterium E. coli, one which is necessary for proper body functioning and one which is a dangerous toxin.

Ⓐ They are
Ⓑ It is
Ⓒ Only
Ⓓ There are

2 By the mid-1980's, ________ that there were between twelve and fifteen million people of Spanish origin here.

Ⓐ estimated
Ⓑ there was estimated
Ⓒ it was estimated
Ⓓ to be estimated

3 ________ Tito's Partisans who deserved the credit.

Ⓐ There was
Ⓑ To be
Ⓒ It had
Ⓓ It was

4 In habitats untouched by human activity ________ a greater balance between the number of species present and the resources available.

Ⓐ there is
Ⓑ it is
Ⓒ to be
Ⓓ are there

5 The reason is that ________ very special conditions to make a fossil and a lot of luck to find one.

Ⓐ taking it
Ⓑ takes it
Ⓒ it takes
Ⓓ to take it

6 Franklin initiated many improvements in the city of Philadelphia, _______ one of the world's first cities to have paved and lighted streets.

Ⓐ making it
Ⓑ it makes
Ⓒ be made it
Ⓓ makes

7 _______ that General Sherman and his army began its famous "march to the sea".

Ⓐ From New York was
Ⓑ To be New York
Ⓒ There was from New York
Ⓓ It was from New York

8 _______ constant irritation over relations with the countries of eastern Europe.

Ⓐ It was
Ⓑ There was
Ⓒ Because they have been
Ⓓ To be

9 In Colorado's Mesa Verde National Park, _______ an impressive structure called the Cliff Palace.

Ⓐ there is
Ⓑ it is
Ⓒ is there
Ⓓ has

10 _______ the great influx of people that built up California and led to its becoming a state of the United States in 1850.

Ⓐ There was
Ⓑ There
Ⓒ To be there
Ⓓ It was

■ 정답 p333

5 Make Possible

Outline

make possible 구문은 자주 출제되는 구문으로 make가 하나의 목적어와 그 목적보어로 possible(다른 형용사가 대신 할 수 있음)을 가지며, 목적어의 종류에 따라 가목적어 it이 삽입되거나 어순이 바뀔 수 있다.

- 목적어로 명사/동명사가 올 때!
- 목적어로 to부정사/that절이 올 때, 가목적어 it 사용!
- 목적어로 앞에 나오는 명사를 받아서 실제 대명사 it이 올 때!
- 목적어가 수동태로 앞으로 나가서 과거분사구문이 될 때!

Hackers Grammar

❺.1 Make + 형용사

· make + 형용사(possible, impossible, easy, difficult, visible...)

'it' 이 안 쓰일 때	· make + 명사목적어 + possible(형용사) The Bessember converter ***made the mass production of steel possible.*** · make + possible(형용사) + 명사목적어 The Bessember converter ***made possible the mass production of steel.***
'it' 이 쓰일 때	· make + it + possible(형용사) + to 부정사 The Bessember converter ***made it possible*** for the steel industry ***to produce more steel than before.*** · make + it + possible(형용사) + that절 The Bessember converter ***made it possible that the steel industry could produce more steel than before.***

The invention of the telegraph made ______ almost instantaneous communication.

Ⓐ it is possible
Ⓑ possible
Ⓒ it possible
Ⓓ possibly

Tip 'made' 뒤에 'it' 이 받을 수 있는 to부정사나 that절이 없으므로 'it' 이 필요없다. 그리고 'made' 의 목적보어로 형용사 'possible' 이 와야하므로 답은 Ⓑ이다.

Hackers Skill

1. make동사가 나오고 선택지에 possible, visible, easy와 같은 형용사가 나오면, make possible 문제임을 유의한다.
2. make possible 구문은 단 한 개의 목적어가 필요하므로 목적어가 몇 개인지 확인해야 한다.
3. It을 포함한 대명사들은 make + possible(형용사) + 대명사의 어순이 불가능하고, make + 대명사 + possible(형용사) 어순이 가능함에 유의한다.
   즉 make possible it 은 불가능하다.
4. It은 뒤에 오는 to부정사구/that절을 받으나, 뒤에 오는 명사구를 받을 수 없음에 주의한다.

Hackers **Practice** | 연습문제 |

다음 문장에서 문법적으로 틀린 부분이 있으면 (I) 를, 틀린 부분이 없으면 (C)를 쓰시오.

1 ______ There has been a series of remarkable genetic advances that have it made possible to cultivate high-yield varieties.

2 ________ Railroad made it the transportation of perishable freight possible.

3 ________ Architects made living as comfortable as possible.

4 ________ The process of de-institutionalization has been made it possible by the improvement in antipsychotic drugs.

5 _______ Kepler made possible for astronomers to predict mathematically the positions of the earth, sun, and planets.

6 _______ Invention of the telescope in the Netherlands about 1608 made possible further discoveries.

7 _______ Space sickness makes it difficult for afflicted astronauts to do their work.

8 ________ Capital inflows will also tend to increase the international value of the dollar, making more difficult to sell U.S. exports.

9 ________ Another factor is the consistency with which significant patterns occur, which makes possible generalizations about distributions.

10 _______ High-speed photography has made it visible certain aspects of motion never seen before.

■ 정답 p334

Hackers TEST | 실전문제 |

1 Phonograph records, tape recordings, and computers have made _____ to store data conveniently and accurately.

Ⓐ easier
Ⓑ it easier
Ⓒ easier than
Ⓓ it is easier

2 The skull shape of Homo erectus had several characteristics that _______ from modern people.

Ⓐ differently made
Ⓑ made it differently
Ⓒ made it a bit different
Ⓓ made a bit different

3 Indoor heating systems have made ________ for people to live and work comfortably in temperate climates.

Ⓐ it is possible
Ⓑ possible
Ⓒ it possible
Ⓓ possibly

4 Fredrick Jones invented a refrigeration unit that __________ the transportation of frozen foods by truck.

Ⓐ made possible
Ⓑ possibly made
Ⓒ it possibly made
Ⓓ made it possible

5 Droplets and ice crystals behave somewhat like dust in the air ________ in a shaft of sunlight.

Ⓐ made visible
Ⓑ visibly made
Ⓒ it visibly made
Ⓓ made it visible

6 Four visible weaknesses of the articles, apart from those of organization, ________ for Congress to execute its constitutional duties.

Ⓐ made possible Ⓑ it made possibly
Ⓒ made it impossible Ⓓ possibly made

---

7 The House bill would make ________ to apply for political asylum, both for those who apply upon entry into the United States and for those already on U.S. soil.

Ⓐ much more difficultly
Ⓑ it much more difficult
Ⓒ it much difficulter
Ⓓ much more difficult it

---

8 One of the problems that have ________ for Chicanos to succeed in the United States is the language barrier.

Ⓐ made it difficult
Ⓑ difficult made
Ⓒ made difficult that
Ⓓ made difficult

---

9 The automobile has contributed to the weakening of neighborhood ties ________ to keep up friendship.

Ⓐ by making easy
Ⓑ by easy it making
Ⓒ by making it easily
Ⓓ by making it easy

---

10 Congress and state legislators obliged and, in January 1920, ________ to buy or sell alcoholic drinks.

Ⓐ made unlawful
Ⓑ making it unlawful
Ⓒ made it unlawful
Ⓓ made it for unlawful

11 China's two distinct geographic regions allow regular production of various food crops, _______ to feed the largest population in the world.

Ⓐ possible make for the country
Ⓑ making possible for the country
Ⓒ making it possibly for the country
Ⓓ making it possible for the country

---

12 Painting, like other arts, exhibits universal qualities that ____________ for viewers of all nations and civilizations to understand and appreciate.

Ⓐ making it easy
Ⓑ make it easy
Ⓒ easy make
Ⓓ make easy

---

13 In 1922 a high tariff on foreign goods ________ to gain market share.

Ⓐ made easier for local manufactures
Ⓑ made it easily for local manufactures
Ⓒ made easy for local manufactures
Ⓓ made it easier for local manufactures

■ 정답 p334

동사의 as 선택

Outline

동사의 목적 보어 앞에 전치사가 허용 되는가를 가리는 것이 이 문제 유형의 초점이다. 따라서 보어 앞에 전치사가 오는 동사와, 오지 않는 동사를 구분하여 숙지하여야 한다. 특히 수동태 구문에서 보어 앞 전치사의 허용여부에 주목하도록 한다.

Hackers Grammar

❻.1 두개의 목적어를 갖는 동사

· 명사 목적어를 두 개 갖는 동사 : 수동태에서 직접목적어 앞에 전치사 없다.

수여동사	(능동) 주어 + 동사 + 간접목적어 + 직접목적어 : 간접목적어 앞에 전치사가 올 수 없다. (수동1) 간접목적어+동사의 수동형+직접목적어+by 주어 (수동2) 직접목적어+동사의 수동형+전치사+간접목적어 + by 주어
buy, give, award, grant, send, lend, bring	(능동) Robin ***gave*** the dog a bone. (수동) The dog ***was given*** a bone by Robin. (수동) The bone ***was given*** to the dog by Robin.

❻.2 목적어와 목적보어를 갖는 동사

(1) 명사 목적어와 명사 보어를 갖는 동사 : 수동태에서 목적 보어 앞에 전치사가 없다.

Call류 동사	(능동) 주어 + 동사 + 목적어 + 보어 (수동) 목적어 + 동사의 수동형 + 보어 + (by 주어)
call, name	(능동) They ***called*** the baby Jean. (수동) The baby was ***called*** Jean by them.

FOOTNOTE
여기서 name은 '명명하다'의 뜻으로 사용될 때이다.
ex. The Peruvians ***named*** a southward-moving current El Niño, boychild.

(2) 목적 보어 앞에 as를 수반하는 동사 : 수동태에서 목적 보어 앞에 전치사 as가 있다.

Regard as류 동사	(능동) 주어 + 동사 + 목적어 + as + 보어 (수동) 목적어 + 동사의 수동형 + as + 보어 + (by 주어)
regard - as, describe -as **define-as, identify -as**	(능동) We all ***regarded*** Kathy ***as*** an expert. (수동) Kathy ***was regarded as*** an expert.

(3) 목적 보어 앞에 as를 수반하는 구동사 : 수동태에서 목적 보어 앞에 전치사 as가 있다.

Think of -as류 동사	(능동) 주어 + 동사 + 전치사 + 목적어 + as + 보어 (수동) 목적어 + 동사의 수동형+ 전치사 + as + 보어 + (by 주어)
think of -as, **refer to -as**	(능동) In terrestrial affairs we ***think of*** "big" ***as*** being complicated. (수동) In terrestrial affairs "big" ***is thought of as*** being complicated.

(4) 목적 보어 앞에 to be나 as를 수반하거나 생략이 되는 동사
: 수동태에서 목적 보어 앞에 to be나 as가 오거나 생략된다.

Consider류 동사	(능동) 주어 + 동사 + 목적어 + (to be/as) + 보어 (수동) 목적어 + 동사의 수동형 + (to be/as) + 보어 + (by 주어)
consider (to be/as)	(능동) Most people ***consider*** success and failure (to be/as) opposites. (수동) Success and failure are ***considered*** (to be/as) opposites.

Tip · Consider 또는 Regard A as B 문형에서 반드시 as 이하에 명사만 나오는 것이 아니라, 형용사도 올 수 있다.
ex. Beaches are considered ***clean*** if there is no plastic waste on the shores.

(5) 목적 보어 앞에 as를 수반하거나 생략이 되는 동사
: 수동태에서 목적 보어 앞에 as가 오거나 생략된다.

Elect류 동사	(능동) 주어 + 동사 + 목적어 + (as) + 보어 (수동) 목적어 + 동사의 수동형 + (as) + 보어 + (by 주어)
elect (as)	(능동) They ***elected*** Hussein (as) Secretary-General of the party. (수동) Hussein ***was elected*** (as) Secretary-General of the party.

Tip · 보어가 (직책이 아니라) 단체일때는 elect to와 같이 전치사 to를 사용한다.
ex. In 1762 John Dickinson ***was elected to*** the Pennsylvania legislature.

Innovation is ______________ new development in business field.

Ⓐ referred as the most exciting
Ⓑ referred as to the most excited
Ⓒ referred to the most excited
Ⓓ referred to as the most exciting

Tip refer to A as B의 수동태는 A be referred to as B의 형태를 갖게 되어 답이 Ⓓ가 된다.

Structure

www.goHackers.com

Hackers **Practice** | 연습문제 |

다음 문장중 밑줄 친 부분이 문법적으로 틀렸을 경우 (I)를, 그렇지 않을 경우 (C)를 쓰시오.

1 ________ King James considered her a genius.

2 ________ Mrs. Sanderson was elected President.

3 ________ America was referred to "a melting pot", a place where people of all types could blend together.

4 ________ They described her attacker as a tall dark man with a beard.

5 ________ Energy can be defined the ability to do work.

6 ________ After tests, they identified the metal as gold.

7 ________ The decade of the 1920's is sometimes called as the Jazz Age.

8 ________ Both legends and myths can be classified as folks tales.

■ 정답 p335

Hackers **TEST** | 실전문제 |

1 M. Weber defined sociology ____________ which seeks to interpret the meaning of action.

Ⓐ a science
Ⓑ with a science
Ⓒ like a science
Ⓓ as a science

2 Lasers are now also used in high-speed printing and in the creation of three-dimensional images, __________.

Ⓐ called as holograms
Ⓑ they are called holograms
Ⓒ called holograms
Ⓓ being called as holograms

3 Blood cholesterol used to be thought _________ only for adults.

Ⓐ as a problem
Ⓑ of a problem
Ⓒ of as a problem
Ⓓ of being a problem

4 The large rise in drag as the plane approaches the speed of sound is referred _________ the sonic barrier.

Ⓐ to with
Ⓑ as
Ⓒ to as
Ⓓ being

5 The Ming emperors were very anxious to have a palace complex worthy of rulers ___________ Sons of Heaven.

Ⓐ considered themselves
Ⓑ who considered them
Ⓒ considered themselves as
Ⓓ who considered themselves

---

6 The native blacks were mostly Bantu-speaking, belonging to a language group that identified _______________ a migration that began centuries earlier.

Ⓐ them as part of
Ⓑ as part of
Ⓒ them part of
Ⓓ themselves part of

---

7 By mid-century Ferdinand __________ Holy Roman Emperor, leaving no doubt that he had claim to recognition as the strongest figure in central Europe.

Ⓐ being elected
Ⓑ was elected
Ⓒ electing
Ⓓ elected as

---

8 The people living in East Asia thought __________ the Middle Kingdom, the center of the universe, surrounded by other lands.

Ⓐ themselves as inhabiting
Ⓑ of themselves inhabiting
Ⓒ themselves inhabiting
Ⓓ of themselves as inhabiting

■ 정답 p335

병치 · 짝짓기

Outline

병치 유형의 문제는 나열된 구문이 품사, 구조, 의미의 측면에서 일관성을 유지하는가를 묻는 문제이다. 짝짓기 유형문제는 상관접속사 둘이 짝을 이루는 문제이다. 일반 접속사 뿐만아니라 상관접속사와 전후로 연결된 구조도 병치를 이루어야 한다.

따라서, 짝짓기는 병치가 이루어질 수 있는 틀을 찾는 것이고, 병치는 그 틀 속에서, 일관성을 유지하는 것이 주된 내용이다.

- **일관성을 깨지 않는 병치구문 찾기!**
- **같이 어울리는 상관접속사의 짝짓기!**

Hackers Grammar

7.1 병치

■ 문장에서는 같은 품사, 같은 구조, 같은 의미를 갖는 것끼리 짝을 이루어야 한다. 병치는 접속사(and, or등)를 사용해 열거할 때 지켜져야 한다.

■ 각각의 나열들이 올바른 병치관계를 이루고 있느냐, 즉 일관성이 유지되고 있느냐는 다음의 세 부분에서 파악될 수 있다.

- **품사병치 : 같은 품사의 병치**
- **구조병치 : 동명사 and 동명사, to 부정사 and to 부정사, 절 and 절**
- **의미병치 : 인간명사 and 인간명사, 분야명사 and 분야명사**

❼.2 짝짓기(상관접속사)

· 상관접속사는 호응하는 단어와 짝을 이루어서 그 구성요소를 나열할 수 있는 틀을 제공하는 것이다.

· 올바른 짝짓기가 이뤄져야 함은 물론이며, 그 나열된 것들이 병치관계를 이루고 있어야 한다.

both … and	either … or	neither … nor
whether … (or)	too … to	such … as
비교급 -er/more …than	not only … but (also)	not … (but)
from … to	between … and	

Dinosaurs may have become extinct because of either the eruption of volcanoes ____________ .

Ⓐ or the impact of a meteor.
Ⓑ and a meteor's impact
Ⓒ or a meteor impacted
Ⓓ nor the impact of a meteor

Tip · 예문에서 'either' 뒤에 'or' 가 없으므로 선택지에서 'or' 를 찾는다. 그리고 'either' 뒤에 나오는 구의 구조와 일치하여야 한다. 그러므로 답은 Ⓐ이다.

Hackers **Practice** | 연습문제 |

다음 문장에서 병치구문이 틀렸으면 (I) , 맞으면 (C)를 쓰시오.

1 __________ In Budapest the nationalists were strong enough to declare independence, draw up a constitution, and forming a national army.

2 __________ Either the Hungarians or are the Slaves had to be brought into the empire as full partners, rather than subjects.

3 __________ Engineers were the people who ran the factories, supervised the businesses, and hired and fired employees.

4 __________ Since many populations establish along waterways, cholera can be spread along the waterways to one community to the next community downstream.

5 __________ Farmers normally grow cabbage one year, store it during the winter, and replant it in the spring to produce seed.

6 __________ The study of isolated roots has provided an understanding of the relationship between shoots but roots in intact plants.

7 __________ The worker bees, which rarely live more than a few months, collect nectar for the hive's winter food store of honey, built honeycombs, and bring pollen to the hive to feed the young larvae.

8 __________ Such compulsive behavior often seems irrational not only to outside observers, but also to the person himself, though he usually finds himself unable to control his actions.

■ 정답 p335

Hackers TEST | 실전문제 |

1 At the war's conclusion some 20,000 people lay dead and another 10,000 were arrested, shot, or ________ .

Ⓐ send into exile
Ⓑ sending into exile
Ⓒ to send into exile
Ⓓ sent into exile

2 Robert Owen hoped to prove that it was possible to both make profits and ________ with dignity.

Ⓐ which treats workers
Ⓑ treating workers
Ⓒ treat workers
Ⓓ to treat workers

3 The communist Manifesto, published in 1848, threatened not only the economic order as it was ________, and social stability.

Ⓐ also religional, government
Ⓑ but religional also government
Ⓒ and religion, government
Ⓓ but also religion, government

4 The new immigrants fit into an economy that now depended more on growing coffee ________ the sugar to sweeten it.

Ⓐ as on producing
Ⓑ to produce
Ⓒ than on producing
Ⓓ or to be produced

5 Towns offered women and men opportunities to pick up supplies, to sell their crafts, _________, and to visit a tavern.

Ⓐ to read a newspaper
Ⓑ that read a newspaper
Ⓒ who read a newspaper
Ⓓ reading a newspaper

---

6 It was in this world in 1500 that the majority of Indian populations were either still in hunting and gathering societies _________.

Ⓐ as in an agricultural economy
Ⓑ nor in an agricultural economy
Ⓒ than in an agricultural economy
Ⓓ or in an agricultural economy

---

7 Cordoso turned the economy around, collecting more revenue, cutting government expenses, and _________ existing trade barriers.

Ⓐ was stroken down
Ⓑ to strike down
Ⓒ striking down
Ⓓ not to strike down

---

8 The Constitution reduced the powers of the king and permitted him only to suspend action for a time, _________ passed by the legislature.

Ⓐ not veto a law
Ⓑ but to veto a law
Ⓒ which vetoing a law
Ⓓ not to veto a law

---

9 _________, who made their living as merchants and craftmen or as professionals, such as engineers, bankers, lawyers, or doctors.

Ⓐ Wealthy bourgeoisie
Ⓑ Had been wealthy bourgeoisie
Ⓒ Some were wealthy bourgeoisie
Ⓓ That some were wealthy bourgeoisie

10 Liberalism in the 20th century stressed individualism, freedom from oppressive government, and the right for men and women to speak, publish, and __________.

Ⓐ worshiping as they wanted
Ⓑ as they wanted to worship
Ⓒ for worshiping as they wanted
Ⓓ worship as they wanted

---

11 Railroads were built, coal mines were opened, and ________ under construction.

Ⓐ put iron and steel mills
Ⓑ was put iron and steel mills
Ⓒ iron and steel mills were put
Ⓓ iron and steel mills to be put

■ 정답 p335

ch3 Mini TEST | 실전문제 |

1 _______ that lured the British and French to the Americas, for the Atlantic coast had no precious metals.

Ⓐ Agriculture and fur trapping were
Ⓑ What was agriculture and fur trapping
Ⓒ Agriculture and fur trapping
Ⓓ It was agriculture and fur trapping

2 For the men and women of Italy, _________ to recover from the war between the Byzantines and Ostrogoths.

Ⓐ there was centuries
Ⓑ if it took centuries
Ⓒ it took centuries
Ⓓ it was taken centuries

3 Not until ________ did a woman serve on the nation's highest judicial body.

Ⓐ President Reagan appointed Sandra to the Supreme Court
Ⓑ did President Reagan appoint Sandra to the Supreme Court
Ⓒ did President Reagan appointed Sandra to the Supreme Court
Ⓓ President Reagan appointed to Sandra to the Supreme Court

4 Ernest has a bigger problem ________.

Ⓐ than Martin does
Ⓑ of Martin
Ⓒ Martin did
Ⓓ than that Martin

5 Only when it was evident the child would survive, at two or three years of age, ________.

Ⓐ the parents gave it a name
Ⓑ which the parents gave it a name
Ⓒ been the parents given it a name
Ⓓ did the parents give it a name

---

6 Along with advantages, ________ certain disadvantages in traveling alone.

Ⓐ are there
Ⓑ it is
Ⓒ there are
Ⓓ are

---

7 The availability of so much easy credit does ________ to get over your head in debt.

Ⓐ make simple
Ⓑ made it simply
Ⓒ being made it simple
Ⓓ make it simple

---

8 From India ________ which, when they later came into Europe, were known as Arabic numerals.

Ⓐ did the numerals come
Ⓑ was the numerals
Ⓒ the numerals came
Ⓓ came the numerals

---

9 Pope Paul III asked Jeanne Bigard to design the apse and dome of St. Peter's, which he wanted to be ________ envisaged by Donato Bramante, the principal architect.

Ⓐ higher much than that
Ⓑ that much higher
Ⓒ much higher than that
Ⓓ much than higher that

10 _________ of Chinese prosperity was the great naval expeditions funded by the Ming emperors from the year A.D. 1403 onward.

Ⓐ Most evident sign
Ⓑ The most evident sign
Ⓒ Sign most evident
Ⓓ The more evident sign

---

11 The use of guns _________ to prey upon the peoples of the interior for captives that could be sold into slavery.

Ⓐ made easy for the Ashante and other coastal nations
Ⓑ made it easy for the Ashante and other coastal nations
Ⓒ was made it easy for the Ashante and other coastal nations
Ⓓ made it easily for the Ashante and other coastal nations

---

12 _________, swamps and marshes were drained, and the plowman moved over higher up the mountainside.

Ⓐ Been cleared by
Ⓑ With forests been cleared
Ⓒ Clearing forests
Ⓓ Forests were cleared

---

13 To pollute means to contaminate—to spoil something by introducing impurities _________ to use.

Ⓐ making unfit or unclean
Ⓑ that made it unfit or unclean
Ⓒ to be made unfit or unclean
Ⓓ that make it unfit or unclean

---

14 The Spaniards considered _________ of God's favor and were convinced that they had a obligation to convert the Indians to Christianity.

Ⓐ their conquest to be a sign
Ⓑ as their conquest to be a sign
Ⓒ their conquest about a sign
Ⓓ to their conquest as a sign

15 The tree producing the dye was ______ and gave its name to the country.

Ⓐ called as brazilwood
Ⓑ called brazilwood
Ⓒ calling to be brazilwood
Ⓓ been to call brazilwood

---

16 Europeans could feel enough to congregate in towns, _________, and to govern themselves in political and economic affairs.

Ⓐ for public buildings constructing
Ⓑ constructing public buildings
Ⓒ that construct public buildings
Ⓓ to construct public buildings

---

17 More difficult to attain ______ that nationalists set before themselves, the quest for a united Germany.

Ⓐ the task was
Ⓑ the task
Ⓒ was the task
Ⓓ be the task

---

18 One of the most controversial programs of the Works Progress Administration was the Federal Arts Project, a program to employ artists full-time at ______ painting murals and teaching various techniques of art.

Ⓐ tasks as such
Ⓑ as tasks such
Ⓒ as such tasks
Ⓓ such tasks as

---

19 Horace Mann, probably the most famous of the reformers, felt that there was _________ excuse in a republic for any citizen to be uneducated.

Ⓐ none
Ⓑ without
Ⓒ not
Ⓓ no

■ 정답 p336

2부

H A C K E R S **T O E F L**

Written Expression

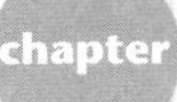

HACKERS **TOEFL**

Written Expression

동사구

이 chapter에서는 동사와 관련된 문제들을 다룬다. 특히 동사에 밑줄이 있을 경우, 주어와의 수 일치, 시제문제, 형태문제 등, 이 chapter에 나와있는 순서대로 점검하도록 훈련하고 to 부정사와 동명사의 사용에 대해 숙지하도록 한다.

TOEFL에서 실제로 출제되는 문장들을 기본으로 하여, 문장내의 구조, 문장간의 구조를 문장의 기본규칙과 공식들로 파악하는 것이 chapter의 목적이다.

1 주어와의 수 일치

Outline

주어가 단수인지 복수인지에 따라 단 · 복수 동사를 사용하는 것을
동사의 수 일치라 한다.

정동사	주어
단수동사	**단수형 명사**, to**부정사**, **동명사**, **명사절**, or**로 연결된 두 개의** idea
복수동사	**복수형 명사**, and**로 연결된 두 개의** idea

수 일치	Checking Points
명사와의 수 일치	수식어를 제외한 실제 주어를 찾아서 동사와 수 일치되었는지 확인
수량표현과의 수 일치	단 · 복수를 결정하는 수량표현과 동사와 수 일치 확인
수량표현+명사와 수 일치	수량표현을 따라오는 명사와 동사의 수 일치 확인
선행사와의 수 일치	선행사와 관계절의 동사의 수 일치

Hackers Grammar

명사와 동사의 수일치

1. 단수취급

단위명사	a flock of sheep, a school of fish, a herd of cattle a pride of lions, a swarm of bees	
시간, 거리, 금액	seconds, minutes, hours, inches, feet, miles, cents, dollars	
형태는 복수 취급은 단수	학문분야	linguistics, physics, mathematics, economics, statistics, ethics
	병명	measles, mumps, herpes, rabies, diabetes
	추상명사	news
	책,잡지,영화 국가 이름	Arabian Nights(책), Times(잡지), Star Wars(영화) the United States(국가)

2. 복수취급

형태도 복수 취급도 복수	한 쌍인 명사 복수추상명사	clothes, trousers, pants, jeans, sunglasses, scissors thanks, pains, manners
항상 복수	people, cattle	cf. buffalo의 복수 : buffalo/buffalo(e)s ex. ***Many cattle are*** suffering from a disease called BSE.

FOOTNOTE

1. 복수형 명사도 단수 단위와 함께 쓰이면 단수동사와 쓰일 수 있다.
   ex. ***A pair*** of glasses ***was*** purchased in L.A.
2. police는 미국영어에서 일반적으로 복수이며, 단수를 취하려면 a policeman(a police officer) 이라고 표현한다.
3. 인종, 언어, 문화를 공유할 때, 단수인 a people을 사용할 수 있고, 따라서 peoples도 가능하다.

3. 단 · 복수 모두 가능

집합명사 (집합체 의미 + 단수동사 / 개별체 의미 + 복수동사)	audience, class, committee, family, jury, team, army
단 · 복수의 형태가 같은 명사	means, species, series, headquarters fish, trout, sheep, deer, bison, offspring
국민과 언어	the + Chinese/English/French (국민) + 복수동사 Chinese/English/French (언어) + 단수동사 The English language (언어) + 단수동사

FOOTNOTE

1. 집합명사가 여러 집합을 나타내는 경우 복수형으로 쓴다.
   ex. The neighborhood consisted of mostly middle-class ***families***.
2. 주의해야 할 명사의 복수형 : child→children, man→men, woman→women, foot→feet, tooth→teeth, mouse→mice, analysis→analyses, cactus→cacti

Hackers Grammar

수량표현과 동사의 수 일치

1. 수량표현에 따라 동사의 수가 바뀐다.

단수동사사용	the number of + 복수 명사, each/every + 단수명사
복수동사사용	a number of + 복수 명사

ex. ***A number of*** special conditions ***are*** necessary for patients.
With Turkey and later Bulgaria joining the conflict, ***the number of*** Central Powers ***was*** complete.
Each boy and girl ***has*** a locker.

2. **수량표현 + 명사의 경우, 명사의 수가 동사의 수를 결정한다.**

all of, some of, most of, part of, a half of, the rest of,
30 percent of + 단수명사/복수명사

ex ***All of*** the food ***was*** prepared by the new cook.
All of the meals ***were*** prepared by the new cook.

Hackers Grammar

주의해야 할 동사의 수일치

1. **주격관계대명사의 선행사와 관계절의 동사와의 수 일치**

단수동사	단수 선행사 + 주격관계사 + 단수동사
복수동사	복수 선행사 + 주격관계사 + 복수동사

ex The knights were ***a German religious order*** which ***was*** founded to garrison the Holy Land.

2. **as well as, in addition to, together with, along with, accompanied by**
부가구문으로 주어가 될 수 없으니 그 부분을 제외하고 실제 주어의 명사를 찾아서 수일치를 시킨다.

ex The division of labor, along with language and religion, ***creates*** social solidarity.

3. **there이나 here구문에서 동사가 보어 (의미상 주어)와 수일치됨에 주의한다.**

ex There ***are*** also breaks for television commercials.

4. **동사가 주어 앞으로 도치된 구문에서 주어 동사 수일치에 주의한다.**

ex Writing in English ***were*** the novelists Charles Dickens and Willam Makepeace Thackery.

Hackers Skill

1. there 이나 here 구문은 동사가 보어와 수 일치 됨에 유의한다.
2. 도치 구문은 주어 · 동사의 수 일치에 주의한다.

Hackers **Practice** | 연습문제 |

다음에서 괄호 안에서 적절한 동사형태를 선택하시오.

1 Every man, woman, and child (is/are) an important being.

2 Let me open the mail which (were/was) delivered this morning.

3 In every one of the nations of Latin America, there (exist/exists) an elite that has its origins in the colonial past.

4 In all major towns there (are/is) numerous public libraries and museums.

5 Outside the capital, the number of government administrators (were/was) actually too few.

6 A large number of goods and animals (were/was) stored in temple warehouses, for the religious establishment was a large landowner.

7 The acquisition and the exchange of costly items in the upper class (was/were) major sources of class differentiation.

8 One of the most famous lyres, which were found in an ancient tomb, (has/have) a bull' s head on it.

9 A large number of students (become/becomes) discouraged and leave school.

10 The police also (help/helps) the homeless in the United States.

11 The women and children who (was/were) left behind could manage their households only by using slaves.

■ 정답 p337

Hackers **TEST** | 실전문제 |

1 Many kinds of patent medicine (A) were available and was (B) claimed to be cures (C) for any (D) disease or condition.

2 Regulated competition (A) is the sort of peaceful conflict which are (B) resolved within a (C) framework of agreed rules. (D)

3 One of the distinguishing features (A) of humans were (B) the long period between the birth of a child and (C) its ability to care for itself. (D)

4 Another student of the slave trade (A) hold (B) that one out of (C) five persons died while on the ships crossing (D) the Atlantic.

5 Each year every large and small town celebrate (A) a fiesta, a colorful (B) holiday that brings (C) out the whole population for sports, dancing (D), and religious processions.

6 The number of nuclear tests of the United States, Great Britain, and France have now (A) reached 250, leaving (B) a (C) permanent scar on the (D) Pacific Islands.

7 The migration of large numbers of Europeans into the Americas, Australia, and other parts (A) of the world were (B) the other major event (C) of the (D) century.

---

8 Vitamins are a major group of organic compounds (A) that regulates (B) the mechanisms by which (C) the body converts food into energy. (D)

---

9 Another element (A) contributing to (B) the rise of western European prosperity were (C) the (D) independent spirit of its merchants.

---

10 Economics have (A) so (B) closely connected the two factors in society that what happens in one directly (C) affects the other. (D)

---

11 Twenty-four hours were (A) all that was needed, because (B) the small San Salvador island in the Bahamas appeared (C) on the horizon. (D)

---

12 For Americans, the (A) simple pumpkin has (B) come to symbolize everything that are important (C) and meaningful about autumn. (D)

■ 정답 p337

2 동사의 시제 일치

Outline

동사의 수 일치가 동사와 주어와의 관계라면, 동사의 시제 일치는 동사와 시간을 나타내는 부사 및 부사구와의 일치라 할 수 있다. 실제 문제에서는 문장의 내용에 의한 분석적인 시제 일치보다는 다음의 몇 가지 시제일치 신호에 따라 동사의 시제를 일치시켜 주면 된다.

시제일치	Checking Points
시간 부사(구)	시간 부사구와 동사의 시제 일치
과거사건	과거 사건과 과거시제 일치

Hackers Grammar

시간부사와 동사의 시제 일치

과거	in + 과거연도/세기, yesterday, last + 시간표현, ago, in those days, once
현재	today(오늘날), (in) these days, nowadays, recently, lately, at present
미래	tomorrow, someday, next + 시간표현, in the future

ex ***Last spring*** Gurerra ***faced*** 15 years in prison.
Some people ***consider*** Vitamin C a good deterrent to colds ***in these days.***
This letter ***will facilitate*** your getting an appointment with the Director ***tomorrow.***

Since의 현재완료 선택과 과거사건의 과거시제 선택

Since는 현재까지의 기간을 나타내므로 현재완료와 일치시키나, during+과거시간은 과거시제와 일치시킨다.

ex Ontario in Canada ***has had*** colleges ***since the late 18th century.***

Creches ***were*** organized in France to care for the children of working mothers ***during the late spring of 1920.***

FOOTNOTE
그러나 during the past three years처럼 현재를 포함시에는 현재 완료를 사용한다.

과거의 사건은 과거시제와 짝짓는다.

ex ***War between Greek cities stopped*** the ancient games only twice in one thousand years.

FOOTNOTE
first telegraph등 역사적 사건은 과거시제와 짝 짓는다.

종속절과 주절의 시제일치

주절의 시제에 따라서 종속절의 시제를 일치시켜 주고 before나 after와 같은 시간의 전후관계를 나타내는 부사절에서는 부사절의 시제에 따라 주절의 시제를 일치시킨다.

ex After the accident ***occurred,*** it ***took*** Ferrari a moment to grasp the reality of how badly his car was damaged.

If, when이 이끄는 시간 및 조건 부사절에서는 현재 시제가 미래시제를 대신할 수 있다.

ex The landlord ***will*** put your apartment deposit in an escrow account and return it to you when you ***move*** out.

Hackers Grammar

제안이나 의무를 나타내는 표현 뒤에 오는 종속절의 동사는 원형을 취한다.

제안이나 의무를 나타내는 동사가 주절 동사이면 그것의 목적어인 명사절에 Should등의 조동사 없이 원형 동사가 나온다. 동일 내용이 적용되는 형용사도 있다.

제안 동사	advise, recommend, ask, demand, require, decide, command, order, suggest, propose, insist, decree
의무의 형용사	important, urgent, necessary, essential, imperative

ex The committee ***required*** that all the candidates ***present*** their views.
Before renovation could continue, it was ***imperative*** that the owner ***suggest*** additional improvement.

Hackers Grammar

가정법의 종속절과 주절의 시제를 일치시켜 준다.

가정법은 문제에서 직접적으로 답이 되도록 출제되기 보다는 도치나 다른 문제를 푸는데 도움이 되기 때문에 알아둘 필요가 있다.

가정법과거 [현재사실 반대]	If + S + 과거동사, S + would/could / might + 원형동사. S + would rather that S + 과거동사 If it were not for /Were it not for …
가정법과거완료 [과거사실 반대]	If + S + 과거완료, S + would/could/might + have + 과거분사 If it had not been for /Had it not been for …

ex If he ***were*** qualified for the job, I ***would employ*** him.
If he ***had helped*** me take some photos, I ***would have given*** him some money.

Hackers Skill

1. 'In + 과거 연도'이면 과거 시제를 확인하고 문제 풀기를 시작한다.
2. 'Since + 시점'이 나오면 주절에 현재완료가 왔는지 확인하고 문제 풀기를 시작한다.

Hackers Practice | 연습문제 |

괄호 안에서 알맞은 동사의 시제를 고르시오.

1 In the summer of 1979, Boston Red Sox first baseman Carl Yastrzemski (had become/became) the fifteenth player in baseball history to reach the three thousand hit plateau.

2 Whereas immigration (was/has been) somewhat restricted during the 1940s and 1950s, another surge in immigration (occurred/has occurred) in the 1970s.

3 When the Europeans arrived, North America (has been/was) uninhabited.

4 Example Art (was/has been) delighting children with its animation technique since 1953.

5 I paused for a little while to consider what I had better (said/say) next.

6 The major provision ordered that the prince of a territory (decided/decide) the religion of his subjects.

7 Selecting the name Clement V, the pope proposed that he (was/be) crowned at Lyon rather at Rome.

8 One of Babe's most famous moments (come/comes/came) during the 1932 World Series when the game was tied four-to-four.

9 Lucas and Spielberg both (have achieved/achieved) fame as the brightest young talents in Hollywood in the late 1970s and early 1980s.

10 Alexander's troops demanded that Alexander (gave up/give up) his ambition to conquer the world.

■ 정답 p337

Hackers **TEST** | 실전문제 |

1 In the past 30 years peasant's uprisings appeared (A) in (B) the (C) Central American countries of (D) Guatemala, El Salvador, and Nicaragua.

2 The constitution makers (A) insisted that the new "Emperor of the Germans" is (B) dependent on (C) popularly elected (D) representatives.

3 In 1769 Newcomen's engine is improved (A) upon by (B) the Scotsman James Watt, who (C) patented (D) a new form of the device.

4 Since the (A) Neolithic period, human settlements clustered (B) in (C) the major river basins (D).

5 In the (A) thirteenth century the Danes send (B) expeditions into the eastern Baltic, to Estonia, where (C) they founded (D) the city of Reval.

6 A quarrel between Frederick and (A) the pope over (B) the marriage was suspended on the news that (C) Jerusalem has fallen back (D) into Muslim hands.

7 During the eleventh century several new vegetables from Asia and North
A B
Africa have been first brought into Europe.
C D

---

8 The extraordinary growth of wealth and population in northern Italy during
A
the Middle Ages is the result of increased agricultural production.
B C D

---

9 Among upper-class women the code of chivalry required that they
A B
were treated with respect.
C D

---

10 Since Evans finished his work, many other archeologists worked in Crete
A B C
where proven sites number in the hundreds.
D

---

11 By 1900 the industrialization of Germany has reached the point that it
A B C
surpassed Great Britain's economy.
D

---

12 Until the 1760's, England has not overly interfered in colonial life, for the
A B C
Americans were far away.
D

■ 정답 p338

3 동사의 형태 · 선택 문제

Outline

동사에 밑줄이 있으면 동사의 형태를 정하는 신호에 따라 동사 형태의 옳고 그름을 파악한다.

형태 · 선택	Checking Points
to/**조동사** + **동사원형**	to/조동사 다음에 동사의 원형이 왔는지 확인
전치사 + **동명사**	전치사 다음에 동사 + ing 형태인지 확인
have + **과거완료**	have/had 다음에 올바른 과거분사형태가 왔는지 확인

Hackers Grammar

옳은 형태와 틀린 형태

조동사나 to 부정사 다음에는 원형 동사가 온다. 이 원형동사는 시제나 수일치를 하게 되면 틀리며, to 부정사는 전치사의 목적어가 될 수 없다.

형태	옳은 예	틀린 예
to **부정사** + **원형 동사**	to have , to do, to be paid	to having, to does, to paid
전치사 + **동명사**	by doing , for studying	by to do, for studied
조동사 + **원형 동사**	could help, may be done	could helped, may doing
have(had) + **과거분사**	have worked, had been made	have work, had being made

실제 문제에서는 신호와 동사 사이에 부사가 있거나, 도치가 일어나 혼돈을 주는 예들이 있다.

ex An opportunity ***has*** never ***diminished*** its potential for devastation to other women.
Neither so simple nor so obvious ***does*** natural behavior ***become*** as we once thought.

Hackers Grammar

자동사와 타동사선택

자동사는 목적어를 취할 수 없고 수동태도 될 수 없다. 따라서 자동사와 타동사가 바뀌어 쓰인 것을 주의하라.

	자동사			타동사		
현재	lie	rise	sit	lay	raise	set
과거	lay	rose	sat	laid	raised	set
과거분사	lain	risen	sat	laid	raised	set
현재진행	lying	rising	sitting	laying	raising	setting

ex A dress ***lays*** on the floor. (lays → lies)
She ***rose*** her eyebrows in surprise. (rose → raised)
I was ***setting*** at my desk reading. (setting → sitting)

Hackers Skill

'전치사 + ______ + 목적어'의 경우 ______ 에 동명사가 왔는지 확인하라.

Hackers **Practice** | 연습문제 |

괄호 안에서 올바른 표현을 찾으시오.

1 Unlike most earlier immigrants who were willing to (learn/learning) English and wanted to "melt" into American life, many of today's immigrants don't see the need.

2 Corn grew so quickly that farmers could (got/get) two crops a year from the same field.

3 The dualistic theology argued that the true believer must (free/freed) the soul from matter by strict asceticism.

4 Between 1830 and 1850 over 8,000 miles of railroad track were (lain/laid).

5 In feudalism, peasant seldom meant that the economic surplus was (rose/raised) by landlords through rent.

6 Both groups considered it in their interest to keep the monarchs impotent so that their own power and wealth could (enhanced/be enhanced).

7 The "weeping god" had apparently (became/become) the most popular divinity of the Peruvian Indians.

8 The constant need for captives to (sacrificed/be sacrificed) to the Toltec gods meant that few tears were shed.

9 Frederick (lay/laid) plans to unite the Norman kingdom of Sicily to the Holy Roman Empire.

10 King Bela IV (rose/raised) an army to meet them, but it was defeated, and the king fled to a Dalmatian island.

■ 정답 p338

Hackers TEST | 실전문제 |

1 Carolyn Brady then uses the information gave by the camera in an individual and intuitive fashion.
(A) the (B) gave (C) in (D) individual

2 It's so easy to taken out a loan at the bank.
(A) so (B) easy (C) taken (D) at

3 A budget is a working plan for allocated the family finances during the year.
(A) allocated (B) family finances (C) during (D) the

4 If present trends continue, Guatemala will become the first Latin American country to having a Protestant majority.
(A) continue (B) will become (C) having (D) a

5 The worst offenders, those who had a prior conviction and then returned to their heresy, might be sentenced to death by burn at the stake.
(A) The (B) their heresy (C) be sentenced (D) burn

6 The fish should be washed, dried, and lay out on the newspaper.
(A) The (B) be (C) lay (D) on

7 Each family held several strips of land about the size of an acre, the amount of land that could efficiently is plowed in a day.

A: strips / B: land / C: is / D: a

---

8 More recently, the question of altruism over egoism has been risen by theories of exchange and reciprocity.

A: More / B: over / C: risen / D: of

---

9 The postal system is not dependable, and governments have no money for introduce modern equipment.

A: postal system / B: no / C: for introduce / D: equipment.

---

10 While the country might still known as Prussia, and the people who lived there Prussians, the name now refers to German colonists.

A: While / B: known / C: who / D: refers to

■ 정답 p338

4 태

Outline

타동사는 목적어를 가져야 하지만, 수동태가 되면 목적어가 주어자리로 이동하므로 타동사가 목적어를 가진다는 규정을 벗어날 수 있다.

동사에 밑줄이 그어있으면, 목적어의 유무에 따라 동사의 태를 확인한다.

태(voice)	Checking Points
능동태	타동사의 능동태는 적어도 한 개 이상의 목적어를 갖는다. 목적어로는 명사구, 동명사, to 부정사, 그리고 명사절만 가능하다.
수동태	목적어가 없으면 수동태임을 의심하라. by가 나오면 수동태임을 의심하라. 목적어를 두개 갖는 동사(4형식), 한 개의 목적어와 명사보어를 갖는 동사(5형식)는 수동태 동사 뒤에 명사가 나올 수 있다.

Hackers Grammar

능동 : 타동사 능동태는 목적어를 갖는다.

한 개의 명사목적어를 갖는 동사	주어 + 타동사 능동태 + 명사목적어
두 개의 명사목적어를 갖는 동사	주어 + 타동사 능동태 + 명사목적어 + 명사목적어
명사목적어와 명사보어를 갖는 동사	주어 + 타동사 능동태 + 명사목적어 + 명사보어

ex In the past, steel ***made*** by a slow and expensive process of heating, stirring, and reheating iron ore. (made → was made)

Tip · 타동사 능동태는 목적어를 취해야 하는데 목적어가 없으므로, 'made'를 수동태인 'was made'로 바꾸어야 한다.

Hackers Grammar

수동 : 수동태는 목적어가 빠진다.

한 개의 명사목적어를 갖는 동사	주어 + 타동사 수동태 + 전치사구(by + 명사)
두 개의 명사목적어를 갖는 동사	주어 + 타동사 수동태 + 명사목적어
명사목적어와 명사보어를 갖는 동사	주어 + 타동사 수동태 + 명사보어

ex She ***is described*** the quality of light as being very important in her work.

Tip · 동사의 수동태는 목적어를 취하지 않는데, 예문에는 목적어가 있으므로 'is described' 가 아니라 'describes' 가 맞는다.

FOOTNOTE

By가 대부분의 경우에는 수동태 신호로 쓰이지만 몇몇 경우에는 "-함으로써"라는 수단의 의미로 사용될 수 있다.

ex. Scientists can create new and useful materials ***by making use of*** forces that assemble molecules into natural crystals.

Hackers Grammar

수동태 변화시 주의해야 할 동사

대부분의 경우에서 동사가 수동형이면 뒤에 목적어가 없어야 하지만, 목적어 외에도 목적어의 보어를 취하는 동사가 있으므로 주의해야 한다.

call **동사**	주어 + 동사 + 목적어 + 보어
call, name	→ 목적어 + 동사의 수동형 + 보어
regard ~ as **동사**	주어 + 동사 + 목적어 + as + 명사
regard ~ as, describe ~ as, identify ~ as, define ~ as	→ 목적어 + 동사의 수동형 + as + 명사
think of ~ as **동사**	주어 + 동사 + 전치사 + 목적어 + as + 명사
think of ~ as, refer to ~ as	→ 목적어 + 동사의 수동형 + 전치사 + as + 명사

Hackers Skill

동사의 목적어가 없으면 수동태임을 의심하라.

Written Expression

www.goHackers.com

Hackers **Practice** | 연습문제 |

괄호 안에 있는 동사의 적절한 형태를 빈 칸에 넣으시오.

1 A collection of fascinating tales called The Arabian Nights (introduce) __________ into Europe by the French scholar Antoine Galland.

2 The drum and flute music once heard in the streets has (replace) __________ by noisy radios and cassette players.

3 By copying material from Hitler's speeches and medical reports, a man (write) __________ the Hitler diaries.

4 Originally, dolphins (use) ______ as messengers or to answer calls for help.

5 Ordinary matter (construct) __________ of the basic atomic building blocks of protons, neutrons and electrons.

6 Parties which do not view the ruling party as legitimate (refer to as) __________ "revolutionary parties".

7 Credit cards (issue) ______________ by banks, travel agencies, and credit associations of all kinds.

8 A primitive artist (carve) __________ a crude portrait on the side of a rock in northern Norway.

9 They thought that the heavens (hold up) __________ by four great trees and that unseen creatures filled the sky in the day and the night.

10 In 1919 Babe (make) __________ his first record by hitting 29 home runs in one season, more than any previous major-league player.

■ 정답 p339

Hackers **TEST** | 실전문제 |

1 The Senator Edward Kennedy thought the (A) President should remove (B) on application of a (C) majority of the state legislatures (D).

2 Communication within the body (A) and the consequent integration of behavior were considering (B) the exclusive province of the nervous system up to (C) the beginning of the present century (D).

3 Modern chemistry (A), aiding (B) by increasingly (C) sophisticated instruments, studies materials as small as (D) single atoms.

4 Sociologists claim that the average person more or less (A) puts up with a job because of (B) private and family needs that considered (C) to be more important, such as (D) food, clothing, and shelter.

5 A special (A) computerized camera, called as a (B) Dykstraflex, was designed (C) to give the illusion of real screen (D) movement.

6 Time (A) can be regarded (B) neither a biological nor (C) a physical absolute but (D) a cultural invention.

7 The impetus for the passage of laws protecting workers first was come from humanitarian and religious figures.

(A) The (B) for (C) protecting (D) was come

8 The rulers of England, France, and the Spanish Christian kingdoms was not welcome any diminution of their sovereignty by an Italian pope or a German emperor.

(A) was not welcome (B) diminution (C) their (D) an

9 Wealthy Romans were expanded their holdings by purchasing the farms of veterans and joining them into large estates, latifundia, run with slave labor.

(A) were expanded (B) their (C) joining (D) slave labor

10 It is estimated that fully one third of the population had decimated by the dreaded disease.

(A) fully (B) the (C) had decimated (D) dreaded disease

11 For the first time in medieval history, a pope had publically humiliated by a secular monarch.

(A) For the first time (B) in (C) publically humiliated (D) secular

12 The olive tree, a small evergreen, has cultivated since the beginning of historical times in its native Asia Minor.

(A) small evergreen, (B) has cultivated (C) the beginning (D) native

■ 정답 p339

5 분사

Outline

지금까지는 동사가 정동사로일 때, 출제될 수 있는 부분을 배웠다.
5장과 6장에서는 동사가 준동사로일 때, 문제에 접근하는 법을 배운다.

분사	Checking Points
현재분사 vs. **과거분사**	현재분사나 과거분사에 밑줄이 있으면 '현재분사 → 과거분사', '과거분사 → 현재분사'가 아닌지 확인한다.
축약분사구문	축약된 분사구문이 완전한 것인지 확인한다.

Hackers Grammar

타동사의 분사형

1. 동사의 행위의 주체가 사람인 경우(명사를 직접 수식하는 경우)

현재분사 (-ing)	수식 받는 명사가 행위의 주체
과거분사 (p.p.)	수식 받는 명사가 행위의 객체(피동체)

ex The lady cleans the floor.
→ The ***cleaning*** lady scrubbed the floor.
→ The lady left the ***cleaned*** floor to dry.

ex 과거분사의 예
baked potato, ***signed*** contract, ***injured*** hand,
frozen meat, ***lost*** puppy

2. **동사의 행위의 주체가 사람이 아닌 경우**

동사의 행위의 주체는 일반적으로 사람으로서 현재분사의 수식을 받는데 아래의 경우는 주체가 사람이 아닌 경우이다.

사물 주체 사람 객체	사물 주체 사람 객체	사물 주체 사람 객체
amusing - amused	exciting - excited	interesting - interested
confusing - confused	boring - bored	discouraging - discouraged

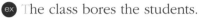

ex The class bores the students.
→ the ***boring*** class [지겨운 수업] : class가 주체
→ the ***bored*** students [지겨워 하는 학생들] : students 객체

Hackers Grammar

자동사의 분사형(명사를 직접 수식하는 경우)

현재분사	진행의 의미를 갖음
과거분사	상태의 의미를 갖음

ex a ***fallen*** leaf [상태:떨어진 잎]
a ***falling*** leaf [진행:떨어지는 잎]
an ***escaped*** prisoner [상태 : 탈주한 죄수]
an ***escaping*** prisoner [진행 : 탈주하는 죄수]

Hackers Grammar

분사구문으로 사용될 때

현재분사	분사구문의 생략된 주어는 주절의 주어와 동일하며 분사구문의 주체
과거분사	분사구문의 생략된 주어는 주절의 주어와 동일하며 분사구문의 객체

ex **_Originated_** with the Persian santir, dulcimers have been around since ancient times.

Tip · originated의 의미상의 주어는 주절의 dulcimers이며, 어디서부터 비롯되었다는 의미므로 dulcimers가 능동관계인 **originating**으로 바뀌어야 한다.(자동사 능동)

ex According to data **_obtaining_** from radioactive dating, the oldest rocks found on earth are approximately 500 million to 4 billion years old.

Tip · data가 obtain하는 것이 아니라 obtain되는 객체이며, data which are obtained from ~에서 생략된 형태이므로 **obtained**로 고쳐야 한다.(타동사 수동)

ex For three days Paris was the scene of battles between the army and citizens **_supported_** reform.

Tip · reform이라는 목적어가 있는 것을 고려해 볼 때, who supported라는 관계절이 축약된 것이다. 이 문장에서 축약된 형태인 **supporting**으로 바꾸어야 한다. (타동사 능동)

Hackers Skill

분사구문에서 현재분사인지 과거분사인지 파악하기 위해서 절을 축약하기 전으로 원상복구하여 의미를 파악한다.

Hackers Practice | 연습문제 |

괄호 안에 있는 동사의 적절한 형태를 빈칸에 집어넣으세요.

1 On May 13, 1607, three frail ships (bear) ___________ 105 colonists from England were moored to trees off the shore of a peninsula.

2 It grew into a large metropolis (hold) ________ nearly a million people.

3 Bulgaria, first defeated by the Serbs, was also a (divide) ____ nation when the Turks appeared.

4 Special (computerize) ________ cameras were invented and miniature models of spaceships and cities were designed.

5 Finally the station managers put Oprah on an early morning talk show (call) ________ People Are Talking.

6 "Smog" is a composite word (form) ________ from the first letters of smoke and the last letters of fog.

7 The 300-mile gorge (cut) ________ by the Colorado River is 4,000 to 6,000 feet deep.

8 (Live) ________ comfortably on this food supply, the newcomers spread out.

9 In the far southwest a lake (surround) _______ by gardens provided a place for enjoying leisure.

10 In the city Chandragupta built himself a magnificent palace (set) _______ among grounds planted with every kind of tree and shrub.

■ 정답 p340

Hackers **TEST** | 실전문제 |

1 The integral connection between vassal <u>and</u> serf <u>depicting</u> in conventional accounts <u>was</u> destined to come <u>under</u> intense scrutiny among a new breed of analysts.
(A: and, B: depicting, C: was, D: under)

2 A <u>unifying kingdom</u> collapsed as <u>did</u> the empire <u>because of</u> dissension among the Fermans themselves and <u>foreign invaders.</u>
(A: unifying kingdom, B: did, C: because of, D: foreign invaders.)

3 <u>Within</u> a short time Cluny <u>attracted</u> a large number of novices <u>interesting</u> in <u>joining a</u> community that enjoyed such privileges.
(A: Within, B: attracted, C: interesting, D: joining a)

4 <u>For</u> twenty years cowboys pushed <u>cattles</u> from Texas to Kansas, until a commination of drought, terrible winters, and <u>falling prices</u> in 1885 and 1886 put <u>an</u> end to the drives.
(A: For, B: cattles, C: falling prices, D: an)

5 Foremost <u>among</u> concerns of the <u>landowning class</u> was to be sure that the farms <u>were held</u> in the family name <u>should be</u> passed on intact to the next generation.
(A: among, B: landowning class, C: were held, D: should be)

6 Tools and weapons <u>were made of</u> bronze replaced those of copper, <u>yet</u> it was only about 1500 B.C. that any kind of metal <u>became known</u> <u>in</u> Scandinavia.
(A: were made of, B: yet, C: became known, D: in)

7 Anyone violated the rules of caste was punished with a beating and ostracism
A B
from the community, which could well mean death.
C D

---

8 The conquest linked England much more closely to continental affairs
A B
because the Norman kings were always interesting in events in France.
C D

---

9 The disease was caused by a bacillus carrying by fleas that lived in the fur of
A B C
a particular kind of black rat.
D

---

10 Jews who had lived quietly in the midst of Christians became victimizing by
A B C
popular prejudice against anyone who was not a believer.
D

■ 정답 p340

6 동명사와 to부정사

Outline

동명사가 쓰일 상황과 to 부정사가 쓰일 상황을 숙지하여 동명사와 to 부정사를 선택한다.

동명사는 명사에 더 가까운 반면에 to 부정사는 동사에 더 가깝기 때문에 쓰이는 용법이 제한적이다. 따라서, 쓰일 수 있는 상황을 미리 파악함으로써 to 부정사와 동명사의 선택문제를 해결할 수 있다.

동명사/to 부정사	Checking Points
동사/형용사의 종류에 따라 구별	동명사가 목적어로 오는 동사/형용사의 종류, to 부정사가 목적어로 오는 동사/형용사의 종류를 확인

Hackers Grammar

동사 신호에 따라 구별하기

1. 동사 바로 뒤에 동명사나 to 부정사가 올 때,

동사 + 동명사					
admit	appreciate	avoid	can't help	consider	delay
deny	enjoy	finish	mind	miss	postpone
practice	quit	report	resent	resist	resume
risk	suggest				
동사 + to 부정사					
agree	attempt	claim	decide	demand	desire
fail	hope	intend	learn	offer	plan
prepare	pretend	refuse	seem	strive	tend
wish					

ex Spectators ***enjoyed watching*** knights kill other knights in tournaments.
A great number of wild birds ***seem to carry*** the virus without showing any evidence of illness.

2. 동사 + 목적어 뒤에 'to 부정사' 나 '전치사 + 동명사' 가 올 때,

동사 + 목적어 + to 부정사					
advise	allow	ask	cause	convince	challenge
encourage	enable	expect	force	hire	instruct
invite	need	order	permit	persuade	remind
require	teach	tell	want	warn	

동사 + 목적어 + 전치사 + 동명사			
accuse ~ of	blame ~ for	congratulate ~ on	discourage ~ from
prevent ~ from	punish ~ for	stop ~ from	thank ~ for

ex Trimeters ***allow*** students ***to*** graduate early.
They ***accused*** the man ***of*** stealing money.

Hackers Grammar

의미에 따라서 동명사와 to 부정사 선택하기

1. 의미변화가 없이 동사의 목적어로 둘 다 사용가능

동사 + 동명사 또는 to 부성사						
begin	cease	commence	continue	decline	dread	hate
loathe	like	love	prefer	start		

ex I ***like listening/to listen*** to music at night.

2. 의미변화가 생길 때의 동명사와 to 부정사

동사 + 동명사 또는 to 부정사	
능동으로 수동의미를 나타낼 때	need, deserve, want, require
과거성(동명사)과 미래성(to 부정사)	forget, recall, regret, remember
기타	try, stop

※실제로 to 부정사와 동명사 사용에 따른 의미의 차이를 묻는 경우는 없으므로, to 부정사와 동명사가 모두 사용될 수 있음을 알고 있으면 된다.

ex Your car needs ***repairing***.(수동)
Your car needs ***to be repaired***.(수동)
I always ***forget to lock*** the door.(해야 할 일)
I will never ***forget meeting*** Dr. Stowel in L.A.(과거에 일어난 일)

Hackers Grammar

형용사 신호(signal)에 따라서

형용사 + to 부정사					
anxious	boring	dangerous	difficult	easy	good
hard	pleased	prepared	ready	strange	usual
형용사 + 동명사					
busy	worth				

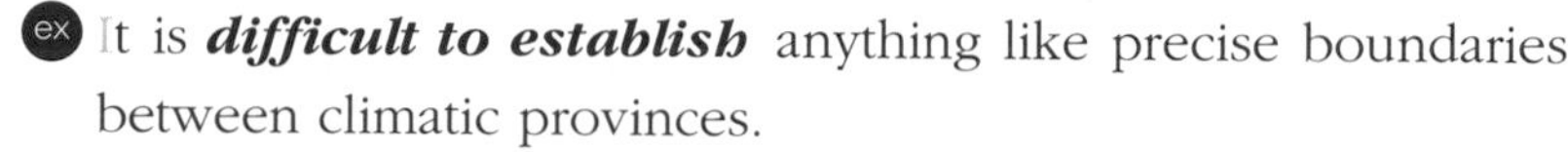

ex It is ***difficult to establish*** anything like precise boundaries between climatic provinces.

It is ***worth noting*** that workers in America were less alienated than others.

Hackers Grammar

to + 명사

'to'가 부정사가 아닌 전치사로 쓰였으므로, 그 다음에는 동사원형이 아니라 명사(동명사)가 나와야 한다. 전치사의 목적어로는 명사(동명사)만 올 수 있기 때문이다.

동사 + to + 명사		
belong to + 명사	contribute to + 명사	lead to + 명사
look forward to + 명사	object to + 명사	
형용사/분사 + to + 명사		
accustomed to + 명사	compared to + 명사	confined to + 명사
opposed to + 명사	related to + 명사	

ex Over 200 teams ***belonged to*** a national association of "Baseball Players".

Dinosaurs were ***confined to*** a relatively small area.

I am not ***accustomed to*** being interrupted.

Hackers **Practice** | 연습문제 |

괄호 안에서 알맞은 단어를 찾으시오.

1 In 1994 Gaston's poems began (to be/being) published once again in Cuba.

2 The varied racial and ethnic groups have learned (living/to live) together in peace and harmony.

3 After that disappointment, Edison decided not (working/to work) on any invention.

4 It seeks to enable them (to choose/choosing) between a career and the home.

5 He thinks the book is just an excuse to avoid (to look/looking) for a job.

6 Teachers say it is hard (judging/to judge) all men by one heel.

7 Nothing he could say or do would persuade his ex-boss (rehiring/to rehire) him.

8 Doctors and tutors could prepare students (to be/being) examined for degrees.

9 Along the New England coast, industries related to (shipbuild/shipbuilding) developed.

10 Change has been painfully slow and obstructed by men who are unwilling (to share/sharing) their power.

■ 정답 p340

Hackers **TEST** | 실전문제 |

1 <u>If</u> the teacher expects <u>little</u> of the child, the child learns he is dumb and soon
A B
quits <u>to bother</u> to tell the testers <u>what</u> they want to hear.
C D

2 Doctors might feel <u>more comfortably</u> prescribing aspirin <u>because of</u> the slight
A B
possibility <u>that</u> warfarin may lead to <u>internal bleeding.</u>
C D

3 No one <u>has</u> been able <u>explain</u> how or why <u>the</u> Moon <u>sporadically</u> sparks.
A B C D

4 The delegates <u>had been</u> instructed <u>by</u> the Continental Congress <u>revising</u> <u>the</u>
A B C D
old Articles of Confederation.

5 Some of them have <u>an</u> <u>open-admissions policy</u> that allows anyone <u>who</u> has
A B C
graduated from high school <u>attending.</u>
D

6 They have worked <u>to</u> encourage the government <u>establishing</u> and <u>enforce</u> a
A B C
national minimum <u>drinking</u> age.
D

7 The species composition of the community remains (A) the same because (B) all the species present successfully reproduce (C) themselves and invading species fail gaining (D) a foothold.

8 Some nobles actually were (A) willing limiting (B) the chronic problems brought (C) on because (D) of the liberum.

9 The landowners threw free peasants off (A) their farms (B), causing (C) them wandered (D) the countryside as day laborers.

10 New weapons were developed (A), such as (B) the bow and arrow, that allowed the early humans killing (C) more elusive (D) animals.

■ 정답 p340

ch1 Mini TEST | 실전문제 |

1 Much of the cotton that(A) pearls are wrapped in when not in use(B) are(C) treated with an(D) acid.

2 Young men, taking as(A) slaves, were(B) brought into the country and then rose(C) through the ranks until they became(D) military commanders.

3 A number of(A) improvement(B) were made(C) during(D) Khubilai's time.

4 The president's career comes(A) to an(B) unexpected conclusion in 1954 when(C) he committed(D) suicide.

5 Thousands of Cubans has fled(A) to the(B) United States, allowing(C) Castro to be rid of(D) his opposition.

6 That a Christian school could founded(A) in Bulgaria in the late ninth century(B) testifies(C) to the conversation of the Bulgaria khan some decades earlier.(D)

7 Most of the Andalusian towns was located(A) along(B) the road system that(C) the Romans had built.(D)

8 Metternich was very concerned [A] to keep a lid on potential troubles causing [B] by liberals and nationalists [C] in central Europe. [D]

9 Party politics were [A] vigorous [B] in Greece where [C] democracy was first born [D].

10 Tradition ruled more than the leaders who [A] were not allowed to make [B] any [C] decision without obtain [D] the universal consent of their council of advisors.

11 There [A] was one other migration [B], as European men and women moved to every other continent [C], brought [D] their culture with them.

12 In the [A] United States, public-health policies require that students are [B] vaccinated for some disease before [C] they [D] may be enrolled in school.

13 Judo involves [A] a complex system [B] of physical and mental skills that helps [C] produce both mental and [D] physical fitness.

14 By the thirteenth century, at [A] the very edge of the rain forest, several town [B] appeared [C] with markets for the exchange of forest products [D].

15 The ideology of the [A] state encouraged people [B] offering [C] Jerry's statue [D] divine honors.

■ 정답 p341

HACKERS TOEFL

Written Expression

명사구

이 chapter에서는 명사, 대명사, 관사 등에 관련된 유형을 공략한다. 관사나 명사는 가장 난이도가 높은 부분이므로 각 문법을 정확히 이해하고 적용하는 훈련이 필요하다.

1 명사

Outline

동사와 함께 문장의 골격을 이루는 명사는 문장에서 주어, 목적어, 보어, 그리고 동격의 자리에 나타나며, 단독으로 쓰이기 보다는 관사, 형용사등과 함께 명사구를 이루어 사용된다.

실제 문제에서 명사에 밑줄이 그어 있으면, 다음의 순으로 검토한다.

명사(noun)	Checking Point
1. 수 일치	부정관사와의 수 일치 수량 형용사와의 수 일치 동사와의 수일치('동사 편 수일치' 부분 참조)
2. 명사자리	명사자리에 다른 품사가 들어간 경우
3. 인간 vs. 추상	인간명사와 추상명사를 바꾸어 놓은 경우
4. 복합명사	복합명사의 수식명사는 단수이어야 한다.
5. 어순	복합명사의 어순, 형용사와의 어순

Hackers Grammar

수일치

부정관사와의 수 일치 : a + 단수명사

ex A ***books*** was imported from England.

Tip · 부정관사는 '하나의' 라는 의미가 있으므로 명사의 복수형과 충돌이 이뤄지기 때문에 함께 사용될 수 없다. 동사 was가 단수형이므로 books를 book으로 바꾼다.

수량표현과의 수일치

복수표현 + 복수명사	few, a few, many, several, various, numerous, hundreds of, a couple (of), a / the number of, a great many (of), a dozen (of), a score of
단수표현 + 단수명사	each / every / another + 가산명사 단수 a great deal of / a large amount of / much / (a) little + 불가산명사 단수
단 · 복수 표현 + 단 · 복수 명사	all, most, some, any, no, two and a half of, the rest of, 30 percent of, a lot of + 불가산명사 or 가산명사 복수 뒤에 나오는 명사에 따라 동사의 수를 결정

ex A chemist can normally find many molecules of ***various shape.*** (shape → shapes)
By signing the work in pencil, an artist could guarantee and personalize ***each prints***.(prints → print)

FOOTNOTE
a. type, kind 다음에는 관사 없이 명사가 단수 혹은 복수로 나올 수 있으며, 동사의 결정은 일반적으로 type의 수와 일치하나 type/kind of + 복수명사일 경우는 복수 동사를 사용한다.
ex. types of rice + 복수형 동사
b. all, several, many가 대명사로 쓰일 경우, 뒤에 복수동사 사용

Hackers Grammar

명사자리

명사가 들어가야만 하는 자리에 다른 품사를 사용해서 틀리는 문제이다.

주어자리	명사나 동명사 중 적절한 명사가 우선
목적어자리	동사의 목적어 및 전치사의 목적어(형용사나 부사는 동사나 전치사의 목적어가 될 수 없다.)
보어자리	be 동사 및 목적어의 보어에서 형용사와 명사의 선택
___ of **명사자리**	the ______ of + 명사일 때, 빈 칸에 들어갈 수 있는 요소 1. 명사 : 형용사나 부사가 나오면 명사로 바뀌어야 한다. 2. 목적어 없는 동명사 : 동명사에 the가 붙으면 명사로 간주되어야 한다. 3. 명사가 생략된 형용사의 최상급 : of 이하 명사의 반복으로 명사 생략 **ex.** Jane was the prettiest of her sisters.

ex They supplemented foraging by ***the hunting*** sea mammals.
Tip · hunting이 관사 the와 함께 사용되면 명사로 간주되어 목적어를 가질 수 없다. 따라서 the hunting은 동명사인 hunting으로 고치든가 the hunting of 으로 고쳐져야 한다.

인간 vs. 추상

명사의 선택에서 답이 되는 경우는 직업이나 분야를 나타내는 추상명사와 그것에 종사하는 사람을 혼동하여,

1. 인간명사를 의미상 분야에 대해서 언급할 때
   분야에 대해 언급하면서 인간 명사를 이용할 때
2. 병치구조로 의미상 인간명사나 분야명사로 이어지지 않고
   의미병치가 깨졌을 때

인간명사	추상명사	인간명사	학문분야
surgeon	surgery	physicist	physics
poet	poetry	biologist	biology
photographer	photography	mathematician	mathematics
editor	editorial	musician	music
electrician	electricity	astronomer	astronomy
criminal	crime	geologist	geology
humorist	humor	geographer	geography
philosopher	philosophy	financier	finance
administrator	administration	athlete	athletics
		chemist	chemistry
		architect	architecture
명사	**명사+hood**		
child	childhood		
neighbor	neighborhood		
adult	adulthood		

ex Faced with a multitude of preoccupations, women in our time could not manage without ***endurance, patience*** and ***optimist.***

Tip · A, B, and C의 병치관계에서 optimist가 추상명사로 바뀌어야 하는 의미 병치이므로, optimist를 **추상명사인** optimism으로 고쳐야만 한다.

ex William Broyles Jr., former ***editorial*** of Newsweek magazine, needed a new challenge.

Tip · Comma 사이에 들어간 주어 동격으로 앞에 William과 같은 사람을 나타내야 하므로 인간명사 **editor**로 바꿔야 한다.

복합명사

다른 명사를 수식하는 수식명사는 단수여야 한다.

복합명사 : 단수명사 + 명사

ex two desks lamp → two desk lamps
a twelve pages assignment → a twelve page assignment
two hundreds people → two hundred people
three hundreds dollars/miles → three hundred dollars/miles
hundred of people → hundreds of people

Tip 앞에 숫자가 있으면 hundred나 thousand등은 복수를 사용하지 않는다.

FOOTNOTE
수식명사가 복수인 복합명사
ex. a clothes shop, a savings account, an admissions office, arms control, a sports car, athletics training, an economics degree

시간, 거리, 금액을 나타내는 명사의 복합명사

숫사표현 + 시간, 거리, 금액의 복수형(years, days, inches, feet, pounds, dollars) + 형용사
숫사표현 + 시간, 거리, 금액의 단수형(year, day, inch, foot, pound, dollar) + 명사

ex 단위명사가 다른 명사를 수식하지 않을 때

One hundred feet long — **cf.** one hundred foot long(×)
One hundred feet in length — **cf.** one hundred foot/feet length(×)
7 years old — **cf.** 7 years age(×)

ex 복합명사를 이룰 때

a one-hundred-foot-long bridge
a 7-year-old boy

어순

수식명사나 형용사가 피수식명사를 수식할 때 수식명사나 형용사가 피수식명사의 앞에 와야한다. 실제 문제에서는 수식명사나 형용사가 피수식명사의 뒤에 와서 피수식명사 앞으로 옮기는 것이 답이다.

ex A ***reservoir multipurpose*** is designed to satisfy a combination of community water needs.
(reservoir multipurpose → multipurpose reservoir)
These instructions are written in such ***language concrete*** that they are easy to follow.
(language concrete → concrete language)

Hackers Skill

1. '명사 + 명사'에 밑줄이 있으면 복합명사문제, 어순문제 순으로 의심한다.
2. 명사의 어순 문제는 밑줄이 있는 두 명사를 바꾸어 놓은 후의 어순이 맞으면 그것이 답이다.
3. '명사 + 형용사'에 밑줄이 있으면 어순문제임을 의심하라.

Hackers **Practice** | 연습문제 |

다음 문장에서 틀린 문장은 (I) 를, 올바른 문장에는 (C)을 쓰시오.

1 _______ News was released about the hostage.

2 ________ In the Middle Ages, there had been a few episode when popular imagination caused people to seek out someone who caused a flood.

3 ______ The origin of the horse go back to eohippus, the "dawn-horse" of the Eocene, only 10 to 20 inches tall.

4 ______ There are several kind of acids that pearls may come in contact with.

5 ______ John had a pairs of small blue eyes which were astonishingly shifty.

6 ______ This news were slightly disconcerting to Amy personally.

7 ______ Dr. Rita Colwell is a microbiologist who wears several different hat.

8 ______ Nuclear power plants efficiently produce large amounts of electrician without polluting the atmosphere.

9 _______ In the early years of the twentieth century several man who had amassed vast fortunes likewise became great philanthropists.

10 _______ An upsurge in mining during the twelfth century affected economic expansion.

11 _______ Elsewhere Justinian's army regained parts of Spain from the Visigoths and several of the large Mediterranean islands.

12 _______ Hundreds of priest served in the temples that dotted the Egyptian countryside.

■ 정답 p342

Hackers **TEST** | 실전문제 |

1 Divergent thinking tends away from a center, perhaps in several direction at once, seeking avenues of inquiry rather than a particular destination.
(A: tends / B: direction / C: at once / D: rather than)

2 High-ranking women in both Egypt and Assryia wore fake beards during official court business to show their equal authorization with men.
(A: and / B: during / C: to show / D: authorization with men)

3 Certainly one of the most intelligent and best educated women of her day, Mercy Otiose Warren produced a variety of poet and prose.
(A: Certainly / B: the most intelligent / C: her / D: poet)

4 Because different tree species adapted to different climates and soil types have evolved over millennia, many kind of forests occupy the earth today.
(A: Because / B: tree species / C: have evolved / D: kind of)

5 The first complete American dictionary of the English language were compiled in 1821 by the lawyer and lexicographer Noah Webster.
(A: The first / B: were compiled / C: by / D: lawyer)

6 In England and Wales, the official statistics used to estimate the criminal rate are based on the recording by the police of notifiable offences.
(A: to estimate / B: criminal rate / C: on / D: notifiable)

7 In Sweden, growth population encouraged colonists to move eastward, making their home in southern Finland.
(A: growth population / B: to move / C: eastward / D: making)

8 Matt also had hundreds of aide to assist him headed by a chancellor and six
A B C
other major ministers.
D

---

9 Louis Sullivan, the pioneer architecture of skyscrapers, built the first building
A B
in Chicago in 1884.
C D

---

10 The various Rockefeller foundation support research as well as
A B
humanitarian causes in the United States.
C D

---

11 The officials of the empire wanted to be sure that every farmers was working
A B C
and easy to locate.
D

---

12 Sculptors found models in the nude athletics who were in the peak of
A B C
physical fitness and attributed poise and serenity to them.
D

---

13 Numerous self-appointed general rose up to lead ragtag armies of peasants to
A B C D
Constantinople.

---

14 Detroit' s many ethnic groups are the Greeks, many of whom live in a
A B
neighbor called Greektown.
C D

---

15 There are basically three kinds of material that may erupt from a volcano
A B C
: lava, rock fragments, and gas.
D

■ 정답 p342

부정관사

Outline

영어는 원칙적으로 관사가 사용되는 언어이고 관사가 사용되지 않는 명사는 예외라는 개념에서 시작하여야 관사문제를 근본적으로 해결할 수 있다. 특히 한정되지 않은 단수가산 명사의 경우는 부정관사가 사용된다.

부정관사(article)	Checking Points
1. a/an	a/an은 뒤에 오는 단어의 발음에 따라 정해진다.
2. Naked Noun	영어의 명사는 naked noun으로 나올 수 없다. 특별한 경우가 아니면, 반드시 관사나 복수라는 옷을 입고 나와야 한다.
3. 명사와 수일치	a/an은 단수가산명사 앞에 사용 되어야 한다.

Hackers Grammar

a/an 부정관사

a **문제**	a + 자음 발음 단어 a university, a unit, a union, a utility, a uniform, a usage, a hospital a yacht, a yawn, a yard, a yardman, a year, a yoke
an **문제**	an + 모음 발음 단어 an umbrella, an uncle, an hour, an heir, an honest answer

FOOTNOTE

a. a, c, i, o로 발음되는 단어 앞에서 무조건 부정관사 an
b. h, u로 시작되는 단어 앞에서 [h] / [ju]로 발음될 때 a을 사용하고,모음으로 발음되면 an을 사용
c. 발음 따라 결정되기 때문에 a one-way ticket, an X-ray machine으로 쓰일 수 있음에 주의하자.

Naked Noun

명사는 몇몇의 특수한 상황을 제외하고는 관사를 가져야 하며, 한정되지 않는 단수가산 명사는 반드시 부정관사를 가져야 한다.

ex Jim placed ***a book*** on ***the shelf.***

Tip - Jim은 (대화자들이 서로 알고 있는) 선반 위에 (대화자들이 잘 알지 못하는 어떤) 책을 놓았다.

단수일 때 부정관사의 의무적 사용

a/an 사용	a great many of, a great number of, a series of a great deal of, a large amount of a lot of, a great quantity of, a wide variety of

FOOTNOTE

number, amount, quantity, lot, variety는 복수형인 numbers, amounts, lots, varieties, quantities으로 사용될 수 있으나 복수형이 없는 many와 deal은 복수로 쓰일 수 없다.

human류 명사

	단수	복수
1. Human : person	a human	humans
2. Human being : person	a human being	human beings
3. Humankind : people	humankind	humankind

ex ***Humankind*** has made great technological progress in the past one hundred years.

부정관사를 사용하지 못하는 특수한 상황(복수도 불가)

추상명사	advice, information, knowledge, news, courage, fun, wealth, evidence research, progress, permission, luck, ignorance, proportion
물질명사	money, cash(←cents, dollars) / equipment(←cars, tents), furniture(←desks, tables, chairs)
리씨형제	machinery, jewelry, poetry, scenery, weaponry
언어	English, Chinese, Japanese, Spanish
병명	appendicitis, measles cf. catch a cold
교통수단	by car/by bus/by bicycle/by tube/by boat, on foot/on horseback

Hackers Grammar

명사와의 수일치

a/an은 단수 가산 명사와 쓰인다. 특히 관사와 명사 사이가 멀 때, 관사와 명사의 수 일치에 주의해야 한다.

ex The operation on her back was ***a*** terribly painful ***ordeals,*** but it was necessary for her health.

Tip · 관사와 명사 사이에 부사와 형용사로 관사와 명사의 거리가 멀지만, 부정관사는 단수명사를 받아야 한다. 따라서, ordeals를 단수로 고쳐야 한다.

Hackers Grammar

부정관사가 특별하게 사용될 때

a /an이 시간, 거리, 금액의 명사와 같이 쓰여서 per의 의미를 가질 때

ex once ***a*** week : 일주일에 한 번, twice ***a*** yard : 1야드마다 두 번

a height of/***a*** weight of + 숫자일 때

ex The cassowary, one of the world's largest and least known birds, grows to ***a height of*** 6 feet and ***a weight of*** 120 pounds.

Hackers **Practice** | 연습문제 |

필요하면 빈칸에 부정관사를 넣으시오.

1 Ragtime was basically _____ pianistic style involving a flexible syncopation.

2 For the first time O'Keeffe created art with ________ unique style, unlike anything she had been taught in school.

3 Thelonious Monk became ______ important composer and performer during the 1950's.

4 He authored _______ series of works urging reform and better opportunities for education.

5 The sugar maple tree is a tall tree, reaching _____ height of 75 to 100 feet.

6 In the sixteenth century Russia was _______ strange and foreign country to West Europeans with customs more Asian and European.

7 Negro merchants from the forest regions placed _______ quantity of goods nearby.

8 Certain eunuchs gained the ears of the emperors and frequently gave ______ knowledge that promoted only their own interests.

9 Oprah was _____ unwanted child whose parents never married.

10 In 1441 European participation in the slave trade began when ______ small number of blacks were brought to Portugal

■ 정답 p343

Hackers **TEST** | 실전문제 |

1 Luther's own religious training made him scrupulous to a extreme, for in his
A B C
own estimation he could never reach perfection.
D

2 One of the world's great waterfalls is on the Zambezi: Victoria Falls trembles
A B C
from height of 335 feet.
D

3 If an unbalanced force acts upon a body, the momentum of the body
A
changes in a proportion to the force and in the same direction as the force.
B C D

4 Far from civilization, a small group of Georgia pioneers developed an unique
A B C
way of life.
D

5 The importance of Spanish discoveries were to give Charles an immense
A B
source of wealth to carry on his many wars in Europe.
C D

6 All of western Europe was never united under an single political structure,
A B
but religious belief for centuries provided a bond for its people.
C D

7 Archaeological investigation are a principal source of knowledge of prehistoric, ancient, and extinct cultures.
(A: Archaeological investigation, B: a, C: knowledge, D: cultures)

---

8 An French woman author, Christine de Pisan, published The City of Women which argued that there was as much talent in a community of women as in one composed of men.
(A: An, B: which, C: as, D: men)

---

9 Curiosity, sparked by the Renaissance fascination with things distant, made the study of the geography extremely popular.
(A: sparked by, B: the, C: the geography, D: extremely)

---

10 The pecan has a average height of 75 feet, although some wild trees have grown as tall as 160 feet.
(A: a, B: have, C: grown, D: tall)

---

11 European's long ships with their brightly colored square sails unfurled could race across the waves at close to 11 miles the hour.
(A: their, B: brightly, C: could race, D: the hour)

■ 정답 p343

정관사

Outline

부정관사와 달리 정관사는 가산명사뿐 아니라 불가산 명사와도 함께 사용할 수 있다. 이 과에서는 무관사로 쓰이는 명사와 정관사가 쓰이는 명사들을 숙지하도록 한다.

정관사(article)	Checking points
1. the vs. **무관사**	정관사를 쓸 수 없는 표현을 파악하기
2. the vs. **소유격**	사람목적어 + 전치사 + the + 신체부분 소유격 + life time/ ages / career

Hackers Grammar

정관사와 무관사의 선택

관사를 사용하지 못할 때

고유명사	호수, 산, 섬 이름	Lake Superior, Mount Everest, Haiti
	단수형 나라 이름	Spain, Canada
	대륙 이름	Asia, Africa, Europe, South America
	주, 도시, 거리 이름	Florida, Los Angeles, Broadway, Palms Street
추상명사	학문분야	literature, history, biology, architecture
	운동	baseball, tennis
	추상명사	love, liberty, literature, nature(자연), space(우주), society
기타	소씨 형제들	oxygen (산소), hydrogen (수소), nitrogen (질소)
	행성	Venus, Mars, Mercury cf. the Earth
	이중표현	day after day, husband and wife, arm in arm, inch by inch, with hat and coat, on land and sea, with knife and fork

무관사로 사용되는 명사라도 전치사구나 관계대명사로 수식을 받아 한정적 표현으로 바뀌어 the를 사용할 수 있다.

ex ***The literature*** of the sixteenth century, ***the history*** of America, ***the geography*** of Asia, ***the oxygen*** of the atmosphere

정관사를 사용해야 할 때

고유명사	바다, 강	the Pacific Ocean, the Hudson river
	복수의 호수, 복수의 섬(군도)	the Great Lakes, the Hawaiian Islands
	복수의 산(산맥)	the Rocky Mountains
전체표현	종족대표	***The dog*** is the cutest animal.
	the + 형용사(복수취급)	the young (people), the French (people)
한정적 표현	하나밖에 없는 존재	the moon, the sun, the world, the universe
	서수 앞	the First World War, the second page cf. World War I
	최상급 앞	the funniest movie, the smartest boy
시간 · 사물의 부위	시간의 부위	the morning, the afternoon, the evening cf. at night
		the past, the present, the future cf. at present
		the beginning, the middle, the end
	사물의 부위	the front, the center, the back, the top, the bottom
of 으로 연결된 이름들	국가명	the United States of America cf. Japan
	주명	the state of Indiana cf. Indiana
	학교명	the University of Oxford cf. Harvard University
기타	복수형태의 국가명	the Philippines, the Netherlands
	세기나 연대 앞	the 1950's, the twenty-first century
	수량표현	all/ most/ any/ some/ one + of + the + 명사
		ex. all/ most/ some + of the students

FOOTNOTE

1. 바다에 the가 사용되고 바다와 연결된 강에도 the가 사용된다. 그러나 바다와 연결되지 않은 호수에는 the가 사용되지 않는다. 복수의 호수의 경우는 너무 넓어서 바다라고 착각하고 the를 사용한다.
2. 유일한 존재가 모두 the가 사용되는 것은 아니다. Venus 나 Mars등 혹성은 유일하나 the가 사용되지 않는다.
3. all/most/any/some/one + of + (the / 소유격 / 대명사) 모두 가능

ex The student read most of ***the*** books / ***his*** books / ***them***.

ex The southern ***California*** (X)

→주 이름인 California를 the가 수식 불가능하므로 the 삭제

The southern ***part*** of California (○)

→ the는 California가 아닌 part를 수식하므로 맞는다.

The West (○)

→ the West는 서부지역의 뜻

Hackers Grammar

정관사와 소유격의 선택

동사 + 목적어 + 전치사 + the + 목적어의 부분
사람목적어와 동일한 신체부분이 전치사로 따라올 경우, 그 신체 부분에는 소유격이 아니라 정관사 the를 사용한다.

ex John's wife punched Tim in ***his*** face. (his → the)
Tim caught Mary by ***her*** neck. (her → the)
Your comments hit the nail on ***its*** head. (its → the)
cf. Jane waved ***her*** hands.

문장에서 사용된 명사(life, ages, career 등)의 소유자가 확실히 정해져야 할 때 정관사가 아니라, 소유격을 사용해야 한다.

ex John wrote many songs in ***the*** lifetime.
Tip · 누구의 lifetime인지 정확하게 하기 위해 소유격 his를 사용해야 한다.

ex Jane studied abroad in ***the*** twenties.
Tip · 누구의 20대 혹은 30대 등 나이를 나타내기 위해서 소유격 her를 사용한다.
the twenties는 20년대의 뜻으로 사용된다.

Hackers Grammar

기타 주의해야 할 정관사 용법

계절 앞의 the는 생략 가능하다.

ex winter / the winter

무관사의 명사도 후치 수식을 받으면 관사가 사용될 수도 있다.

ex the water in the bucket

Hackers Skill

관사문제는 a/an문제, 수일치 문제가 나온 문제에서 그것이 틀렸을 경우, 발견 즉시 답으로 정하고, 다른 종류의 관사문제는 다른 답이 있는지 먼저 확인하고 최후의 답으로 선택한다.

Hackers **Practice** | 연습문제 |

필요시 정관사를 넣으시오.

1 The land of China extended over a large territory in ______ East Asia.

2 ______ highest is 209 feet tall and almost 35 feet in diameter.

3 The egalitarian nature of Islam proved attractive to the people at ____ bottom of the caste system.

4 They populated ______ North America long before the continent was settled by Europeans.

5 In fact, the price of farm produce grew threefold in ______ first two decades of _____ century.

6 _____ African history can best be studied by looking at one region at a time.

7 _____ poor wear fine linen and the laundryman will not carry his burden.

8 The cell demonstrates all of _____ major characteristics of the cells of higher animals.

9 The precipitation north of _____ Appalachian Mountains is about 40 percent less than that south of them.

10 In the Southern Hemisphere the seasons are reversed, and February, which is wintertime in the United States, is summertime in _____ Australia.

11 Many of _______ raw materials that the nation's industry needed were in foreign hands.

■ 정답 p343

Hackers TEST | 실전문제 |

1 An Italian astronomer named Giovanni Riccioli used a telescope to map
A B C
moon 350 years ago.
D

2 Articles and books have been written by environmentalists and organizations
A B
interested in the ecology.
C D

3 Since a late 1950s California law has enforced the use of antipollution devices
A B C
on cars, trucks, and buses.
D

4 In 20th century, cultivation of bottle gourds, finger millet, and Galla potatoes
A B
is on the decline.
C D

5 The materials that are archaeology's subject of the research and study include
A B
everything made or used by human being.
C D

6 Colonization was especially attractive for the farmers who did not own their
A B C
own land and for unemployed.
D

7 The unpredictability of [Yellow River]A [has]B never allowed [it]C [to be]D tamed.

---

8 After [successful pollination]A, the pollen germinates [on surface]B of the pistil and [produces]C a tube [that]D grows down through the style to an ovule.

---

9 Thomas Malthus, [who an]A English economist, [developed]B a theory that became [widely]C accepted in [the nineteenth]D century.

---

10 The history of the Iditarod goes back to 1925 when a doctor in Nome, Alaska, [was]A [desperate]B in need of medicine to stop the spread of a [deadly]C disease [called diphtheria]D.

---

11 Some of [most promising]A advances [in]B Africa [have]C been made [in education]D.

---

12 At [beginning]A, town meetings [were]B intended [to operate]C on eventual differences between the village-dwellers [and]D outlying farmers.

■ 정답 p343

대명사

Outline

실제 TOEFL시험에서 명사의 반복사용을 피하기 위하여 대명사가 나올경우, 문장에서 대명사가 가리키는 명사(선행사)가 반드시 존재한다. 따라서 대명사에 밑줄이 그어져 있으면, 선행사를 찾아 수·성 일치, 재귀대명사 여부, 주어·목적어 반복등을 확인할 필요가 있다.

대명사(Pronoun)	Checking Points
1. 일치	선행사와 수일치및 성일치
2. 형태(격)	대명사의 주격, 목적격, 소유격, 소유대명사를 확인한다.
3. 재귀대명사	같은 절의 주어를 받는 대명사는 재귀대명사를 사용해야 한다.
4. 주어 · 목적어 반복	명사와 대명사의 주어반복, 관계대명사와 주어 / 목적어반복

명사와의 일치

대명사가 가리키는 명사의 수(단수, 복수)와 성(남성, 여성, 중성)을 일치시킨다.

ex The boy will cause trouble if you let ***them***.
them → him (the boy) : 수일치
A scientist bases ***its*** work on hypotheses that have been checked through careful experimentation.
its → his (scientist's) : 성일치

Hackers Grammar

대명사의 형태

밑줄 친 대명사의 문장에서의 위치(기능)에 따라 적절한 형태인지 파악한다.

격	용법	인칭변화
주격	대명사 + 동사	I, you, he, she, we, they, it
목적격	동사/ 전치사 + 대명사	me, you, him, her, us, them, it
소유형용사	대명사 + 무관사 명사	my, your, his, her, our, their, its
소유대명사	주어, 목적어, 보어자리	mine, yours, his, hers, ours, theirs
재귀대명사	목적어, 보어자리	myself, yourself, himself, herself, itself, themselves, ourselves

ex Everyone except ***he*** agreed.

Tip · 전치사 뒤에는 목적격 대명사가 오므로 he를 him으로 고친다. 동사 앞이라는 이유로 목적격이 아닌 주격으로 쓰지 않도록 주의한다.

Hackers Grammar

재귀대명사의 선택

대명사의 선행사가 동일 절의 주어이면, 그 대명사는 재귀대명사로 사용되어야 한다.

ex John killed ***himself.*** (동사의 목적어 자리)

Tip · 동일절의 주어가 John이므로 재귀대명사 himself를 사용한다.

Many birds follow a migration route to protect ***itself*** against severe cold during the winter.

Tip · protect하는 의미상의 주어가 many birds이므로 그것의 목적어는 재귀대명사가 되어야 한다. 수일치를 시키면, themselves가 되어야 한다.

목적어나 보어의 위치에 있지 않은 대명사가 선행사를 강조하기 위해서 선행사 뒤에서 '바로 자신' 정도의 의미로 사용된다.

ex They ***themselves*** may become identified with the status quo.(목적어나 보어 이외의 자리)

주어 및 목적어 반복

주어 반복	주어 + (삽입구/ 절) + 주어반복 + 동사 주격관대 + 주어반복 + 동사
목적어 반복	목적격관대 + 주어 + 동사 + 목적어반복

ex The history of taste, which is part of the history of art, ***it*** is a continuous process of discarding established values and rediscovering neglected ones.

Tip · 삽입절인 which이하의 관계절을 거둬내면 앞에 the history와 뒤에 it의 주어중복이 일어나므로 it을 삭제한다.

ex Businessmen who ***they*** took their companies public sold stock as another means of capital expansion.

Tip · who이하 관계절에 they라는 주어가 다시 나오므로 주어반복이 일어났으므로 they를 삭제하여야 한다.

ex The Sterns sued and regained custody of the little girl they called ***her*** Melissa.

Tip · 목적격 관계대명사가 생략된 관계절 이하에서 한 개의 명사와 명사 목적보어를 갖는 동사인 call동사의 생략된 목적격 관계대명사 whom이 있으므로 중복된 her를 삭제한다.

Hackers Skill

삽입구로 문장이 복잡해지면 주어와 동사사이의 거품을 걷어내고 주어의 반복을 확인한다.
관계절에서 주어나 목적어에 밑줄이 있으면 관계대명사를 원상복귀시켜서 확인한다

Hackers **Practice** | 연습문제 |

다음 문장에서 틀린 문장에는 (I) 를, 올바른 문장에는 (C)를 쓰시오.

1 _______ Europeans erroneously considered them the first settlers in North America.

2 ______ Ideology works in a manner analogous to naming a person or hailing him or her in the street.

3 _____ Protecting pearls properly can make themselves last for centuries.

4 _____ On the contrary, each region sets his table with a different specialty.

5 ______ New Orleans is known for its jambalaya, a spicy dish of rice, ham, shrimp, and tomatoes.

6 _______ Jefferson also drew up the constitution for his state, Virginia, and served as her governor.

7 ______ Even before the United States became a nation, some of its people began to move west.

8 _____ The Chicanos bring some pleasure into his hard life.

9 _____ They describe themselves as political activists.

10 _____ Each Spartan had their Messenian helot family to supply his food.

11 _____ The Assyrians began to assert themselves only in about 1350 B.C.

12 _____ Chinese culture extended to an area much larger than the country it.

■ 정답 p344

Hackers **TEST** | 실전문제 |

1 The classic Neanderthals, who they (A) lived between about 70,000 and (B) 30,000 years ago, shared a number of (C) special characteristics (D).

2 Jazz trumpeters (A) and saxophonists departed from (B) written notes in order to express (C) them (D).

3 John Alden ends up marrying (A) Priscilla Mullins himself, and it takes (B) time for him (C) friendship with Miles Standish to recover (D).

4 Joseph Nicephore Niepce put some paper dipped (A) in a light-sensitive chemical into (B) his camera obscura which she (C) left on (D) a window.

5 Each Pueblo community closely (A) organizes their (B) political and social life and also maintains (C) the (D) old religious ceremonies.

6 Many (A) of these newcomers have worked very hard to establish (B) himself (C) in their (D) new land.

Written Expression

www.goHackers.com

7 Cesar Chavez was particularly well-known for their leadership of farm workers.
A: particularly B: their C: of D: farm workers

---

8 Part of the problem is the size and complexity of the job market himself.
A: is B: the C: job market D: himself

---

9 The Indians evolved quite different techniques for human survival in adapting them to local conditions.
A: human survival B: in adapting C: them D: to

---

10 The American Revolution settled the issue when the United States took their place as an independent nation.
A: settled B: when C: their place D: an

---

11 The generation after Alexander's death was very turbulent as the generals who they accompanied him struggled among themselves for precedence.
A: after B: turbulent C: who they D: among themselves

---

12 Before Greece reached their golden age in the Western world, it first had to pass through the Dorian invasions.
A: Before B: their golden age C: to pass D: the

■ 정답 p344

1 Few observer (A) would have (B) expected the Bolshevik rise to power (C) in (D) Russia.

2 The Iconodules formed (A) party (B) that insisted that icons have a (C) place in (D) the churches and in the worship of the church.

3 A series of hammer (A) attached to the gears of the mill replaced (B) human feet in the (C) process of fueling, cleaning, and thickening wool (D).

4 Holding (A) one end of the pole between alligator's tooth (B), Loon would imitate (C) the animal's deep growl (D).

5 Ethiopia produced an (A) unique form of the Christian religion in (B) eastern Africa that was remarkably vital (C), despite (D) its isolation.

6 Interplanetary craft will be built (A) to carry explorers to the (B) Mars and perhaps one day to other planets (C) in (D) our universe.

7 In Gaul the invading (A) Germans belonged to (B) a variety of tribe (C), and the largest (D) and most important were the Franks.

8 New office buildings are constructed (A), factories are expanded, the (B) machinery is purchased, and workers are hired - all to be (C) ready for a great surge of consumer buying (D) power.

9 Every nation had their(A) favorite authors and poets(B) in an(C) age where romanticism flourished in literature(D).

---

10 Ferdinand de Lesseps, a French engineers(A), proposed building(B) a canal through the Suez Isthmus to unite(C) the(D) Mediterranean and Red Seas.

---

11 Although English(A) colonized areas throughout the New World, their most important(B) foreign holdings turned out(C) to be the 13 colonies along(D) the Atlantic coastline of North America.

---

12 Homeostasis enables the(A) body to maintain(B) their(C) internal biological systems under variable environmental stresses(D).

---

13 Watson's theory inspired a tremendous(A) increase in research on(B) how humans and animals learn from their(C) infancy to early child(D).

---

14 Many historic and architecturally(A) significant building(B) are maintained(C) in the French Quarter, the oldest(D) section of the city.

---

15 The amount of vitamin in a given solution(A) can be measured, under carefully(B) controlled conditions, by observing(C) the multiplication of a particular kinds(D) of bacterium.

■ 정답 p345

chapter 2

HACKERS TOEFL

Written Expression

수식어구

이 chapter에서는 수식어구인 형용사, 부사, 관계사, 그리고 전치사와 접속사를 공략한다. 형용사나 부사 관련해서는 특히 형용사 부사의 선택문제, 어순문제를, 관계대명사는 각 관계대명사의 용법을, 그리고 전치사와 접속사를 각각의 용법뿐 아니라 전치사와 접속사를 문장에서 구별해서 쓰도록 훈련을 한다.

1 형용사와 부사

Outline

형용사와 부사는 수식어로서 형용사는 명사를, 부사는(대)명사 이외의 것을 수식한다. 형용사와 부사의 선택문제, linking verb뒤에 형용사/명사 선택문제등이 출제된다.

형용사 & 부사	Checking Points
1. 형용사 vs. 부사	형용사와 부사의 적절한 선택 형용사와 부사의 혼동하기 쉬운 형태
2. 형용사 vs. 명사	linking verb 뒤에 형용사/명사 선택하기
3. 어순	부사 + 형용사 + 명사의 어순 빈도부사의 위치 부사 + 전치사 또는 접속사

Hackers Grammar

형용사와 부사의 선택

형용사 선택	
명사앞	형용사는 명사를 수식 ex. (관사) + 형용사 + 명사
Linking verb의 보어	주어 + linking verb + 형용사 (주어수식)
형용사 병치	형용사, 형용사, (and/or) 형용사

FOOTNOTE
Linking verb : feel, look, smell, sound, taste
appear, be, become, prove, remain, seem, go
(go crazy 처럼 become 의 뜻일 때)

형용사 : **주어 수식**(no action)

1. John looks nice
Sub. Adj.
2. John seems unusually nice
Sub. Adv. Adj.

ex The candy tastes ***sweetly.***
The couch looks ***comfortably.***

Tip · sweetly와 comfortably가 동사를 수식하는 것이 아니라 각각의 주어를 수식하므로 sweet와 comfortable로 바뀌어야 한다.

부사 선택	
명사이외의 앞	부사는 (대)명사를 제외한 모든 것을 수식한다. ex. 부사 + 관사 + 명사
동사를 수식	일반동사 + 부사 (동사수식)
부사 병치	부사, 부사, and/or 부사

부사 : 동사 수식(action)

John spoke nicely.
Verb. Adv.

ex Jane spoke to me ***blunt.***

Tip · blunt는 동사를 수식하므로 부사인 bluntly로 고쳐야 한다.

ex Cells can exist ***independent*** of other cells.

Tip · independent가 명사를 수식하지 않으므로 부사인 independently로 바꿔야 한다.

ex ***Complete*** aquatic, sirenians inhabit the tropical coastal waters of the West Indies

Tip · complete가 명사를 수식하지 않으므로 부사인 completely로 바뀌어야 한다.

Hackers Grammar

형용사와 부사의 형태

-ly로 끝나는 단어가 형용사인 경우
friendly, ugly, costly, lively, lovely, orderly, etc

ex I thought Joan was a very ***friendly*** person. (friendly가 명사 person을 꾸미는 형용사)

형용사형과 부사형이 같은 경우
early, daily, weekly, monthly, yearly, fast, late, hard, long, etc

ex Like all children living in villages, Dashnyam was used to working from an ***early*** age.

Hackers Grammar

일부 Linking Verb 뒤의 형용사 · 명사 선택

관련 Linking Verb : become, remain, be**동사**

Linking Verb + **형용사**	보어인 형용사가 주어를 수식 Heathcliff remained ***silent.***
Linking Verb + **명사**	보어인 명사가 주어와 동격 Marriage remains ***a popular institution.***

Hackers Grammar

형용사와 부사의 어순

형용사 + 명사의 앞에 오는 수식어는 부사와 형용사가 모두 가능하나 부사나 형용사의 선택은 해석하여 뒤의 형용사를 수식하면 부사가, 뒤의 명사를 수식하면 형용사가 맞다.

명사 앞의 형용사를 수식하는 부사	(관사) + 부사 + 형용사 + 명사
명사를 수식하는 형용사	(관사) + 형용사 + 형용사 + 명사

a specially designed camera ← a camera which is specially designed

a special computerized camera ← a special camera which is computerized

ex ***Distinctively*** American architecture began with Frank Lloyd Wright.

Tip · 뒤의 형용사 American을 수식해 주므로 부사 distinctively가 올 수 있다.
명사 architecture를 수식하려면 형용사 distinctive가 와야 한다.

빈도 및 불특정기간 부사의 위치는 첫 번째 조동사나 be동사 뒤, 혹은 조동사가 없을 때는 본동사 앞에 위치한다.

ex He ***has taken long*** an English course. (→has long taken)
I ***get often*** headaches.(→often get)

부사가 전치사구나 부사절을 수식할 때는 바로 앞에서 수식한다.

ex Latin America remained a part of the European economic system ***after long*** political independence was attained. (→long after)
Before two hours we reached our base camp, a sudden hailstorm pelted it with ice.
(→Two hours before)

Hackers Grammar

부사의 위치

일반적으로 동사를 수식하는 부사는 타동사와 목적어 사이에는 위치하지 않는다.
'동사 + 부사 + 목적어 → 부사 + [동사 + 목적어], 또는 [동사 + 목적어] + 부사'

ex A star and an empty space composed ***really*** a binary star. (composed really → really composed)

문장전체를 수식하는 부사는 일반적으로 문두, 문미, 그리고 동사 앞에 위치한다.
recently(lately) : 문두, 문미
certainly : 문미만 빼고 어느 곳에나 위치

강조부사와 '거의' 의미의 부사는 수식하는 다른 부사나 형용사 앞에 온다.
very, much, too, extremely, almost, nearly, all but, etc.

ex all almost → almost all

Hackers Skill

Linking verb의 품사문제에서 linking verb의 보어가 주어를 수식하면 형용사, 주어와 동격관계를 이루고 있으면 명사이어야 한다.

Hackers **Practice** | 연습문제 |

다음 문장 중에서 틀린 문장에는 (I), 올바른 문장에는 (C)를 쓰시오.

1 ______ The Aztecs of Mexico were probably the first people to domesticate the turkey.

2 ______ The chiefly difference between brown bears and black bears is size, as brown bears on the average are slightly larger.

3 ______ Milk contains hydrocarbons necessary for crude oil and gasoline substitutes.

4 ______ Two theaters in Stratford-upon-Avon and two in London are regular used by the Royal Shakespeare Company.

5 ______ Although square dancing is usually considered a typically American form of dance, its origin can be traced to early European folk dances.

6 ______ Greg stretched out comfortable after reading a book.

7 ______ The holiday is now principally observed as a three-day weekend, the final extended holiday of summer.

8 ______ People moved to westward beyond the Mississippi.

9 ______ Charlie narrow escaped capture by hiding in the Highlands until he was rescued by a French ship.

10 ______ More important, he identified public loyalty to his throne with fidelity to Catholicism.

■ 정답 p346

Hackers TEST | 실전문제 |

1 The emergence of endocrinology as <u>a</u> (A) separate discipline can <u>probable</u> (B) be traced <u>to the experiments</u> (C) of Bayliss and Starling <u>on</u> (D) the hormone secretion.

2 The <u>chief</u> (A) characteristic that distinguished the corporate colony from others <u>were</u> (B) the <u>large measure</u> (C) of self-government <u>it</u> (D) enjoyed.

3 <u>In atherosclerosis</u> (A), small patches of fatty material, <u>composed mostly</u> (B) of cholesterol, <u>forms</u> (C) on the inside lining of <u>the</u> (D) arteries.

4 Dolphins do <u>such</u> (A) dangerous and necessary work <u>as</u> (B) locating explosives <u>hiding</u> (C) in the sea and helping ships <u>navigate safely</u> (D) in war zones.

5 Tomatoes, <u>actual</u> (A) a fruit that <u>is used</u> (B) as a vegetable, began <u>gaining</u> (C) wide acceptance <u>as a</u> (D) food plant in the United States between 1820 and 1850.

6 <u>The</u> (A) government <u>made</u> (B) <u>much</u> (C) new treaties with <u>the</u> (D) Indians.

7 The Irish and others (A) were eager (B) absorbed as construction laborers (C) on roads, bridges, and railroads as well as in (D) factories.

---

8 John D. Rockefeller became fabulous (A) rich through (B) oil refineries (C) and other enterprises (D).

---

9 The Wan Li emperor, who ruled (A) from 1572 to (B) 1620, was completely almost (C) indifferent to (D) government.

---

10 The Indians of South America (A) created a way of life remarkable suited (B) to their (C) environments, living (D) in harmony, not in contest, with nature.

---

11 A careful tended (A) garden was a place that was bound to inspire (B) inward (C) thought (D) for Zen Buddhists.

---

12 The (A) death of so many natives after immediately (B) the conquest caused (C) a chronic labor shortage (D).

■ 정답 p346

2 전치사

Outline

전치사 문제는 구동사에서 전치사 문제와 기본적인 전치사의 용법의 문제가 출제되므로 구동사를 외우고 기본적인 전치사의 용법을 알아두어야 한다.

전치사	Checking Points
1. 전치사 실종	필요한 전치사가 실종된 경우
2. 전치사 선택	명사, 동사, 형용사 등이 잘못된 전치사와 결합된 경우
3. 전치사 사족	필요 없는 전치사가 첨가된 경우

Hackers Grammar

전치사 실종

실종 list	실종 사례
자동사의 전치사 실종	A lack of one vitamin can ***interfere*** the processing of another. → **interfere with**
과거분사 다음에 전치사 없이 나오는 목적어	Public service, widely ***practiced*** other countries, is fairly new concepts in the united state. → **practiced in**
관계대명사의 전치사 실종	An ideal is a standard ***which*** people judge real phenomenon. → **by which**

Hackers Grammar

전치사 선택 (전치사 list는 뒤의 부록 참조)

선택 list	선택 사례
동사의 전치사 선택	Atomic nuclei are believed to ***be composed by*** protons and neutrons. → **be composed of** in/on은 정지동사와, into/onto는 이동/변환동사와 함께 사용됨 Originally, robots were ***found*** only ***into*** science fiction books. → **in** The office was ***organized in*** various departments. → **into**
형용사의 전치사 선택	Network games are very ***popular in*** the youth lately. → **popular with**
전치사의 목적어의 전치사 선택	A storm is moving ***with a slow speed*** of about 30 mph. → **at a slow speed**

Hackers Grammar

전치사 사족

사족 list	사족 사례
부사 앞에서	A group of people moved to ***upward*** fast. → **to 삭제**
타동사의 전치사	Rolland ***entered into*** the room silently. → **into 삭제** (enter into는 '시작하다' 의 뜻)
관계대명사의 전치사 사족	We lodged at the hotel in which Jack ***recommended*** to us. → **in 삭제** (which는 recommend의 목적어로 in which가 될 이유가 없음)

FOOTNOTE

forward, backward, upward, downward, eastward, southward, abroad나 downtown, underground, home등이 부사로 사용될 때는 앞에 전치사가 올 수 없다.

Hackers **Practice** | 연습문제 |

다음 문장에서 틀린 문장에는 (I) 를, 올바른 문장에는 (C)를 쓰시오.

1 _____ Like the CSS Merrimack, the USS Monitor was expected to sink, and it was referred as "Ericsson's Folly"

2 _____ Since Hemin was young, he has always wanted to go to abroad.

3 _____ As soon as I arrived my office, I knew that something was wrong.

4 _____ A water molecule consists two hydrogen atoms and one oxygen atom.

5 _____ Lyric poems were once sung to the musical accompaniment of a stringed instrument called as a lyre.

6 _____ Due as its massive nature the ship's draft stretched twenty-two feet to the bottom.

7 _____ Addition the Confederate fleet included the CSS Tennessee, a 209-foot-long blockade runner with four broadside cannons.

8 _____ The United States can be proud its democratic educational heritage.

9 _____ A small group of cowboys had full responsibility a herd of thousands.

10 _____ The nomadic Plains Indians were dependent the buffalo.

11 _____ Pope Leo X, a true Florentine, continued his predecessor's attention to music and art.

12 _____ Charles tried to deal with all the problems, but each one demanded his full attention.

■ 정답 p346

Hackers **TEST** | 실전문제 |

1 Plant fiber was [A] used to weave baskets with beautiful, intricate patterns [B] that are regarded [C] being among the finest [D] in the world.

2 After [A] the United States took over Louisiana, the Creole cultural identity became a means [B] of distinguishing [C] who was truly native of [D] Louisiana.

3 The [A] reason as [B] the high number of f.p.c. in New Orleans was largely due to [C] the influx of Haitian Refugees into the city [D] in 1809.

4 Due to [A] the racial and cultural complexity of colonial Louisiana, native Americans who were [B] born into slavery were [C] sometimes described [D] "Creoles" or "born in country."

5 The early Mardi Gras consisted [A] citizens wearing [B] masks travelling on foot [C], in [D] carriages, and on horseback.

6 Several [A] writers focused [B] their plight and the moral [C] obligation of the United States to right the wrong that was done [D] to them.

7 In economic [A], the [B] policy in which the government does not interfere with [C] the county's business affairs is [D] called laissez-faire.

8 Many other (A) leaders and sects have founded Utopian communities (B) in accordance (C) their (D) belief.

9 In addition (A) he opposed (B) a strong government because (C) it might interfere (D) ___ people's freedom.

10 Ferdinand and Isabella requested the pope to draw (A) a (B) line of demarcation to separate Spanish finds to (C) those of (D) Portugal.

11 The effect of the silver trade to (A) China and Spain, geographically (B) so far away from each other, demonstrates (C) at the early date the (D) interdependence of the world economy.

12 The only commercial (A) activity carried on was the exportation of wood contained (B) a (C) special kind of dye in demand (D) in Europe.

13 On (A) 1961 the first attacks began (B) on the Europeans, and (C) for the next 15 years the conflict continued (D).

■ 정답 p346

3 관계대명사

Outline

관계대명사 문제는 알맞은 관계대명사를 선택하는 것이 대부분이므로 각 관계대명사의 용법을 알아두어야한다. 관계대명사가 형성되기 전으로 원상복구시켜 문제를 해결하는 훈련을 하도록 한다.

관계사	Checking Points
1. who vs. which	who는 사람 선행사를 받고, which는 사물 선행사를 받는다. → who(사람), which(사물), that(사람, 사물)
2. 원상복구문제	관계대명사 앞에 오는 전치사 선택이나 관계대명사의 격문제는 관계절을 원상복구시켜 해결한다.
3. 주어실종	'전치사 + 관계대명사 + 동사' 에서 주어 실종
4. 관계부사	장소선행사 + where 시간선행사 + when
5. that & what	that은 계속적 용법이나 전치사의 목적어로 사용되지 않으며, what은 선행사를 가지면 안 된다.

Hackers Grammar

who / which 선택 문제

가장 빈도수가 높은 문제 유형 중 하나이다.
사람 선행사일 때 who (whom), 사물 선행사일 때 which 사용

ex A light-skinned individual ***which*** moves to a hot tropical region will develop increased pigmentation in his skin.

Tip · 선행사가 사람(individual)이므로 관계대명사 which를 who로 바꾼다.

Hackers Grammar

원상복구문제

적당한 전치사 선택을 위해 선행사를 관계절 이하에 복원하여 문장을 완전하게 만든다.

ex Bill didn't get the job ***in which*** he applied.

Tip · 전치사 in이 적절한지 확인하기 위해 관계절을 선행사(the job)를 넣어 문장을 복원한다.
'he applied in the job' 으로 복원되는데, 의미상 '지원하다' 일 때는 apply for를 사용하기 때문에 in을 for로 바꿔야만 한다.

ex Empirical studies include the way ***which*** the first five seconds of telephone conversation are structured.

Tip · way는 in the way처럼 in과 함께 쓰이고, ~ are structured in the way로 복원되므로 in which가 되어야 한다.

Hackers Grammar

주어실종

'전치사 + 명사' 가 전치사구로서 주어가 될 수 없는 것과 마찬가지로
'전치사 + 관계대명사' 도 전치사구로서 주어가 될 수 없다.
따라서 [전치사 + 관계대명사 + 동사]로 된 문장은 주어가 실종된것이므로,
[전치사 + 관계대명사 + 주어 + 동사]로 **주어**가 삽입되어야 한다.

ex The spat grew larger by drawing in seawater ***from which*** derived microscopic particles of food.

Tip · 전치사 + 관계대명사는 주어가 될 수 없으므로 from which는 동사 derived의 주어가 될 수 없다.
derived의 주어가 삽입되어야 한다.

Hackers Grammar

관계부사의 선택

선행사가 장소일 때 where를 사용하며 in/at/on which로 대치될 수 있다.

ex It was in a cave near Magdalena, New Mexico, ***where*** the oldest known ears of cultivated corn were discovered.

선행사가 시간일 때 when을 사용하며, in/at/on which로 대치될 수 있다.

ex John's wife graduated from college in 1980 ***when*** their youngest child was born.

Hackers Grammar

주의해야 할 관계대명사 용법

that은 comma뒤에 계속적 용법의 관계 대명사로 사용될 수 없다.

ex Trees attacked by insects may communicate information to neighboring trees, ***that*** act accordingly.

Tip · that은 관계대명사 계속적 용법이 불가능하므로 which로 대치한다.

, that (X)

that절은 전치사의 목적격으로 사용되지 않는다.
(단, 부사절 in that은 예외)

ex Art Clokey used a technique called stop-motion ***in that*** he filmed clay figures.

Tip · that은 전치사의 목적어로 사용되지 못하고, 이유를 나타내는 부사절 in that도 아니므로, in that을 in which로 바꾸어야 한다.

what은 선행사를 갖는 관계대명사로 사용될 수 없다.

ex Studying management is helpful to break it down into planning, staffing, leading, and controlling ***what*** can be organized by the knowledge that underlies those functions.

Tip · what은 선행사를 가질 수 없음에도 planning이하를 선행사로 하는 what 관계절 이하가 형용사절로 되어 있으므로, what을 which로 바꿔야 한다.

Hackers Skill

1. that은 계속적 용법이 없다.
2. that절은 전치사의 목적어가 될 수 없다.
3. what은 선행사를 갖는 관계대명사로 사용 될 수 없다.

Hackers Practice | 연습문제 |

다음 문장에서 틀린 문장에는 (I) 를, 올바른 문장은 (C)를 쓰시오.

1 _____ Algae are aquatic plants who may serve as food for many large and small animals.

2 _____ Radar for fire control differs from ordinary radar chiefly in the precision with which locates targets.

3 _____ There are three main types of sedimentary rocks, which are classified according to the origin and size of their particles.

4 _____ Seahorses have eyes that move independently of each other, that enable them to spot potential food.

5 _____ "Abstract Expressionism" was the movement in painting which originated solely in America.

6 _____ Today the structures in which live and work, the machines that we rely on, the tools with which we create – all of these are dependent on metal.

7 _____ Extra toes became vestiges that was not visible externally.

8 _____ Henry David Thoreau was a writer and naturalist which lived in the nineteenth century.

9 _____ The "market basket" for the consumer price index, who is used to measure inflation in the U.S. economy, is made up of over 80,000 items.

10 _____ Congress also granted the Indian's funds for education, who was to be compulsory.

■ 정답 p347

Hackers **TEST** | 실전문제 |

1 The term "endocrine" contrasts with (A) "exocrine", who (B) is applied to glands that secrete their products (C) through ducts to the site of (D) action.

2 A (A) pound of these crustaceans contains about (B) 460 calories - about the same as (C) shrimp or lobster, in which (D) they are related.

3 Dahlgran guns were massive (A) rifled cannons that (B) were capable to fire (C) a (D) variety of shots.

4 Within (A) the village the Indians lived in (B) dwellings called (C) "long houses" who (D) were up to 300 feet long and 16 feet wide.

5 Many of us which (A) have been in the same job for years suddenly (B) find we must go back (C) to school to retrain in order to meet (D) the advancements made in our field.

6 Although (A) the early colonists were preoccupied (B) with personal goals such as (C) building family and farm, they left descendants who they (D) possessed broader vision.

7 Galaxies have some puzzling features (A), but on the whole (B), they are scarcely most complicated (C) than the stars that (D) compose them.

8 In (A) 1889 Jane Addams established (B) a "settlement house" where (C) she initiated many humanitarian project (D).

---

9 Language has (A) been one of the chief problems (B) of (C) the Puerto Ricans, to which (D) English is foreign.

---

10 Democratic ideas prompted elections to be hold (A) for seats in (B) the assemblies where men (C) freely discussed (D) issues.

---

11 They were not free to leave (A) the (B) estates which (C) they (D) were born or to change jobs.

---

12 In the center of every towns (A), the agora was surrounded (B) by shops called (C) stoa where (D) people came to shop.

---

13 Andalusia was (A) the major channel which (B) western Europe obtained (C) products from (D) Asia and Africa.

---

14 The Berbers were often influenced (A) by marabouts, holy men (B), whom the (C) Arabs thought them (D) to be quite outside orthodox Islam.

■ 정답 p347

4 접속사

Outline

접속사는 두 개의 문장을 이어준다. 두 개의 절을 하나의 접속사로 연결한 후에 다른 접속사가 추가되면 안된다. 접속사와 비접속사를 구별할 수 있어야 한다.

접속사	Checking Points
1. 전치사 vs. 접속사	접속사는 절을 이끌고, 전치사는 구를 이끈다.
2. 접속사 선택	해석을 통해서 의미상 맞지 않는 접속사를 가려낸다.
3. 접속사 중복	두 개의 절은 하나의 접속사에 의해 연결된다.
4. 부사와 어순문제	접속사 + 부사 → 부사 + 접속사

Hackers Grammar

전치사와 접속사 선택문제

뒤에 절(주어+동사)이 오면 접속사, 뒤에 명사나 동명사가 나오면 전치사

	부사절 접속사	전치사(구)
이유	as, because, since, now that, in that	because of, on account of, due to, owing to
대조	although, though, even if, whereas, while	despite, in spite of, regardless of in contrast with
시간	when, while, after, before	at, in, on, during, after, before
장소	where	in, at, on
목적	so that, in order that	so as to, in order to, for the purpose of
조건	if, unless, provided, in case	in case of

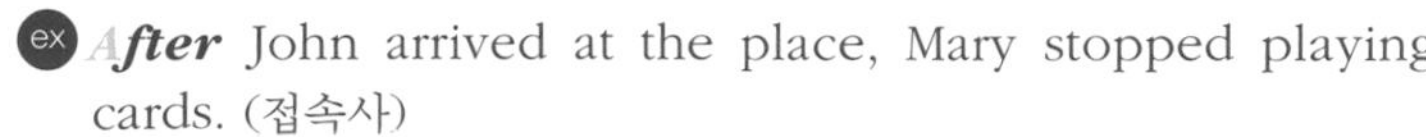

ex ***After*** John arrived at the place, Mary stopped playing cards. (접속사)

Visibility was poor yesterday ***on account of*** air pollution. (전치사)

축약된 절에서는 주어가 생략되고 현재분사나 과거분사, 또는 형용사, 전치사구의 형태가 나온다. 전치사와 접속부사의 구분을 위해 생략된 주어를 살려서 주어동사관계를 확인한다.

ex ***When compared*** with their western neighbors, Americans rank right about in the middle in hours of free time.
(When Americans are compared의 축약절)
When young, Clinton fell in love with his classmate.
(When Clinton was young의 축약절)

Hackers Grammar

접속사선택

접속사의 선택문제에서는 특히 주절과 종속절이 역접관계인지 순접관계를 파악하는데 유의한다.

순접관계	and, so, because, as
역접관계	but, yet, although, even though, whereas, while,

ex ***Because*** most honeybees die in the field while gathering pollen, some bees die in the hives.

Tip · 해석하면 주절과 종속절의 관계가 역접인 것을 알 수 있다. 따라서, Because보다 **Although**가 올바른 표현이다.

Hackers Grammar

접속사 중복

부사절 접속사 + 주어 + 동사, 등위접속사 (또는 비접속부사) + 주어 + 동사의 경우, 두 개의 절을 두 개의 접속사로 이을 수 없으므로, 앞의 부사절 접속사나 뒤의 등위접속사가 빠져야만 한다. 또한 주절을 비접속부사로도 시작할 수 없다. (자세한 내용은 Structure의 '접속사' 편 참조)

ex ***Although*** the candidate made sanctimonious statements about the need for more jobs, ***but*** he didn't create any after he was elected.

Tip · 앞에 although가 이끄는 종속절이 있고, 다시 뒤에 but이 이끄는 등위절이 있으므로 이것은 접속사 중복이므로 **둘 중에 하나는 없어져야 한다.**

ex ***Because*** prisons help protect society from its most dangerous criminals, ***then*** they are important.

Tip · 앞절이 부사절 접속사로 시작하였으므로 주절은 비접속부사(then)없이 주어 + 동사로 시작하여야 한다.

Hackers Grammar

부사와 어순문제 ('형용사와 부사' 편 부사의 어순 참조)

부사(shortly, soon, long, twenty minutes) + 접속사(before, after)

ex The fiscal year ended ***before shortly*** the company reached its target sales.

Tip · 부사(shortly)가 접속사 앞에 와야 하므로 shortly before로 어순이 바뀌어야 한다.

Hackers **Practice** | 연습문제 |

다음 문장중에서 문법상 틀린 문장이면 (I) 를, 올바른 문장이면 (C)를 쓰시오.

1 ______ The age of rock formations can sometimes be determined during paleontologists examine ancient fossilized remains.

2 ______ While associations with left-handedness tend to be negative, those relating to right-handedness are positive.

3 _____ Geysers have often been compared to volcanoes due to they both emit hot liquids from below the Earth's surface.

4 ______ Because of their hardiness, day lilies can be cultivated particularly easily.

5 _____ Because the African tsetse is a serious threat to human health, it helps maintain the delicate balance of nature.

6 ______ While there was an abundance of ammunition and ordinance, there was not a single morsel of food.

7 ______ Some won recognition and a place in the history of the War of Independence by their outstanding service, in spite of most have remained anonymous.

8 ______ Despite of its enormous food potential, little effort was made until recently to farm plankton as we farm grasses on land.

9 _____ While the northern part is bitter cold, the south, near Canada, is damp and mild.

10 _____ With the exception of Angola, the population was able to absorb the losses because the high birth rate among African families.

11 _____ The San hardly fared better, for they were pushed into the inhospitable Kalahari Desert.

■ 정답 p348

Hackers TEST | 실전문제 |

1 In eighteenth century Louisiana, the term Creole referred to locally born persons, regardless status or race, and was used to distinguish American-born slaves from African-born slaves.

(A) eighteenth century (B) referred to (C) regardless (D) distinguish

2 Since their pink color, people often appear as a solid reddish mass when viewed from a ship or from the air.

(A) Since (B) as (C) when (D) the

3 At night desert regions are often quite cool because of heat is lost rapidly after the sun sets.

(A) At night (B) are often (C) because of (D) lost

4 Today, Hay is flourishing again because of a flamboyant gentleman whom has turned the town into the world' s largest secondhand bookstore.

(A) flourishing (B) because of (C) whom (D) largest

5 Powell had made long trips down the Ohio and the Mississippi during his twenties, which his lifelong interest in natural history developed.

(A) had (B) during (C) his (D) which

6 Although Jazz' s melodies and harmonies are influenced by European music, the rhythms have essential a West African origin.

(A) Although (B) are influenced (C) music (D) essential

7 While the infamous Atlantic slave trade, thousands of Muslims from the Senegambia and Sudan were kidnapped or captured in local wars and sold into slavery.
(A: While, B: thousands, C: were, D: into)

---

8 Although the loss of two ships, Joan convinced his crew to sail through the strait at the tip of South America that still bears his name.
(A: Although, B: to sail, C: at, D: bears)

---

9 North America's weather tends being more moderate, whereas much of South America is tropical.
(A: being, B: more moderate, C: whereas, D: much)

---

10 Because he hardly ever left the cloister, Bede became the outstanding scholar of his age.
(A: Because, B: hardly ever left, C: the, D: his)

---

11 The practice of enslaving criminals and prisoners of war taken from neighboring peoples was common in Africa before long the coming of the Europeans.
(A: enslaving criminals, B: taken from, C: was, D: before long)

---

12 Although the apparent simplicity of her work, O'Keefe was the product of a rigorous and formal art education.
(A: Although, B: a, C: and, D: formal)

■ 정답 p348

ch3 Mini TEST | 실전문제 |

1 People on the(A) coast of eastern Africa(B) continued their contact with(C) the trading lively(D) world of the Indian Ocean.

2 The most serious(A) challenge at(B) the Roman Empire of the(C) fifth century came from the never-ending war with(D) the Persians.

3 By the time the army reached friendly territory(A) in early December, half a million soldier(B) lay(C) beneath the ground, covered(D) by Russian snow.

4 African wood carvings, especially(A) of masks, became a(B) major influence with(C) twentieth century European art(D).

5 The influence of Theravada Buddhism was evident(A) everywhere in Burma, when(B) the kings lavished(C) the wealth of the nation on(D) the construction of temples.

6 Depredations by the Patzinaks caused one group of Magyards to move(A) to westward(B) until they settled(C) on(D) the great plain of the middle Danube.

7 The loyal courtiers were in charge(A) the city at(B) the time the Crusaders approached(C) Jerusalem in(D) A.D. 1095.

8 Despite (A) the soil is generally quite (B) fertile, low rainfall can make (C) farming difficult (D) for those located in the west away from the major waterways.

---

9 Dirk Stroeve was one of those persons (A) whom, according (B) to your character, you cannot think of them (C) without derisive laughter or an embarrassed (D) shrug of the shoulders.

---

10 At (A) August 4, German armies crossed (B) the border, with (C) guns firing (D).

---

11 Holy places and temples were (A) scattered all over (B) the empire when (C) priests received people's offerings and sacrifices of (D) grain and animals.

---

12 There are (A) nine planets which (B) orbit the Sun and one should be familiar at (C) the names of these planets and their relative (D) locations.

---

13 Tundra is a cold area consisting (A) of flat, treeless plains where the ground is almost always (B) frozen except for a few centimeters (C) of the surface while (D) the short summer season.

---

14 When (A) complete (B) satisfied with its new mobile home, the hermit crab will emerge one last (C) time, turn (D) the shell over and make a final entrance.

---

15 Reverend William allowed his church and his home to be (A) used as a meeting place for a number of organizations (B) dedicated to (C) the education and socially (D) advancement of blacks.

■ 정답 p349

chapter 4

HACKERS TOEFL

Written Expression

구문

이 chapter에서는 병치, 짝짓기, 비교급과 최상급, so~that 구문을 공략한다. 각 과의 요점으로 쉽게 공략이 가능한 부분이니, 각 유형별 요점을 하고 숙지토록 한다.

병치

Outline

병치는 문장에 나열되는 문법단위들이 동일한 품사나 구조를 가지고, 연결관계의 일관성을 유지해야 한다는 것이다.

A, B, and C의 형태로 끊임없이 출제되는 문제 형식이므로 comma와 등위접속사(and, or, but)의 신호를 보고 병치를 파악하는 훈련이 필요하다.

병 치	Checking Points
1. 품사병치	명사, 형용사, 부사 병치
2. 구조병치	절, 동명사구, to 부정사구 병치
3. 의미병치	인간 vs. 추상

Hackers Grammar

품사병치

문장에서 나열시 동일 품사가 나열되어 병치를 이루어야 한다.

명사, 명사, and/or 명사
형용사, 형용사, and/or 형용사
부사, 부사, and/or 부사

ex The creative photographer perceives the essential qualities of the subject according to his judgment, taste, and ***involved.***

Tip · 명사간의 병치이므로 involved를 **involvement**로 바꿔야 한다.

Hackers Grammar

구조병치

병치구조에서 나열되는 항목들은 동일한 구조로 연결되어야 하지만, 동일한 전치사를 명사목적어가 같이 공유할 때는 전치사 생략이 가능하다.

동명사, 동명사 and/or 동명사	to 부정사, to부정사, and/or to 부정사
전치사구, 전치사구 and/or 전치사구	절, 절, and/or 절

ex Reading, writing, and ***to calculate*** are important skills to learn.

Tip · 동명사로만 병치관계를 이루어야 하므로 to calculate을 **calculating**으로 고친다.

Hackers Grammar

의미병치

병치 구조에서 가장 까다로운 부분으로 품사 및 구조병치를 완벽하게 이루었다고 하더라도 의미상 병렬관계가 아니라면 병치가 이루어지지 않은 것이다.

인간명사, 인간명사, and/or 인간명사	분야명사, 분야명사, and 분야명사

ex Chemical engineering is based on the principles of physics, ***chemists,*** and mathematics.

Tip · 같은 명사간의 병치라도 분야명사를 열거하는 중에 chemists라는 인간명사가 들어가면 의미병치가 성립되지 않으므로 **chemistry** 로 바꾸어야 한다.

Hackers Skill

Comma가 많거나 등위접속사(and, or 등), 혹은 짝짓기 접속사(상관접속사)가 오면 병치구조문제가 아닌가 의심한다.

Hackers **Practice** | 연습문제 |

아래의 문장에서 병치가 제대로 이루어지지 않은 문장은 (I), 제대로 이루어졌으면 (C)를 쓰시오.

1 Cooks, farmers, and butchers all do different tasks in food production.

2 Each person would have to master many trades just to satisfy the basic needs of food, clothing, and shelter.

3 During the first stage of creating a work, one can envision Michelle arranging her still-life materials and her flowers, selecting camera angles, and to wait until the light is perfect.

4 The history of metals in the hands of humans encompasses fire, pain, frustrate, and triumph.

5 Tiny amounts of some hormones can modify our moods and our actions, our inclination to eat or drink, our aggressiveness or submissiveness, and our reproductive and parental behavior.

6 A lady could easily find outlets in such obvious activities as decorating the pastor's study, carrying baskets to the poor, sewing for missionaries, or to take flowers to the sick.

7 Salaries, for instance, may be received weekly, biweek, or monthly.

8 The pioneers saw them as places for mining, for cattle-raising, and farming.

9 The Indians were accustomed to common ownership of tribal lands and to tribal units rather than to independent family living.

10 Some years swarms of locusts flew in like a dark cloud, settled on the field, and devouring every green leaf.

■ 정답 p350

Hackers **TEST** | 실전문제 |

1 Worker bees labor [A] for the good of the hive by collecting [B] food, caring [C] for the young, and to expand [D] the nest.

2 The creation of a map is a composition of [A] what will be [B] shown, what can [C] be shown in terms of map design, and which [D] we would like to include.

3 Hawks [A] can spot their [B] prey from a [C] great distance and attack swiftly, quietly, and accuracy [D].

4 By 1988 Gordon Parks had made two documentary films, wrote [A] two best-selling books [B], and [C] had accrued thirty years of experience [D] in still photography.

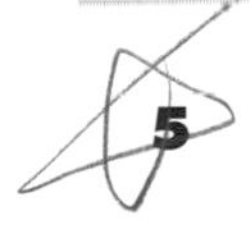

5 The zircon, a semiprecious [A] stone, occurs [B] in many shades [C] of red, green, and bluish [D].

6 Bricks are made from clay that is processed into a workable [A] consistency, form [B] to standard [C] sizes, and then [D] fired in a kiln.

7 Josh Billings roamed the country as a laborer [A] when he was a young man, but settled down [B] in his later life [C] to become a humorist and lecturing [D].

8 From dawn <u>to</u> dark the farmers performed <u>their</u> duties, rounding up the <u>cattle</u>, branding them for identification, and <u>repaired</u> equipment.
A B C D

9 <u>In spite</u> of all this progress, careers for women <u>were</u> largely restricted <u>to</u> teaching, <u>nurse</u>, and office work.
A B C D

10 The upper classes <u>with</u> <u>country estates</u> still <u>spent</u> much time hunting, fishing, <u>to ride</u> to the hounds, or giving lavish entertainments.
A B C D

■ 정답 p350

2 짝짓기

Outline

상관접속사는 두 개의 단어가 짝을 이뤄야 하며, 단독으로는 존재할 수 없다.
또한 짝짓기 구조 안에서 열거되는 항목들은 병치를 이룬다.

짝짓기(pairing)	Checking Points
짝 짓기 문제	같이 연결되는 상관접속사 찾기
짝짓기 구조내의 병치문제	상관접속사 구조 안에서 병치 이루기

Hackers Grammar

짝 짓기 문제

문장에서 상관접속사의 한 부분이 나오면, 그것의 짝이 나와야 한다.

both ... and	between ..... and	
whether ...(or)	either ... or	neither ... nor
not ... (but)	not only ... but (also)	
such ..... as	as··· as	as well as
so... that	such··· that	too .... to
비교급 ~er/more ... than	from ..... to/until	

※from··· to는 시간과 거리에, from··· until은 시간에만 사용한다.

ex **Whether** in analog **and** digital form, the signal is subsequently routed to a modulator.

Tip · whether는 or와 짝을 이루므로 and를 or로 바꿔야 한다.

ex Doctorates are awarded in **both** arts **but** sciences.

Tip · 'both A and B' 의 형태로 사용되므로 but을 and로 고친다.

짝짓기 구조내의 병치문제 ('병치' 편 참조)

상관 접속사로 연결하는 항목의 병치관계를 확인한다.
both A and B, either A or B, neither A nor B, not A but B, not only A but also B, B as well as A 등에서 A와 B는 병치구조를 이룬다.

ex Since the detainees can keep jobs, part of their salaries can be paid out either ***as fines*** or ***as compensating*** to victims.

Either A or B의 형태로 either와 or가 짝을 지어야 할 뿐 아니라, A와 B, 즉 fine과 compensating 이 병치구조를 이루어야 하므로 compensating 이 fine과 같은 일반명사인 **compensations**로 바뀌어야 한다.

FOOTNOTE

'not A, but B' 에서 but을 사용하지 않고 'B, not A' 의 형태로 바꿀 수 있다.

ex. The earliest use of the steam engine was **not to make** cloth **but to pump** water from mines.
→ The earliest use of the steam engine was **to pump** water from mines, **not to make** cloth.

Hackers **Practice** | 연습문제 |

괄호 안에서 알맞은 단어를 고르시오.

1 Eohippus died out about 50 million years ago in (from/both) North America and Europe.

2 The pieces of rock fragments can range in size from tiny bits of dust (and/to) large rocks.

3 Female cowbirds can (either/neither) sing nor teach songs to their babies by responding to certain chirps more than to others.

4 The jazz musician has to decide with lightning speed which notes to play, (what/whether) to play many or a few.

5 The marine biologists discovered that by raising the temperature of the water they could induce oysters to spawn (whether/not only) in the summer but also in the fall, winter, and spring.

6 Today, other techniques of water management are also possible, (as such/such as) tapping underground reservoirs and diverting rivers (until/from) one basin into another.

7 Most of these plants and animals are (very/too) small for the human eye to see.

8 The Feminist movement has focused on economic rights (as such/such as) "equal pay for equal work".

9 The difference between your assets (as well as/and) liabilities is your net worth.

10 Edward Hopper's paintings were composed in such a way (with/as) to create a somber, melancholy mood.

■ 정답 p350

Hackers **TEST** | 실전문제 |

1 The innovative poetry [A] of Walt Whitman motivated later [B] poets to experiment with [C] both meter or [D] subject matter.

2 According [A] to cognitive theories of emotion, anger occurs when individuals believe that they have been [B] harmed and that the harm [C] was either [D] avoidable and undeserved.

3 Throughout [A] history, shoes have been worn [B] not only for [C] protection and [D] also for decoration.

4 A marketing firm must be able [A] to evaluate the sales potential [B] in future markets as well in [C] markets that the firm currently serves [D].

5 Of all the famous American jazz musicians [A] of the [B] 20th century, none [C] was more resourceful, prolific, or durable as [D] Duke Ellington.

6 Throughout American history [A], Afro-Americans have had to decide whether [B] they belonged [C] in the United States and [D] they should go elsewhere.

7 Their great attraction [A] for suburban dwellers [B] is only proximity [C] but also ample parking [D] space.

8 Among the fixed expenditures are such budgetary items to rent, food bills, and the mortgage.

A: fixed, B: are, C: to, D: food bills

9 Alexander's goal was not only to complete the project of his father but also breaking the Persian hold on southwestern Asia.

A: was, B: his, C: also breaking, D: southwestern Asia

10 Male servants as such a butler or a coachman were signs that a family had arrived.

A: as such, B: or, C: were, D: a

■ 정답 p350

3 비교급과 최상급

Outline

비교급과 최상급의 형태

비교급과 최상급	Checking Points
1. 비교급 짝짓기	the + 비교급, the + 비교급 짝짓기 more/ ~er...than 짝짓기
2. 비교급, 최상급 형태	2음절에서 ~er/more , 3음절 이상에서 more 사용 '형용사 + ly'형 부사의 비교급/최상급은 more/less, most/least사용 the + 최상급
3. 비교급 vs. **최상급선택**	비교급 신호 : than, of two… 최상급 신호 : of 복수표현, in 집합표현, that절
4. 강조표현	원급, 비교급, 최상급의 강조 부사

Hackers Grammar

비교급 짝짓기

짝짓기 list	**짝짓기 예**
The **비교급**.., the **비교급**…	***The hotter*** the food is, ***the harder*** it is to eat.
형용사/부사의 ~er than	There are ***cheaper*** plastic baskets on the shelf ***than*** wooden ones.
more **형용사/부사** than	The present king is ***more*** popular ***than*** the last one.
more than … (~ **이상**)	***More than*** half of demonstrators crowded into the park.
less than… (~ **이하**)	***Less than*** two months after the work was finished we had to prepare it.

'The 비교급, the 비교급' 형태에서 be동사가 생략되어 동사가 없는 문장이 만들어지면 'the 비교급 + the 명사, the 비교급 + the 명사' 가 가능하다.

ex ***The more expensive*** the hotel, ***the better*** the service.

의미상 비교되는 대상, 즉 than 이하를 알 수 있는 경우 than 이하가 생략될 수 있다.

ex The art of making land ***more productive*** is practiced throughout the world.

Hackers Grammar

형 태

비교급 · 최상급의 형태는 원칙적으로 2음절일 때 형용사 · 부사의 '~er / ~est' 형태, 3음절 이상에서 'more / most + 형용사, 부사' 의 형태이다.

ex happy - happier, foolish - more foolish
pure - purest, famous - most famous

'형용사+ly' 형 부사는 'er' 이나 'est' 를 붙여서 비교급이나 최상급을 만들지 못한다.

more quickly, more cheaply, more beautifully, most easily, etc

FOOTNOTE
a. '명사+ly' 형 형용사의 비교급, 최상급
costly - costlier - costliest / friendly - friendlier - friendliest
b. '형용사 + ly' 가 아닌 형용사 · 부사의 비교급, 최상급
early - earlier - earliest

불규칙 변화형태

원급	good, well	bad, badly	little	many, much	far
비교급	better	worse	less	more	farther, further
최상급	best	worst	least	most	farthest, furthest

비교급과 최상급의 written 문제는 짝짓기문제와 비교급과 최상급 선택문제임에 특히 숙지해야 한다.
최상급은 'the + 최상급' 의 형태여야 하나, 최상급의 피수식어가 명사를 포함하고 있지 않거나 소유격+ 최상급+명사에서는 the가 생략된다.

ex Some engineers have predicted that automobiles will be made ***most completely*** of plastic. (명사를 포함하지 않는 경우)
I asked for a copy of ***his most recent*** catalog.(소유격을 포함한 경우)
Peter was ***the smartest*** of his brothers (smartest one 의 생략이므로 이 경우는 the 사용)

Hackers Grammar

비교급/최상급 선택

비교급 신호	비교급 + than, the + 비교급 of (the) two …
최상급 신호	최상급 + of 복수 · 집합단수, in 장소/집합표현, that/who/which/ …(ever), 최상급 + in the world, the world' s + 최상급

＊비교대상이 둘 뿐일 때에는, 비교급 앞에 the를 사용한다.

| 비교급의 선택

ex Brazil's future may well be ***brighter than*** its many unsolved problems might admit.
The Bay Bridge is ***the larger of the two*** suspension bridges.

| 최상급의 선택

ex Mexico is the fourth ***largest*** oil-producing nation ***in the world.***
After two strikes, Ruth hit the ***longest*** home run ***that*** had ever been hit in Chicago's Wrigley Field.

Hackers Grammar

강조표현

원급 강조	too, very
비교급 강조	far, much, by far, still, even/rather, somewhat, slightly
최상급 강조	by far, much, even

ex The age of the universe is ***too*** long to be measured.
The suitcase is ***far*** heavier than any other bag.
The president made a difficult situation ***even*** the worst.

Hackers **Practice** | 연습문제 |

다음 문장에서 비교급과 최상급의 형태를 올바르게 고치시오.

1 _____ Mercury is the most small planet in the solar system and the closest to the Sun.

2 ______ Sarah Hale became one of the famousest magazine editors in the United States during the 1800's.

3 _____ The force of gravity is stronger at the North or South Pole that at the equator because the poles are nearer to the Earth' s center.

4 _____ Some insects hear ultrasonic sounds more than two octaves than higher humans can.

5 ______ Meadowlarks are about the same size than robins, but they have heavier bodies, shorter tails, and longer bills.

6 ______ Most critics agree that William Shakespeare was the greater writer in the English language.

7 _______ The Soay sheep, the old breed of sheep in existence, has changed little since 3500 B.C.

8 _____ The spacecraft is traveling 50 times as faster than the speed of a pistol bullet.

9 _____ Most babies will grow up to be as cleverer as their parents.

10 _____ Their rule is considered to be the more notable in Byzantine history.

11 _____ The life of poor women was lesser restricted than that of the wives of aristocrats.

12 _____ The more outrageous the charge, the most people were likely to be swept by mass hysteria

■ 정답 p351

Hackers **TEST** | 실전문제 |

1 The most easiest process for mining gold is panning, which involves using a circular dish with a small pocket at the bottom.
(A: most easiest, B: involves using, C: dish, D: at the bottom)

2 The Victorian constructions of Haight-Ashbury are among the fewer architectural survivors of the San Francisco earthquake in 1906.
(A: among, B: fewer, C: survivors, D: in 1906)

3 Columns may be circular or polygonal in cross section, and are generally at least four times more taller than they are wide.
(A: Columns, B: circular, C: at least, D: more taller)

4 Certainly one of the most intelligent and better educated women of her day, Mercy Otiose Warren produced a variety of poetry and prose.
(A: Certainly, B: better educated, C: her day, D: a variety)

5 Until the mid-nineteenth century, a greater number of migrants arrived in the boomtown from northern states such as New York and Pennsylvania that from the Old South.
(A: the, B: a, C: such as, D: that)

6 People can remember more information for higher periods of time when they use more than one sense in the process of learning.
(A: higher, B: when, C: than, D: in)

7 Ironclad ships began to roll out of ship yards than more often their wooden counterparts.
(A: to roll, B: than more often, C: their, D: wooden)

Written Expression

www.goHackers.com

8 More <u>comfortably</u> houses were built, and the women tried to <u>bring</u> some beauty as <u>well</u> as convenience <u>into</u> the home.
(A: comfortably, B: bring, C: well, D: into)

---

9 Medieval people owed more to the <u>patient donkey</u> <u>than</u> any other <u>animals</u> <u>for getting</u> about.
(A: patient donkey, B: than, C: animals, D: for getting)

---

10 The eighteenth century provided <u>farther</u> opportunities <u>to enhance</u> their position as junior partners of the Turks <u>in</u> managing <u>the</u> government.
(A: farther, B: to enhance, C: in, D: the)

---

11 The country <u>was much</u> more dependent <u>on</u> events <u>occurring</u> in Europe <u>as</u> the Spanish colonies were.
(A: was much, B: on, C: occurring, D: as)

■ 정답 p351

So That / Such That구문

Outline

so~that구문은 결과를 나타내는 부사절의 한 형태이고,
너무 ~ 해서 ~ 하게 되다'로 해석된다.
such~that과 구분할 수 있어야 한다.

so that	Checking Points
so that vs. such that	so + 형용사 / 부사 + that
	such + 형용사 + 명사 + that
so that의 틀린 표현	so that 구문의 형태를 벗어나는 오류를 파악할 것.

Hackers Grammar

So that과 Such that 선택

so와 that사이에 형용사가 들어가며, such와 that사이에 명사가 들어가야 하는 것이 가장 중요한 부분이다.
그러나 '수량형용사 + 명사' 의 경우는 so ~that이 사용된다.

so that vs. such that	문장 구조
so……that S+V	so + 형용사/부사 + that
	so + many/much/few/little + 명사 + that
such…that S+V	such + a/an + 형용사 + 단수명사 + that
	such + 형용사 + 복수명사 / 불가산명사 + that

ex The milk was ***so*** good ***that*** he couldn' t stop drinking it.
There are ***so*** many people in the auditorium ***that*** we could barely get in the front door.

ex It was ***such*** a pretty view ***that*** he took a photograph.
It was ***such*** good milk ***that*** he couldn' t stop drinking it.

Hackers Grammar

So that의 오류 찾기

that절을 신호로 하여 that절 앞에 형용사만 있고, 형용사앞에 too/very/such가 온다면 모두 so that 구문을 잘못 쓴 예이다.

too / very / such / so much + 형용사 + that

→ so + 형용사 + that

ex Mushrooms are ***very*** fragile ***that*** they are seldom preserved for long

Tip · '형용사 + that' 이 왔으므로 very를 **so**로 고쳐야 한다.

so that이 목적을 나타내는 부사절 접속사 일 때는 so와 that을 붙여 사용한다.

ex An accordion is pressed in from each side ***so that*** the air is forced through holes.

Hackers Grammar

such as의 용법

such as는 보기(example)를 유도하며, such as와 as such를 혼동하는 문제가 출제된다.

Such as	명사 + such as + 앞 명사의 보기 such + 명사 + as + 앞 명사의 보기
As such	as such + 명사 없음 as such가 보기를 유도하면 틀림 '가령 그와 같은'의 뜻으로 as such는 문장 뒤에 쓰인다.

ex. Typical of mammalian structure, the human body shows ***such*** characteristics ***as*** hair, mammary glands, and highly developed sense organs.

ex Astronomers are scientists that study heavenly bodies ***as such*** the sun, moon, stars, and planets.

Tip · 보기를 유도하는 것은 such as 이므로 as such는 **such as**로 바뀌어야 한다.

Hackers Practice | 연습문제 |

괄호 안에서 알맞은 단어를 찾으시오.

1 The Mesabi deposits were (so/too/such) near the surface that they could be mined with steam shovels.

2 The problem has become (too/so/such) serious that some oyster beds have vanished entirely.

3 It was published in 1936 and proved to be (too/so/such) a huge success that Mitchell's life was irrevocably altered.

4 Most of these are crustose lichens, which grip the rock (very/too/so) tightly that they cannot be removed intact.

5 Mushrooms are (so/such/too) fragile that they are seldom preserved for long.

6 The rings reflect the effects of earthquakes, (such as/as such) tilting, the disruption of root systems, and breakage, as well as shifts in environments.

7 The Carnival season eventually became (very/too/so) wild that the authorities banned street masking by the late 1830's.

8 Durkheim was concerned to understand the universal functions of religious systems for the continuity of society (as such/such as).

9 Attractive neighborhoods were found to be (very/such/so) costly that the cities could not do it unaided.

10 There were (so/such) wealthy resources that they were believed to be endless.

■ 정답 p352

Hackers **TEST** | 실전문제 |

1 It is a history of curious, creative people sweating(A) and struggling through thousands of years over materials(B) too mysterious(C) that their craft was(D) viewed with superstition.

2 If the krill can feed such huge creatures(A) as whales, many scientists reason, they must certainly(B) be contenders as a new food sources(C) for humans(D).

3 The(A) empty space is known(B) as a "black hole," a star with so(C) strong gravitational force that no light is able to(D) get through.

4 Today, ironclad ships are so advanced(A) that they(B) are scarcely more big(C) than the ironclads used(D) in the Civil War.

5 Some types of(A) ferns resemble(B) trees and some are too(C) small that they look like(D) moss.

6 Inventions earned(A) Edison such much(B) money that he was able to establish(C) a laboratory for(D) inventions.

7 Jane Addams was such(A) distressed about the misery of(B) the poor that she left home to spend(C) her(D) life in the slums of Chicago.

8 Many Mexican-Americans have succeeded in <u>entering</u> various professional <u>fields</u> <u>as such</u> <u>teaching</u> and law.
(A: entering, B: fields, C: as such, D: teaching)

9 Some lakes and rivers <u>have</u> <u>became</u> <u>so</u> contaminated that the fishes in them <u>die</u>.
(A: have, B: became, C: so, D: die)

10 At this time Chinese culture was <u>very</u> strong in Manchuria that, <u>except</u> for language, <u>it was</u> difficult to distinguish Chinese <u>from</u> Manchus.
(A: very, B: except, C: it was, D: from)

11 Bust periods in history <u>were</u> caused by <u>excessive</u> expansion of such new industries <u>with</u> shipping, railroad-building, and <u>auto-manufacturing</u>.
(A: were, B: excessive, C: with, D: auto-manufacturing)

12 Colonists <u>established</u> <u>distinctive</u> American customs <u>such</u> widely accepted that <u>they</u> superseded regional differences.
(A: established, B: distinctive, C: such, D: they)

■ 정답 p352

1 In Orthodox Christian denominations, <u>there is</u> (A) a great emphasis <u>placed</u> (B) on preserving as <u>more</u> (C) traditions as <u>possible</u> (D).

2 Blacks <u>neither caused</u> (A) nor even <u>benefit</u> (B) <u>significantly</u> (C) from the rampant legislative corruption of <u>the</u> (D) period.

3 Providence, <u>Rhode Island,</u> (A) is <u>a</u> (B) busy manufacturing city <u>and</u> (C) seaport, <u>as well</u> (D) state capital.

4 Constantinople <u>could win</u> (A) the battles but not <u>the</u> (B) war, <u>for</u> (C) there were <u>very</u> (D) many Bulgarians for Greeks to rule.

5 Franz Josef, emperor <u>after 1848,</u> (A) proved to be <u>the longer</u> (B) reigning sovereign of any European <u>state</u> (C) <u>in modern times</u> (D).

6 Shakespeare composed an average <u>of</u> (A) one or two plays <u>each year</u> (B) <u>to</u> (C) <u>his</u> (D) death in 1616.

7 <u>At</u> (A) the town meeting, voters acted <u>upon</u> (B) <u>so</u> (C) matters as the appropriation of money for schools and highways; and the selection of local government <u>officials</u> (D).

8 The colors were very (A) strange that words could hardly (B) tell what (C) a troubling emotion they (D) gave.

9 The problem has become (A) such (B) serious that some oyster beds have vanished (C) entirely (D).

10 Railroad managers not only learned how to lay (A) rails, and (B) they discovered ways of manipulating (C) legislatures to guarantee favorable treatment (D).

11 A farther (A) division of animals often used in zoology (B) is (C) between carnivores and (D) herbivores.

12 By the time he was 50, Ellington had (A) earned such (B) much money that he could have withdrawn (C) from the rigors of life on (D) the road.

13 Electronic (A) mail is more far (B) expensive than the postal system (C), as (D) it must compete for transmission space on satellite, telephone, and cable links.

14 Foresters make (A) maps of forest areas, estimate the amount (B) of standing timber and future growth (C), and managing (D) timber sales.

15 By 1740, about 4,000 Acadians, as they were then called, had settled (A) in the wetlands surrounding (B) the mouth of the (C) Mississippi River, living by fishing, trapping fur-bearing animals and raise (D) sugarcane.

■ 정답 p352

chapter 5

HACKERS TOEFL

Written Expression

Word Choice & Word Order

이 chapter에서는 other/another 등의 단어선택과 enough 등의 어순 문제들을 다룬다. 어순 문제는 다소 기계적인 측면이 있어서 요점을 숙지하면 쉽게 공략할 수 있다. 단어의 선택 문제는 예문을 이용하여 각 단어의 용례를 충분히 숙지토록 한다.

단어선택A

Outline

비슷한 형태이거나, 의미상 혼동하기 쉬운 단어의 선택 문제가 출제되는데, 출제경향이 정형화되어 있으므로 본문의 표현들을 빠짐없이 익혀야 한다.

Hackers Grammar

Twice vs. Double

Twice	부사. "두 배"	He won a man who was ***twice*** his age.
Double	형용사. "두 배의" 동사. "두 배로 하다"	You had to charge for a ***double*** room. They can't just ***double*** the rent in this year.

Hackers Grammar

Earliest vs. Soonest

Earliest	"시기적으로 가장 빠른" 의 의미	Aborigines have settled in Australia from the ***earliest*** time.
Soonest	"곧, 빨리, 즉시" 의 의미	The doctor told me I' d get better ***soonest.***

Hackers Grammar

Percent vs. Percentage

Percent	숫자 뒤에 쓰이며 복수 불가	The crime rate in the United States rises four hundred *percent.*
Percentage	숫자 뒤에 사용불가	The US is shouldering an enormous ***percentage*** of the financial burden.

Hackers Grammar

Before vs. Ago

Before	과거와 비교된 과거 표현	I washed my face and hands ***before*** I came.
Ago	현재와 비교된 과거 표현	That meat was fresh two days ***ago.***

Hackers Grammar

Around vs. Round

Around	전치사. "둘레에, 사방에"	Satellites are placed in an orbital region ***around*** Earth.
Round	형용사. "둥근 모양의" 명사. "(탄약의) 1발"	His ***round*** eyes grew ***rounder.*** They fired hundreds of ***rounds*** of ammunition.

Hackers Grammar

Near vs. Nearly vs. Nearby

Near	전치사. "(공간적으로) 근처에" 형용사. "(시간적으로) 가까운"	Annie is hitchhiking ***near*** a bridge. David will visit L.A. in the ***near*** future.
Nearly	부사. "거의(almost)"	The Garden runs ***nearly*** half a mile straight across.
Nearby	부사. "가까이" 형용사. "(공간적으로) 가까운"	She gets in bed and puts the candle ***nearby.*** He took his shirt from a ***nearby*** tree branch.

Tip · *near*와 *nearly*의 구분은 *almost*로 대치했을 때 어색하지 않으면 nearly가 올바른 표현이다.

Hackers Grammar

Some vs. Somewhat vs. Somewhere

Some + 단수명사	형용사. "어떤"	Telecommuting is ***some*** form of computer communication.
Some + 복수명사	형용사. "약간의"	Technicians removed ***some*** papers from the safe.
Some	대명사. "약간의 사람/것"	***Some*** of the photons collided with the electrons.
Somewhat	부사. "다소"	The President calmed down ***somewhat.***
Somewhere	부사,명사. "어딘가"	We have to find a safe port ***somewhere*** between here and there.

Hackers Grammar

Able vs. Enable

Able	형용사. "be + able + to 부정사"	Few American painters were ***able*** to achieve the kind of abstract simplicity.
Enable	동사. "enable + 목적어 + to 부정사"	Computers have ***enabled*** people to understand science better

Hackers Grammar

After vs. Afterwards

After	전치사, 접속사 기능	***After*** breakfast, Catherine insisted on my bringing a chair.
Afterwards	부사. "그 후에"	I will take you on a vacation ***afterwards.***

Hackers Grammar

부정표현

No	한정사. 뒤에 무관사 명사 사용	You have ***no*** right to keep us here.
Not	부사. 동사부정 부사 부정 부분 부정 강조	Television was ***not*** invented by any one person. ***Not*** surprisingly, a scientist in California invented the Richter scale used to measure earthquakes. ***Not*** all the conclusions scientists make are accurate. I remember ***not a single*** thing about him.
None	대명사. 명사수식 못함	I have thousands of memories but ***none*** of them are mine.
Never	부사. 동사부정 "결코~않다."	I have ***never*** seen a movie or a television show.

Hackers Grammar

Farther vs. Further

Farther	거리	She was afraid to go ***farther***.
Further	거리 정도	L.A. is ***further/farther*** north than San Diego. Humans ***further*** endanger the cougar.

Hackers **Practice** | 연습문제 |

괄호에 알맞은 단어를 찾으시오.

1 Wilbur Wright delighted thousands of people flying circles (round/around) the Eiffel Tower for two hours.

2 It is (some/somewhat) astonishing to realize that the era of colonialism did not catch on earlier than 1880.

3 Other archaeologists believe that the Sumerians may well have been in the Fertile Crescent long (before/ago) 3500 B.C.

4 The shift reported one sentry returned his weapon to the switch with a (round/around) of ammunition missing.

5 Women constituted about 43 (percentage/percent) of the British labor force in the early 1980s.

6 The way to succeed is to (twice/double) your failure rate.

7 Gertrude Stein had (not/no) interest in anything that was (not/no) aggressively modern.

8 Congress has (not/no) authority to create a holiday in any of the states.

9 Volcanoes occur most frequently (nearby/near) tectonic plate boundaries.

10 Dinosaur tracks (unable/enable) scientists to calculate the animal's weight, stride, and speed.

■ 정답 p353

Hackers **TEST** | 실전문제 |

1 By 1848 near everyone agreed Louis Philippe was dull, and the French
A B C
could not tolerate dull leaders.
D

2 The Tigris and Euphrates Rivers now share a common mouth before entering
A B
the Persian Gulf, but 5,000 years before they emptied into the sea separately.
C D

3 Archaeologists are enable to read the sources of Sumerian history for they
A B
wrote in a script known as cuneiform.
C D

4 Demographers estimate that near 60,000,000 Europeans left their homes from
A B
1815 to 1914 to settle in foreign places.
C D

5 At the beginning of the century, 67 percentage of men over 65 years were
A B C
still employed.
D

6 Stroeve went double a day to the hospital to enquire after his wife, who still
A B C D
declined to see him.

7 The problem has become (A) so serious (B) that somewhat (C) oyster beds have vanished (D) entirely.

8 It was bitterly cold (A), and afterwards (B) an (C) hour or two of uneasy dozing people would tramp the (D) streets again.

9 An increase in (A) the percent (B) of deposits required to (C) be kept on hand would reduce the available money supply (D).

10 No (A) of the rebellions were successful (B) because the number of German communists (C) was (D) still not large.

11 Most (A) sociologists study social phenomena (B) falling some (C) between the two micro- and (D) macro-extremes.

12 Despite (A) extensive archeological research many unanswered questions (B) remain about the soonest (C) inhabitants on the (D) North American continent.

■ 정답 p353

2 단어선택B

Outline

앞 장에서 배운 단어 선택문제보다 비중이 높고, 혼동하기 쉬운
단어선택문제를 파악한다.

Word Choice		Checking Points
1. most vs. almost	most	한정사. most students 최상급. the most famous jazz 대명사. most of the students
	almost	부사. almost half of 200 students
2. do vs. make	make	make + -sion/-tion형 명사 ex. make a contribution, make a decision
	do	do + job을 나타내는 명사 ex. do business, do dishes, do research
3. like vs. alike	like	전치사. like + 명사, 또는 unlike + 명사
	alike	형용사. be 동사 + alike

Hackers Grammar

Most vs. Almost

Most	한정사.	'most + 명사'	'대부분의 ~' 의 뜻
	최상급.	'the most + 형용사/부사'	최상급의 기능
	대명사.	'most of the + 명사' 의 형태	' ~의 대부분' 의 뜻
Almost	부사.	정도표현과 같이 쓰이며 "거의" 의미 almost + every/all/whole/nothing/never/thirty/ half / completely etc.	

almost와 most의 선택은 **almost**를 nearly로 대치해 보았을때, 의미가 통하면 almost를 선택하는 것이 옳다.

ex **Almost** large commercial organizations are limited-liability or corporations.

Tip · almost 가 nearly로 대치될 수 없으므로 almost의 사용은 불가하며 의미상 most가 맞다.

ex After Dickinson died at the age of 56, ***most*** 2000 poems were found among her papers.

Tip · most를 nearly로 대치하여 의미가 통하며, 뒤에 숫자 나오므로 '거의' 의미인 **almost가 사용되어야 한다.**

Hackers Grammar

Do vs. Make(부록 'Do Vs. Make' list 참조)

Make	명사형 어미가 ~tion이나 ~sion로 끝나는 동사 파생명사와 함께 사용 동사형과 명사형이 같은 명사와 함께 사용
Do	동사형 명사와 함께 사용 일이나 작업을 나타내는 명사형과 함께 사용

ex Other companies allow purchasing managers to ***make*** more individual ***decisions.***

Hackers Grammar

Like vs. Alike

like/unlike	'like + 명사'	전치사이므로 뒤에 반드시 명사가 있어야 한다.
alike	'동사 + alike'	서술적 용법으로만 사용되므로 뒤에 명사가 나올 수 없다.

ex ***Like/Unlike*** John, Tom is tall.
John and Tom are alike.

Hackers Skill

1. most/almost 문제에서 nearly 로 대치 가능하면 almost로 정정하는것이 답이다.
2. do나 make에 밑줄이 있으면 do/make 선택 문제임을 의심하라.
3. alike 뒤에 명사가 나오면 alike가 답이다.

Hackers Practice | 연습문제 |

괄호 안에서 알맞은 단어를 찾으시오.

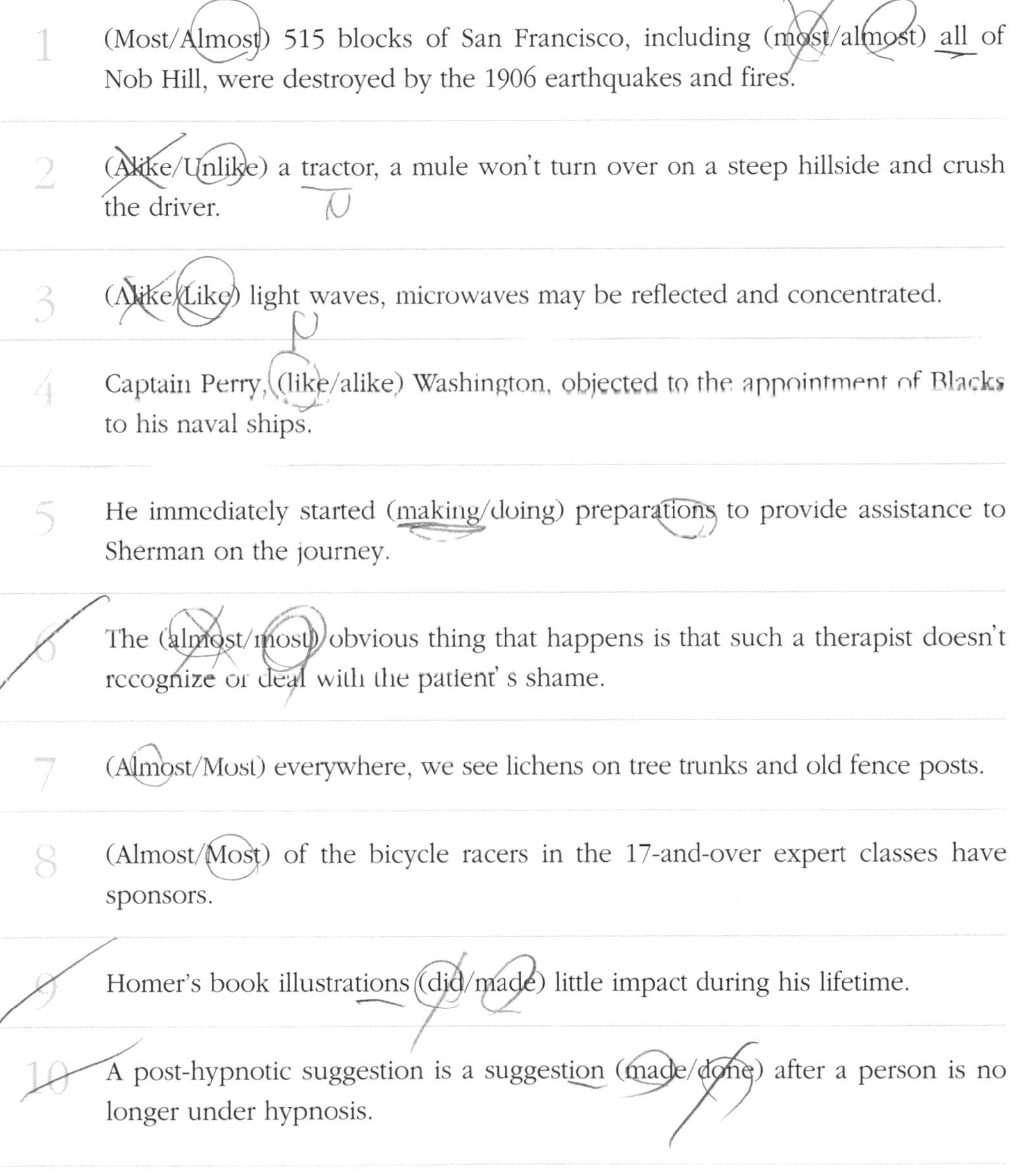

1 (Most/Almost) 515 blocks of San Francisco, including (most/almost) all of Nob Hill, were destroyed by the 1906 earthquakes and fires.

2 (Alike/Unlike) a tractor, a mule won't turn over on a steep hillside and crush the driver.

3 (Alike/Like) light waves, microwaves may be reflected and concentrated.

4 Captain Perry, (like/alike) Washington, objected to the appointment of Blacks to his naval ships.

5 He immediately started (making/doing) preparations to provide assistance to Sherman on the journey.

6 The (almost/most) obvious thing that happens is that such a therapist doesn't recognize or deal with the patient' s shame.

7 (Almost/Most) everywhere, we see lichens on tree trunks and old fence posts.

8 (Almost/Most) of the bicycle racers in the 17-and-over expert classes have sponsors.

9 Homer's book illustrations (did/made) little impact during his lifetime.

10 A post-hypnotic suggestion is a suggestion (made/done) after a person is no longer under hypnosis.

■ 정답 p353

Hackers TEST | 실전문제 |

1 In Cincinnati in the nineteenth century, for example, most fifty thousand Germans lived in a section of the city called "Over the Rhine."

2 Two days after Grant did preparations to move again, Lee had already assessed the situation and informed President Davis that Richmond and Petersburg were doomed.

3 The Center for Disease Control is responsible for the research made in solving or attempting to solve medical mysteries.

4 A drawback common to most all these methods of water management is a need for substantial capital investments.

5 Despite its enormous food potential, little effort was done until recently to farm plankton as we farm grasses on land.

6 Not likely that of iron construction, the technology for constructing buildings with reinforced concrete developed rather rapidly.

7 Most [A] half of the [B] students were [C] beginning college [D] or post-high school study.

---

8 Technological inventions were not of much interest [A] because [B] slaves made [C] the hard work in the [D] Greek world.

---

9 Volcanic eruptions are not under control [A], and in recent years they [B] have made [C] much damage to the [D] Philippines.

---

10 Sarah could take [A] a pop song alike [B] "I Left My Heart in San Francisco" and improvise an [C] inventive second melody to fit all the prescribed chord changes [D].

---

11 A [A] good deal of the work that zoologists make [B] involves [C] the analysis of [D] animal morphology, or anatomy.

■ 정답 p353

3 Other와 관련된 표현

Outline

other은 형용사 혹은 대명사로 사용된다. other/another이 명사와 함께 쓰일 때 명사의 단·복수 선택에 주의한다. 또, 관사가 없는 others는 대명사로서 뒤에 명사가 올 수 없음에 주의한다.

other와 관련된 표현들중에서는 뒤 명사와의 수일치에 따라 other / another를 선택하는 것이 주로 출제된다.

Word Choice	Checking Points
Another	형용사. another + 단수명사 대명사. another이 단독 사용
Other	형용사. other + 복수명사 대명사. others가 단독사용
The other	형용사. the other + 단수·복수명사 대명사. the other (단수형), the others (복수형)가 단독 사용

Hackers Grammar

명사와의 수일치

another(an + other)	부정관사 an과 결합한 형태이므로 언제나 단수취급한다. 형용사로 사용시 단수명사와 결합. 대명사로 단수취급.
other	관사가 없으므로 형용사로 사용시 복수형태의 명사와 결합. 대명사로 사용시 복수형태인 others. (단수 other은 대명사 불가)
the other	단·복수와 무관한 정관사가 사용되었으므로 단복수 명사와 결합가능. 대명사로 사용시 복수는 the others

ex ***Other breakthrough*** was the concept of the stored-program computer.

Tip · 동사가 단수이고 결합되는 명사도 단수 이므로 other을 another로 바꾼다.

ex Animal screams attract another predators.

Tip · 명사가 복수인 predators이므로 another을 other로 바꾼다.

Hackers Grammar

대명사의 용법

another, others, the other, the others는 대명사로 쓰이나, other만으로는 대명사가 될 수 없다.

ex Still ***other*** called for more radical approaches.

Tip · other는 대명사 용법으로 단독으로 쓰일 수 없으므로 대명사형인 **others**가 올바르다.

Hackers Grammar

other의 그 외 표현

other은 원칙적으로 복수명사를 받지만 'some/any/no +other + 단수명사'도 가능하며, 'one other + 단수명사' 만 가능하다.

ex There was ***no other*** hotel of that name in Paris.
Without ***one other*** factor we could have achieved nothing.

'비교급 + than any other + 단수명사' 의 구조는 any를 생략할 수 없고, 단수명사대신 복수명사를 사용할 수 없다.

ex This city is ***bigger than any other*** cites.

Tip · any other는 another와 비슷한 표현으로써 단수형이 와야 하므로, 단수명사의 형태인 any other city 로 바꾼다.

Hackers Grammar

one + 명사 ~ another (대명사) 짝짓기

one + 명사는 대명사 another과 짝을 짓는다.

ex Capital was ***one source*** of market capacity, but skill and education formed ***another.***

Hackers **Practice** | 연습문제 |

괄호 안에서 알맞은 단어를 고르시오.

1 (Another/The other/Others) living expenses should be itemized also: laundry, dry cleaning, transportation, and education.

2 There is not enough room in zoos to house all the (another/other/others) subspecies that need preserving.

3 Psychologists claim that people tend to live up to the expectations of (another/other/others).

4 Lizards lack the built-in body temperature control many (another/other/others) creatures possess.

5 The customary postal system requires messages written on paper to be transmitted physically from one location to (another/other/the other).

6 Some blood types are quite common, (another/the other/others) are regionally distributed, and (another/the other/others) are rare everywhere.

7 A pheromone is a chemical substance released by many kinds of animals to communicate with (another/other/the others) members of their species.

8 Peter is considered to be as efficient as, if not more efficient than, (another/other/others) workers in his office.

9 Compared to (another/other/others) Americans, most Indians are poor.

10 As in almost any (another/other/the others) outdoor activity, common sense is an important part of one's basic equipment.

■ 정답 p354

Hackers **TEST** | 실전문제 |

1 In addition there are specialized public schools for the handicapped and for those with another special needs.
(A: In addition, B: specialized, C: handicapped, D: another)

2 Spanish is used as the language for learning arithmetic and other basic subject.
(A: Spanish, B: is used, C: learning, D: subject)

3 Some are state-supported, others is privately endowed.
(A: state-supported, B: is, C: privately, D: endowed)

4 Glass, bricks, iron, and another construction materials were manufactured there.
(A: bricks, B: another, C: manufactured, D: there)

5 The buffalo and other animal were thoughtlessly slaughtered, sometimes for no purpose but sport.
(A: animal, B: thoughtlessly, C: slaughtered, D: but)

6 Another traditional system of classification establish such categories as literature, the visual arts, and architecture.
(A: Another, B: of, C: establish, D: as)

7 Later(A) in the(B) 18th century, other(C) English astronomer contributed to the telescopic survey of(D) the heavens.

8 The(A) conservationists exerted influence to save(B) the forests and another(C) resources from(D) wasteful use and destruction.

9 Interests have(A) declined, but(B) sociology continues sharing(C) with other.(D)

10 Catherine is other(A) Russian ruler who(B) has had Great added(C) to her(D) name.

11 Another writer(A) who was indebted(B) to Emerson was Walt Whitman, author of the(C) collection of poems(D) Leaves of Grass.

12 A stradivarius violin responds more quickly(A) to(B) the touch than(C) any other violin(D)

■ 정답 p354

4 어순

Outline

각 chapter마다 올바른 어순에 대해서 언급되었지만,
특히 이 과에서는 시험에 출제될 수 있는 어순문제 들에 대해
전반적으로 언급된다.

Hackers Grammar

문법적으로 확연히 드러나는 경우

Word order list	Word order Examples
1. **명사 + 소유격 → 소유격 + 명사**	car Tom's → Tom's car
2. **본동사 + 조동사 → 조동사 + 본동사**	borrow must → must borrow
3. **형용사 + 부사 + 명사 → 부사 + 형용사 + 명사**	cold extremely weather → extremely cold weather
4. **부사/형용사/수량형용사** + almost → almost + **부사/형용사/수량형용사**	entirely almost → almost entirely
5. number + **형용사 + 측정단위** → number + **측정단위 + 형용사**	3 long feet → 3 feet long 16 old years → 16 years old cf. Alaska covers 591,004 ***miles square.*** → Alaska covers 591,004 ***square miles.***(square mile은 '평방 마일' 이란 뜻의 복합단위명사)
6. **의문사 + 동사 + 주어(직접의문문) → 의문사 + 주어 + 동사(간접의문문)**	You should tell me ***why are you*** here. → You should tell me ***why you are*** here.
7. **전치사/접속사 + 부사 → 부사 + 전치사/접속사**	after soon → soon after before shortly → shortly before
8. **선행사 + 관계대명사 + 전치사 → 선행사 + 전치사 + 관계대명사**	the point which at + S + V → the point at which + S + V

Hackers Grammar

형용사나 분사의 전치 수식 경우

형용사나 짧은 축약분사의 경우 대부분 명사의 앞에서 수식한다.

1. 명사 + 형용사 → 형용사 + 명사	students smart → smart students
2. 과거분사 + 부사 + 명사 → 부사 + 과거분사 + 명사	increased greatly salary → greatly increased salary

Hackers Grammar

긴 관계절의 축약 분사구문이 후치 수식을 할 경우

관계절 축약으로 이루어진 긴 분사구문이 명사를 수식할 때, 명사의 뒤에서 수식을 하는 후치수식의 형태를 갖는다.

1. 명사 + (주격관계대명사 + be동사) + 형용사

a solution (which is) necessary to restore backup data

2. 명사 + (주격관계대명사 + be동사) + 과거분사 + 부사

the surface (which is) covered widely with ice

Hackers Skill

두, 세 단어에 밑줄이 그어져 있으면, 어순 문제임을 의심하라.

Hackers **Practice** | 연습문제 |

다음 중 틀린 문장에는 (I), 올바른 문장에는 (C)를 쓰시오.

1 ______ Soon after Ashoka's death, the Mauryan Empire began to fall apart.

2 ______ The Romans thought India must be a place marvelous to live.

3 ______ The Iditarod Trail Sled Dog Race is over 1000 long miles, and is considered the toughest race in the world.

4 ______ Three days before George's high school graduation, he was in an accident that nearly killed him.

5 ______ Pecan trees continue producing nuts when they are over 100 old years.

6 ______ Position France's at the end of the war was ambiguous in the extreme.

7 ______ The stadiums which in colleges and universities play are often called "bowls".

8 ______ Medical progress has led us into unexplored previously abilities.

9 ______ O'Keefe's subjects are always almost derived from nature.

10 ______ The sparsely populated colonies were a wilderness waiting to be developed.

■ 정답 p355

Hackers TEST | 실전문제 |

1 Over (A) the centuries each group ethnic (B) has preserved (C) its history in story and (D) dance.

2 Germany and Australia occupied (A) the country, after soon (B) the Romanian government decided to fight (C) with the Allies (D).

3 The toga, a garment that was (A) 7 wide feet (B), which the men in the upper classes wore, severely (C) restricted their physical activity (D).

4 The long sheet of material (A) was draped (B) over the shoulder and fastened with a pin, but (C) its size made manual labor impossible almost (D).

5 Europeans (A) discovered how could be used gunpowder (B) to project a lead ball (C) out of a container at a great speed (D).

6 Gupta India's culture (A) remained in the collective memory of the (B) century after long (C) the names of its emperors were forgotten (D).

7 Unfortunately (A), when a rural predominantly (B) society such as (C) that in Europe reaches a (D) certain peak, a downward trend develops.

---

8 The Aryans were conscious extremely (A) of the (B) possibility that (C) the native peoples of India might well assimilate (D) them.

---

9 Amin's forces armed (A) murdered over (B) a million of his opponents until (C) he crumbled and went into exile (D).

---

10 Scientists have found (A) strong evidence of (B) an ancestral "first man" whom from (C) all human beings (D) are descended.

■ 정답 p355

5 Enough의 어순

Outline

enough의 어순은 enough 자체의 품사 혹은 enough와 결합하는 단어의 품사에 따라 다양한 어순을 가지고 있으므로 enough의 문법적 특성을 파악하고 어순에 접근할 필요가 있다.

Enough	Checking Points
enough to의 어순	부사. '형용사/부사 + enough + to 부정사' 한정사. 'enough + 명사 + to 부정사'
enough의 용법	한정사. 'enough + 명사' 의 형태 대명사. 'enough of + 명사' 부사. '형용사/부사 +enough'

Hackers Grammar

Enough의 어순

Word order	**예문**
형용사/부사 + enough + to	Most teenagers are ***responsible enough*** to do a good job.
enough + **명사** + to	Clinton had ***enough supporters*** to win the election.
동사 + enough + to	They have ***learned enough*** to make wise decisions.
형용사 + enough + **명사**	Jane has a ***similar enough*** car.

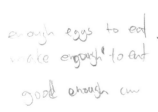

Hackers Grammar

Enough와 명사의 결합시 어순

time, food, room, money와 같은 불가산 명사는 'enough + 불가산명사 + 수식구'가 원칙이나 '불가산명사 + enough + 수식구' 어순을 가질 수도 있다.

명사 + enough	예문
to 부정사 사용시	There was food ***enough to*** last me all day.
that 절 사용시	We have proof ***enough that*** James Bond is a spy.
of 사용시	We have proof ***enough of*** his guilt.

ex There was ***enough room to*** park John's car. (O)
There was ***room enough to*** park John's car. (O)

Hackers Grammar

More Than Enough의 어순

more than enough는 '아주 충분한' 뜻으로 어순문제가 출제된다.

more than enough	예문
보어	The books they bought for the course were ***more than enough.***
명사수식	A few boatloads of machine guns provided ***more than enough*** firepower.

Hackers **Practice** | 연습문제 |

괄호 안에서 올바른 어순을 고르시오.

1 The drops become (heavy enough/enough heavy) to fall as raindrops or snowflakes.

2 Genetic behaviors were (enough no longer/no longer enough) in order to survive.

3 (Enough quickly/Quickly enough) she came to be simultaneously his student, and colleague.

4 Janet had to concoct a foundation that would be (solid enough/enough solid) to 'hold' her empire.

5 Aside from garlic, no herbs have been studied (enough well/well enough) to determine their possible cancer preventive effects.

6 The Germans settled in the Midwest because most of them were skilled farmers with (money enough/enough money) to move there and buy land.

7 Those peddlers who were (lucky enough/enough lucky) to have a wagon added bulkier goods to their stock.

8 Pay was a scant portion of the harvest, (enough hardly/hardly enough) to feed their families.

9 Jobs are (enough tough to/tough enough to) find today.

10 It is adapted to present needs (enough well to/well enough to) maintain life with the least waste of energy.

■ 정답 p355

Hackers **TEST** | 실전문제 |

1 An (A) army was seen by the revolutionaries as a machine of possible corruption, in that (B) it held power enough significant (C) to wield itself (D) against the principles of liberty and democracy.

2 The sand absorbs enough moisture (A) to support drought-resistant plants as such (B) mesquite, as well (C) as several species (D) of grasses.

3 Satellite measurements (A) of crystal blocks are improving (B), and California seismologists believe they may in time be precise enough (C) to allowing (D) earthquake prediction.

4 The Earth, about the same (A) size as (B) Venus, is enough far (C) from the Sun to (D) retain water.

5 In some areas of the ocean, general (A) during the winter season, cooling (B), or net evaporation causes surface water to become (C) dense enough (D) to sink.

6 Until recently (A) the supply of wild oysters and those crudely farmed (B) was enough more than (C) to satisfy people's needs (D).

7 A seemingly (A) natural enough assumption (B) to make is that a rule which (C) generates a certain structure tells you how to form, create, or producing (D) that structure.

---

8 Comprehensive education has not existed for enough long (A) to ascertain its (B) effect (C) on (D) attainment.

---

9 His net worth will probably (A) grow, but (B) it may not increase (C) enough fast (D) to suit you.

---

10 In advanced cases (A) of AIDS, white blood cells are not (B) produced in enough large (C) numbers to fight (D) infections.

---

11 Oil lamps (A) of the (B) ancient world were not bright enough (C) to illuminate a stage at the night (D).

---

12 Because (A) an elaborate worship was required after the death of an Inca, every rulers (B) had to be sure that he made enough conquests (C) to support his cult after death (D).

■ 정답 p355

ch5 Mini TEST | 실전문제 |

1 One of the seismic sea waves rose (A) to a (B) height of 120 feet and took 36,000 lives in (C) the coastal towns nearly (D) Jakarta.

2 Few relatively (A) African slaves came to Mexico (B) because (C) a (D) plantation economy did not exist there.

3 Before he reached (A) the age of 40, James Buchanan earned had (B) enough money (C) to retire from law and to enter politics full time (D).

4 The typewriter was (A) the other (B) invention that changed the position of women (C) in (D) the nineteenth century.

5 The domestication of corn (A) abled (B) the population of Mexico to increase to a point (C) that town life (D) now appeared.

6 When (A) the delegates failed to get (B) a hearing from (C) Michael, they excommunicated the patriarch and two other churchman (D).

7 What (A) might start as a limited conflict between (B) two nations threatened dragging (C) other (D) countries, willingly or not, into war.

8 In the home, washing machines (A) lessened the drudgery of making (B) laundry, while (C) gas and electric stoves made preparing meals easier (D).

---

9 The Belgians held (A) the country with a firm hand during (B) the colonial period, making sure that not (C) native Congolese received any training in politics (D) or economic affairs.

---

10 The alphabet for (A) the Slavic language is known as Glagolitic and made (B) use of invented newly (C) letters to reproduce (D) the Slavic sounds.

---

11 The Khazars, whose (A) upper class had adapted to (B) Judaism, were strong enough to keeping (C) the Muslim Arabs at bay (D).

---

12 The Magyars were expert horsemen (A) and able (B) marksmen but were not enough powerful (C) to ward off the attack of still another (D) people, the Patzinaks or Cumans.

---

13 Alike (A) the settled (B) Chinese farmers, the Mongols were (C) constantly on the move (D).

---

14 The domestication of unknown preciously (A) food plants was (B) one of the most lasting (C) of native American contributions to the world (D).

---

15 Cow skulls and other bare bone (A) found (B) in the desert were (C) frequent motifs in (D) O'Keeke's paintings.

■ 정답 p356

부 록

DO

이익과 손해		
• do good	• do harm	• do damage
일		
• do business	• do one's duty	• do one's job (errand, chore)
• do one's work	• do one's homework	
• do things	• do an assignment	
청소		
• do dishes	• do laundry	
기타 명사들		
• do one's teeth	• do one's hair	• do some shopping
• do one's best	• do a favor	
주의!!		
• do an experiment	• do an exercise	• do research

MAKE

동사에서 파생된 명사		
• make a suggestion	• make a decision	• make arrangements
• make a correction	• make an exception	• make a conclusion
• make a preparation	• make an apology	• make a response
동사와 형태가 같은 명사		
• make advances	• make an attempt	• make a forecast
• make an offer	• make progress	• make a visit
• make a promise	• make an excuse	
• make a phone call	• make a plan	
돈(money) 관련 명사		
• make money	• make a profit	• make a fortune
기타 명사들		
• make a mistake	• make an error	• make a noise
• make peace	• make war	• make a point
• make a bed	• make a journey	• make a difference
• make dinner	• make an effort	

AT
· 장소 at school
· 시간 at 7:30, at night (midnight), at noon, at present
· 주소 at 551 Elm Street
· 기타 at first

FOR
· 목적 Jane went to the store for some cookies.
· 시간 길이 for 4 days
· ~를 위하여 for John
· 가격 I bought a shirts for 15 dollars.

TO
· 방향 They are walking to the beach.
· ~에게 Gregory gave it to her.

IN
· 장소(도시, 나라, 대륙, 주) in Seoul, in the U.S., in Ohio
· 년도, 월 in 2000, in December
· 때 in the morning / in the afternoon / in the evening
· 계절 in the winter
· 미래시간 Sue will be there in a few minutes.
· 장소 in the world
· 세기 in the seventeenth century
· into/in : into는 내부로의 운동이나 방향을 나타내고 in은 단순히 장소를 나타낸다.

ON
· -위에 on the shelves
· 요일 on Saturday
· 특정한 날짜/특정한 날 on March 29
· 교통수단 on a train
· 거리이름 on Saint Street

BY
· 방법 by phone
· 교통수단 by car, by plane (cf. on foot)

동사 + 전치사

accuse of
sympathize with
keep on
look forward to
approve of
boast about
rely on, upon
object to
consist of
find out about
call off
refer to
in charge of
forget about
apologize to, for
respond to
take care of
think about, of
apply to, for
subscribe to
agree with
worry about
be used to
arrive at, in
cooperate with
dependent on, upon
compare to, with
look at, for
compete with
comment on
contribute to
believe in
experiment with
count on
dedicate to
excel in
interfere with
insist on, upon
devote to
major in
forgive for
substitute for
prevent from
take part in
thank for
vote for
prohibit from
participate in
distinguish from
escape from
rescue from
succeed in

형용사/과거분사 + 전치사

afraid of
(un)skillful in
familiar with
similar to
appreciative of
(un)successful in
pleased with
derived from
ashamed of
based on, upon
provided with
different from
aware of
dependent on, upon
patient with
divorced from
bored of
insistent on, upon
satisfied with
far from
capable of
innocent of
alter to
prevented from
careful of
jealous of
attentive to
good at
composed of
made of
close to
anxious about
conscious of
proud of
comparable to
concerned about
envious of
regardless of
dedicated to
confused about
fearful of
sick of
devoted to
happy about
guilty of
suspected of
faithful to
nervous about
hopeful of
thoughtful of
indifferent to
skeptical about
disappointed in
tired of
inferior(superior) to
adequate for
(dis)interested in
tolerant of
opposed to
blamed for
(un)involved in
acquainted with
related to
famous for

명사 + 전치사

pity for
participation in
comparison to
in front of
preference for
pleasure in
devotion to
in honor of
reason for
pride in
dedication to
in search of
responsibility for
satisfaction in
indifference to
instead of
respect for
skill in
objection to
in spite of
search for
success in
opposition to
in terms of
substitution for
approval of
reference to
by means of
sympathy for
choice of
response to
for fear of
authority on
division of
argument about
for the sake of
dependency on
fear of
concern about
make use of
effect on
knowledge of
confusion about
on account of
reliance on
means of
doubt about
because of
ability in
possibility of
ideas about
for the purpose of
belief in
prevention of
ahead of
in addition to
competency in
process of
in case of
in comparison to
confidence in
escape from
in care of
in reference to
experience in
protection from
in charge of
in regard to
failure in
access to
in the course of
due to
faith in
commitment to
in favor of
except for
in accordance with

HACKERS **TOEFL**

정답 및 해설

진단고사 p24

1. **대명사 형태 문제 : W[2-4]**
대명사 it은 명사 host를 수식하므로 소유격이 되어야 한다. human과 human being은 단, 복수가 가능하며 humankind와 humanity는 단수형태만 가능하고 복수 형태는 불가능하다.
답 **D** (it → its)

2. **전치사 문제(동사 용법 문제) : W[3-2]**
serve는 사람이 주어로 오면 "봉사하다, 섬기다, 공급하다"의 의미가 된다. 그러나 사물이 주어로 오고 "~에 도움이 되다, ~에 쓸모가 있다"의 의미일 경우는 serve as가 된다. nearly all : 거의 모든
답 **C** (served → served as)

3. **주어, 동사 문제 : S[1-1]**
주어자리가 비어 있으므로 주어가 될 수 있는 (A)가 답이 된다.
답 **A**

4. **동사의 형태문제 : W[1-3]**
전치사 다음에는 명사상당어구가 온다. 즉, 동사는 올 수 없다. 동사는 명사 형태인 동명사로 고쳐야 한다. (D)번의 its가 가리키는 것은 the spectacular West가 된다.
답 **B** (in depict → in depicting)

5. **비교급 형태문제 : S[3-2]**
동등비교는 as+형용사 또는 부사의 원급+as의 형태가 되어야 한다.
답 **D**

6. **관계대명사 선택문제 : W[3-3]**
environment가 사물이므로 which가 되어야 한다.
the environment이하를 원상복구 시키면, we live and work in the environment가 된다. 여기서 in environment가 앞으로 나가면서 in which가 된 것이다. be used to V : ~에 사용되어지다, be used to ~ing : ~에 익숙하다.
답 **D** (in who ---> in which)

7 **a great deal of + 불가산명사 문제 : W[2-1]**
a great deal of는 불가산명사와 함께 쓰인다.
A : usually는 빈도부사이므로 일반동사 앞, be동사/조동사 뒤에 위치한다.
C : it가 지시하는 것은 volcanic ash가 아니고 volcanic gas입니다. it은 목적어이다. 주어와 목적어가 같다면 목적어는 재귀대명사가 되어야 한다. 주어와 목적어가 다르기 때문에 itself가 아닌 it가 되어야 한다.
D : look like + 명사상당어구
답 **B** (volcanic ashes → volcanic ash)

8. **명사절 접속사 what 문제 : S[2-4]**
what절은 불완전한 문장이어야 한다. (B)번은 주어가 없는 불완전한 문장이므로 답이 된다.
답 **B**

9. **분사 문제 : W[1-5]**
the time which is required이 축약된 형태로 the time이 require의 객체이므로 과거분사형이 되어야 한다.
답 **B**

10. **전치사/접속사 선택문제 : S[2-1]**
전치사구 + 명사 상당어구, 접속사 + 주어 + 동사의 형태가 된다. his ambition은 명사이므로 blank에는 전치사가 들어가야 하므로 답은 (D)가 된다.
답 **D**

11. **like / alike 문제 : W[5-2]**
like는 전치사이므로 뒤에 명사가 와야 하고, alike는 서술적 용법의 형용사이다.
답 **D** (alike → like)

12. **주어(최상급) 문제 : S[3-3]**
주어자리가 비어 있으므로 주어가 들어가야 한다.
답 **D**

13. **최상급 형태문제 : W[4-3]**
the most famousest라는 형태는 없다. the most famous가 되어야 한다. indisputably는 one of ~ century를 수식하므로 부사형태가 된 것이다.
답 **C** (most famousest→ most famous)

14. **단어선택 문제 : W[5-1]**
material ~ conduits까지가 주어. 그러나 동사가 없으므로 large가 동사가 되야한다.
답 **B** (large → enlarges)

15. **관계대명사 선택문제 : S[2-2]**
Pattern 7의 문형(Hackers Grammar p48참조)으로 주어와 동사사이에 관계절이 들어간 형태이다. 선행사가 physicians이므로 관계대명사는 who가 되어야 한다.
답 **A**

16. **수동태문제 : W[1-4]**
문맥상 동사 absorbed의 주어는 green-colored substance이므로 수동태가 되어야 한다.
답 **C** (absorbed → is absorbed)

17. **주어 동격 문제 : S[2-7]**
주어 · 동사 모두 갖춘절이므로 blank에는 거품이 온다. 올 수 있는 것은 부사절, 부사구, 분사구문, 동격 등이다. A novelist와 Frank Norris는 동격이므로 답은 (D)가 된다.
답 **D**

18. **형용사 / 부사 형태 문제 : W[3-1]**
immediately는 명사 occasion을 수식하고 있으므로 형용사형이 되어야 한다.
답 **A** (immediately → immediate)

19. **상관접속사 문제(짝짓기 문제) : S[3-7]**
not only because ~ but (also) because ~
답 **C**

20. **현재분사 / 과거분사 문제 : W[1-5]**
use to V는 주체가 사람이어야 한다. 그러나 the biological term은 사물이므로 수동이 되어야 한다. 따라서 다음과 같이 고쳐져야 한다. Symbiosis is the

biological term (which is) used to describe ~
답 **B** (using → used)

21. **명사의 수문제 : W[2-1/5-3]**
another + 단수명사, other + 복수명사
B : found는 앞에 which were가 생략된 과거분사이다.
답 **A** (bone → bones)

22. **관계대명사절 축약문제 : S[2-6]**
because of 이하의 문장을 원래대로 분석해보면,
The many names were given to early humans and their predecessors (by them.)
← They gave many names to early humans and ther predecessors
because of 이하의 문장은, the many names (which were) given to early humans and their predecessors.
A : to give는 문맥상 적절하지 않을 뿐더러 목적어가 하나이므로 답이 될 수가 없다.
답 **D**

23. **병치구조문제 : W[4-1]**
by sending ~ rather than by twirling ~으로 연결되는 구조 병치이다.
답 **D** (with twirling → by twirling)

24. **동사의 형태문제 : W[1-3]**
조동사 뒤에는 원형동사가 온다. led는 lead의 과거, 과거분사이므로 원형인 lead가 되어야 한다.
답 **B** (can led → can lead)

25. **도치문제 : S[3-1]**
장소, 방향, source(출처, 기원)를 나타내는 부사구가 문두로 나갈 경우 도치가 일어난다. 원래문장은, The Algonquian-speaking people / were / along the eastern seaboard, extending north and west to the Great Lakes. 부사구를 강조하기 위해서 along 이하가 문두로 나가면서 도치가 된 것이다.
답 **B**

Structure

Chapter 1. Rule & Pattern

❶ S + V Rule

Hackers Practice p36

1. ~~As the air shot through the furnace~~, the bubbling metal would erupt ~~in showers of sparks~~.
2. The universe consists of billions of galaxies ~~flying apart as if from an explosion that set it in motion.~~
3. Democratic candidate, ~~General George B. McClellan,~~ promised ~~peace at any price.~~
4. One scientist has estimated that the sea's plankton generates more than twice as much.
5. ~~Growing to two or three inches long,~~ krill provide the major food ~~for the giant blue whale.~~
6. Mercury, ~~closest to the Sun,~~ receives the most solar energy.
7. ~~To describe her research~~ she has written or edited seven books.
8. ~~Despite such an impressive research background,~~ she ~~also~~ enjoys her work ~~in helping guide young scientists~~
9. ~~Like its relatives, the ancient tapir and rhinoceros,~~ eohippus had four toes ~~on its front feet, three on the rear, and teeth adapted to a forest diet of soft leaves.~~
10. Owning a phone ~~in some countries~~ is a well-known status symbol.

Hackers Test p37

1. **동사찾기**
   주어, 주어의 동격, blank , 부사구의 구조
   Cape Cod가 주어, 동사자리가 비어있음. 동사가 있는 (C)가 답
   답 **C**

2. **주어 · 동사찾기**
   부사구, 관계대명사절(형용사절), blank 형용사 and 형용사 구조
   거품을 걷어내면 주어, 동사 자리가 비어있음. 주어, 동사가 있는 (D)가 답
   답 **D**

3. **분사구문거품**
   blank, 절 구조
   문장의 주어 · 동사가 있으므로 blank에는
   Because people were drawn by fresh lands and low taxes, ~의 축약형인 (B)가 답
   답 **B**

4. **동사찾기**
   주어 + blank, 관계대명사절(형용사절) 구조
   주절의 주어만 있고 동사자리가 비어있음. 동사가 들어 있는 (B)가 답
   답 **B**

5. **동사찾기**
   주어, 분사구문, blank + 목적어[보어]구조
   주어는 New Orleans, 분사구문 거품제거후 동사를 찾는다.
   New Orleans는 도시명이므로 단수
   C : 타동사의 목적어로 형용사가 올 수 없으므로 틀림
   답 **A**

6. **동사찾기**
   부사구, 주어, 분사구문, blank, 등위접속사 + (주어, 동사가 생략) + 부사구구조
   부사구와 분사구문은 문장거품이므로 제거하면 동사자리가 비어있음. blank에는 동사가 포함되어야 함
   A : 관계대명사절이므로 was는 주동사가 아님
   B, C : 주어가 들어갔으므로 주어반복
   답 **D**

7. **주어 · 동사찾기**
   부사구, blank + 목적어[보어]구조
   부사구는 거품이므로 주어, 동사가 실종되었으므로 주어 동사로 시작하는 주절인 (D)가 답.
   답 **D**

8. **동사찾기**
   주어 + 부사구 + blank + 목적어[보어]구조
   동사가 실종됨. 목적어가 있으므로 타동사 능동태가 답.
   답 **B**

9. **주어찾기**
   부사구, 부사구, blank + 동사 + 보어구조
   실종 주어가 있는 (D)가 답
   답 **D**

10. **동사찾기**
    주어 + 부사구 + blank 구조
    주어는 있으나 동사가 실종됨.
    동사를 포함하고 주어와 수가 일치하는 (D)가 답
    답 **D**

11. **주어찾기**
    주어 + 분사구문 + 동사 + 부사구구조
    decorated ~ motifs는 관계절 축약이므로 거품. 주어가 있는 (D)가 답.
    답 **D**

12. **전치사구 + there was + 주어 + blank + 관계부사절구조**
    완전한 문장이므로 blank는 부사구 또는 주어를 수식하는 분사구문(형용사)이 되어야 한다.
    a court와 shaped사이에는 which was가 생략되어 있다.
    C : whose shaping의 동사가 없어서 틀리다.
    like는 전치사이고 'Capital I' 는 '대문자 I' 의 뜻이다.
    답 **B**

13. **주어 · 동사찾기**
    부사구, blank + 분사 + 부사구구조
    이 문장의 동사는 picked이고, built는 동사가 아니라 to be built에 쓰인 과거분사이다.
    B : picked의 주체인 Alexander가 built의 대상이 될 수 없으므로 틀리다.
    C : 문장에 정동사가 없어 틀리다.
    D : be앞에 조동사가 없으므로 비문법적 문장이 된다.
    답 **A**

14. **주어 + blank + 동사 + 목적어 + 부사구구조**
    meant는 목적어가 있으므로 과거분사가 아니라 동사가 된다. 완전한 문장이므로 주어와 동사사이에 부사구가 들어간 (A)가 답
    답 **A**

15. **주어 · 동사찾기**
    blank + 부사구구조
    부사구를 제거하면 주어와 동사가 실종되어 있음. 주어와 동사가 있는 (D)가 답
    답 **D**

16. **주어찾기**
    [blank + 목적어 + 부사구] + 동사 + so + 형용사 + that절 구조
    주어구의 목적어를 받는 동명사가 있는 (A)가 답
    답 **A**

❷ Structure Patterns

Hackers Practice p49

1. Pattern **1**
2. Pattern **1-A**
3. Pattern **2**
4. Pattern **3**
5. Pattern **6**
6. Pattern **5**
7. Pattern **7**
8. Pattern **7**
9. Pattern **1**
10. Pattern **3**

Hackers Test p50

1. Pattern 2

blank + 주어 + 동사 + 목적어의 구조이므로 blank에는 부사구가 들어가야 하므로 (B)가 답

D : beginning은 명사로 처음, 최초, 개시. 명사앞 the가 빠졌음

답 **B**

2. S + V Rule

부사구, 주어 + blank + 목적어[보어] + 부사구의 구조

동사자리가 비어 있으므로 동사가 있는 (C)가 답

답 **C**

3. Pattern 1-C / Pattern 6

타동사 know의 목적어를 포함하는 what이 답

답 **B**

4. Pattern 1-C / Pattern 6

전치사의 목적어와 are known as corporate network의 주어역할을 동시에 하는 what이 답

답 **B**

5. Pattern 4

부사구, 주어 + 동사 + 부사구 + as + 주어 + 동사 + 목적어 + blank 구조

as 이하는 부사절이고 완전한 문장이므로 blank에는 문장의 거품이 들어가야 한다.

문장 거품이 들어간 (D)가 답

답 **D**

6. Pattern 3

A : 명사이므로 주어와 동격이 되어야 하나 문맥상 regular supplies와 our capacity는 같지 않으므로 틀림

B : 주어 + 동사가 왔으므로 주어 앞에 종속접속사가 와야 하므로 틀림. 만약 B번이 답이 되려면 our capacity앞에 등위접속사가 있어야 한다.

C : that은 명사절을 이끄는 접속사이므로 완전한 문장의 절이 와야 하나 부사구가 왔으므로 틀림.

답 **D**

7. S+V Rule

after는 접속사와 전치사로 모두 사용됨. 여기서는 after이하에 구가 왔으므로 전치사로 사용되었다.

부사구, blank + 분사구조이므로 blank에는 절이 들어가야 한다.

A : 부가구나 절 뒤에 주절이 시작할 때, 주절은 then과 같은 비접속 부사로 시작할 수 없다.

답 **B**

8. Pattern 5

주절, 관계대명사절의 구조

A : A번이 답이 되려면 the outlines of them앞에 대등절 접속사가 필요하다.

B : which는 선행사 elaborate designs를 받는 관계대명사

C : which가 주격, 혹은 목적격 관계대명사인 경우, which가 이끄는 문장에서 주어 혹은 목적어 사리가 비어있어야 한다. which 다음이 주어나 목적어가 비어있지 않은 완전한 문장이므로 틀렸다.

답 **B**

9. Pattern 6

문장에서 as는 접속사가 아니라 전치사. as가 전치사일 경우는 " ~ 로서" 의 의미로 자격을 나타낸다.

따라서, 주어 the emergence와 동사 can probably be traced사이에 부사구가 삽입된 구조이다.

완전한 문장이므로 blank에는 문장거품이 들어가야 하므로 (B)가 답.

답 **B**

10. Pattern 1

while이하는 부사절이므로 blank에는 주절의 주어가 실종되어 있다.

분사구문의 생략된 주어 주절의 주어가 일치하는 (D)가 답

while working ~ = while he was working ~ 또는 while he worked ~

답 **D**

11. Pattern 4

앞에 주절이 왔으므로 적절한 전치사구가 따라오는 (C)가 답이다.

B : 동명사가 왔으므로 동명사 앞에 동명사를 목적어로 취할 수 있는 전치사가 나와야 한다. which뒤에 구밖에 없어서 틀리다. 이 which 대신에 전치사가 나오면 문장이 성립한다.

D : D도 전치사구이므로 문법상으로는 자격이 되지만 의미상 틀리다.

답 **C**

12. Pattern 6

주절은 완전한 문장이므로 blank에는 분사구문이나 관계대명사절이 들어가야 하므로 (D)가 답

답 **D**

13. Pattern 5

A : 절이 왔으나 접속사가 없다.

C : comma 이하에 to부정사는 올 수 없다.

D : 관계대명사 계속적 용법으로 that은 사용할 수 없다.
㊐ **B**

14. Pattern 1
동사 consider는 5형식동사.
consider A B ⇒ A is considered B
주어가 실종되었으므로 주어가 되는 (D)가 답.
㊐ **D**

15. Pattern 5
앞에 주절이 있고 주절 뒤에 comma가 있으면 따라오는 절은 관계절이나 대등절이다. 관계절인 (C)가 답이다.
㊐ **C**

16. Pattern 5
B : 선행사는 athletes이므로 who가 되어야 한다. many of them이 관계대명사화된 many of whom이 답이다(Structure 2-2참조).
㊐ **D**

17. Pattern 7
주어와 동사 사이에는 관계절, 부사절, 분사구문, 부사구, 동격이 삽입 가능하다. 동격인 (C)가 답이다.
㊐ **C**

18. Pattern 3
뒤에 주절이 왔으므로 앞에 올 수 있는 절은 부사절밖에 없다. 부사절인 (A)가 답이다.
㊐ **A**

Chapter 1 Mini test p54

1. Pattern 1 [1 – 2과 참조]
주어가 될 수 있는 요소중 선택지에는 명사절과 동명사구가 있는데 문법적 형태를 갖춘 동명사구인 (C)가 답이다.
㊐ **C**

2. S + V Rule [1–1과 참조]
주어와 동사가 있고 주어와 동사가 수일치가 되는 (D)가 답이다. 이 문장은 it-that강조구문이다.
원래 문장은 The hardy pioneers built up the American West이며, 여기에서 pioneers가 사람이므로 who를 사용한다.
㊐ **D**

3. Pattern 5[1–2과 참조]
독립절, blank구조
부사구 형태인 (C)가 답
B : comma 이하에 to부정사는 사용불가.
㊐ **C**

4. Pattern 1 [1 – 2과 참조]
주어 + of + blank + 동사 + 보어 + 부사구구조
완벽한 문장이므로 blank에는 주어를 한정하는 명사상당어구가 들어가야 한다.
A : 문맥상 make와 pratice는 같은시제여야 하므로 단순시제가 되어야 한다.
B : 전치사의 목적어로 to부정사는 불가
C : 전치사의 목적어로 that절 불가
D : 동명사는 전치사의 목적어가 될 수 있으므로
㊐ **D**

5. Pattern 4 [1 – 2과 참조]
독립절 + blank구조
A : the cultures와 they사이에는 목적격 관계대명사가 생략되어 있다.
B : 선행사가 사물이므로 who는 which가 되어야 맞는 문장이다.
㊐ **A**

6. Pattern 3 [1 – 2과 참조]
blank, 독립절구조
alternate의 주체가 Hooper이므로 축약부사절이면서 능동형인 (A)가 답
㊐ **A**

7. Pattern 3 [1 – 2과 참조]
blank, 독립절구조
뒤에 주절이 오면 앞에 오는 구조는 부사절, 준동사구문, 부사구 중의 하나다.
C : to 부정사구이고 주절의 주어인 congratulators가 celebrate의 주체가 될 수 있으므로 답
D : 수동분사구문은 수동태문형이므로 목적어가 나올 수 없다.
㊐ **C**

8. Pattern 3 [1 – 2과 참조]
주어의 동격인 (C)가 답
㊐ **C**

9. Pattern 3 [1 – 2과 참조]
comma 이하가 독립절이므로 comma 앞은 구를 이끄는 전치사구인 C가 답
㊐ **C**

10. Pattern 1–A [1 – 2과 참조]
명사절의 동사 is의 주어와 본동사 is의 주어를 동시에 수행할 수 있는 what이 들어가는 (D)가 답
㊐ **D**

11. Pattern 4 [1 – 2과 참조]
In 1927 ~ government는 완전한 문장이므로 생략해도 무방한 거품이 와야하므로 (B)가 답
grant A B : A에게 B를 수여하다.
grant는 4형식 동사로서 수동태가 되어 뒤에 명사 목적어 a commission이 온 것임.
㊐ **B**

12. Pattern 6 [1 – 2과 참조]
The medium which is chosen by the artist ~의 축약형태인 D가 답
㊐ **D**

13. Pattern 5 [1 – 2과 참조]
its protein supplies for energy와 동격 명사구인 D가 답
㊐ **D**

❶ 등위접속사와 부사절접속사

Hackers Practice p61

1. until
2. when
3. While
4. Because/Since
5. Although/While
6. while/because
7. because
8. When
9. Although/While

Hackers Test p62

1. Pattern 5

앞에 주절 + comma가 오면 뒤에 대등절, 관계절이 오지만 부사절이 따라올 수도 있다.

A : 접속사 but과 when이 중복되어 틀리다.

B : until then은 부사구로서 절과 절을 연결하는 접속사로 쓰이지 않는다.

C : in spite of 는 전치사로 접속사가 아니다

D : 부사절을 이끄는 although가 정답이다.

㉤ **D**

2. Pattern 4

앞 문장은 주절이고 뒤 문장은 부사절 형태의 구조이다.

A : 주어가 없다.

C : because of는 전치사구로서 절과 함께 사용할 수 없다.

D : 접속사 which와 because가 중복되었다.

㉤ **B**

3. Pattern 3

뒤에 'comma + 주절'이 왔으므로 앞에는 부사절이 와야 한다.

C : 주어, 동사 중복

㉤ **B**

4. Pattern 5

독립절 + comma 뒤에는 관계절이나 대등절이 온다.

B : 등위접속사 but과 주어 + 동사가 완전하게 갖춰져 있으므로 맞는 답이다.

㉤ **B**

5. Pattern 5

blank이하에 절이 왔으므로 comma이하는 일반적으로 등위절 또는 관계절이 오지만 부사절이 오기도 한다.

(A), (B)번의 how나 whether는 명사절을 이끄는 접속사이므로 등위절이나 부사절이 아니므로 틀리다.

㉤ **D**

6. S + V Rule

comma 앞에 부사절이 왔으므로 뒤에는 주절이 되어야 하고, blank 이하에 주어 + 동사가 없으므로 blank에 주어 + 동사가 들어가야 한다.

B : 답이 되려면 common이 명사로 쓰여야함. commom이 명사일 때의 의미는 문맥상 적합하지 않으므로 답이 되지 않음.

C : 접속사가 when과 so 2개가 되어 '하나의 접속사로 두 개의 절을 연결' 원칙을 위반한다.

㉤ **A**

7. Pattern 5

Pattern 5에서 독립절 + comma뒤에는 일반적으로 관계절, 대등절이 오지만, 부사질이 오는 경우가 있다.

A : despite는 전치사로서 절과 함께 사용할 수 없다.

B : after는 접속사로서 절과 함께 사용할 수 있지만 문맥상 적절하지 않다.

C : the fact = that ~ = duct glands이므로 문맥상 적절치 않다.

㉤ **D**

8. S + V Rule

blank + 등위접속사+절의 구조이므로 blank에는 주어 · 동사가 와야 한다.

A : 주어만 있으므로 틀림.

B : 부사절이므로 틀림

D : 부정사구이므로 틀림

㉤ **C**

9. Pattern 3

A : on account of는 전치사구이므로 절이 올 수 없다.

B : 주어 + 동사의 절이므로 comma 다음에 등위접속사가 와야한다.

C : 부사절로서 적절한 문장

D : for가 대등접속사로 사용될때는 문두에 나올 수 없다.

㉤ **C**

10. S + V Rule

comma 앞은 부사절이므로 comma 이하에 주절이 와야 한다.

주어, 동사가 실종되어 있으므로 주어, 동사가 있는 (C)가 답.

find A B : A를 B로 알다.

B : 주어는 finding이므로 단수

㉤ **C**

❷ 관계대명사

Hackers Practice p67

1. who	6. who
2. who	7. which
3. whose	8. who
4. whose	9. which
5. which	10. who

Hackers Test p68

1. 관계대명사 종류문제 / Pattern 4

recreation seekers는 사람이므로 관계대명사는 who가 되어야 한다.

A : are owned는 수동태이므로 목적어를 받을 수 없다.

B : whose는 소유격 관계대명사로서 뒤에 명사가 나와야 한다.

답 **D**

2. 관계대명사 종류문제 / Pattern 4

A : who이하가 완전한 문장이므로 관계대명사 who의 역할이 없다.

B : 소유격 관계대명사는 뒤에 명사가 나와야 하고 주어역할을 하고 있으므로 맞는 표현이다.

C : that은 주격 관계대명사의 역할을 제대로 수행하고 있지만 동사의 시제가 일치하지 않는다.

D : whose 다음에 명사가 없다.

답 **B**

3. 관계대명사 종류문제 / Pattern 7

선행사는 the classic Neanderthals이고 사람이다. 따라서 주격관계대명사는 who가 되어야 한다.

C : between about 70,000 and 30,000 years ago는 과거표시 부사구이므로 시제가 과거가 되어야 한다.

답 **A**

4. 관계대명사 종류문제 / Pattern 5

선행사가 crusted lichens이므로 관계대명사 which가 되어야 한다.

답 **B**

5. 관계대명사 어순문제 / Pattern 5

A : which의 선행사가 복수인 scorpiones이므로 which are가 되어야 한다.

B : scorpiones는 가산명사이므로 many of which나 most of which가 되어야 한다.

C : 절이므로 앞에 접속사가 들어가야 한다.

답 **D**

6. 관계대명사 종류문제 / Pattern 5

A : in that은 부사절을 이끄는 접속사이므로 뒤에 절이 와야 한다. in that 이하에 주어가 없으므로 틀림.

B : 관계대명사 주격으로 which one은 사용되지 않는다.

C : which의 선행사인 복수 theories와 단수동사 was가 수일치가 되지 않는다.

D : which의 선행사는 theories이고 comma 이하의 주어는 one = theory이므로 단수동사와 수 일치되고 있다. 여기서 one은 지시대명사가 아니고 하나라는 뜻의 수사로 쓰였다.

답 **D**

7. 관계대명사 종류문제 / Pattern 5

관계대명사와 동사의 수 일치에 관련된 문제.
blank 이하에 동사가 왔고 앞에 comma가 있으므로 주격관계대명사가 들어가야 한다.

A : which의 선행사는 sub-systems가 복수인데, 단수동사가 따라와서 주어 동사의 수일치가 되지 않았다.

B :what은 선행사를 받는 관계대명사가 될 수 없다.

C : 두 개의 절을 연결하는 접속사가 없어 틀리다.

D : which역시 선행사는 sub-systems, each는 항상 단수 취급

답 **D**

8. 관계대명사 어순문제 / Pattern 4

The spat grew larger by drawing in seawater.
They derived microscopic parties of food from seawater.
→ The spat grew larger by drawing in seawater from which they derived microscopic parties of food.

답 **B**

9. 관계대명사 종류문제 / Pattern 4

선행사는 German shepherds(개의 한 종류)이므로 주격 관계대명사는 which가 되어야 한다.
German shepherds는 훈련을 받는 객체이므로 수동태 동사가 되는 (D)가 답

답 **D**

10. 관계대명사 종류문제 / Pattern 5

A : 절이므로 앞에 접속사가 들어가야 한다.

B : 소유격 관계대명사이므로 뒤에 명사가 와야한다.

C : what은 선행사를 받을 수 없다.

D : which의 선행사는 the Franklin stove

답 **D**

11. 관계대명사 어순문제 / Pattern 6

주어와 동사 사이에 blank가 있으므로 주어를 수식하는 관계절이 들어가야 한다.
The world is known as the Paleolithic Age or Old Stone Age.
Homo erectus men and women lived in the world.
→ The world in which Homo erectus men and women lived is known as the Paleolithic Age or Old Stone Age.

답 **D**

12. 관계대명사 종류문제 / Pattern 4

Others see Jim as an ambitious man.
His life was dedicated to his own aggrandizement ~.
→ Others see him as an ambitious man whose life was dedicated to his own aggrandizement ~
원래 문장들을 하나로 합칠 경우 위와 같이 된다.

답 **C**

❸ 명사절

Hackers Practice p73

1. That rent control laws inhibit landlords from repairing properties is unfortunate, but true.
2. Sophia realized that the experience caused her to see her world differently.
3. How glass is blown in a cylinder was demonstrated at the Stuart Crystal factory.
4. A top architect lamented that culture uniqueness had been replaced by international sameness.
5. Why consumers hesitated to buy the controversial digital audiotape players is a subject the article ignored.
6. Whom the late Dr. Bishopstone left his fortune to will be revealed this afternoon.
7. Richards claimed that the documents were taken from archives in Portugal.
8. Recent scientific studies show that off-road vehicles can cause damage to desert landscapes.
9. What they found when they got there was very disappointing.
10. He knew that the Federal forces held more than a modest advantage in terms of men and supplies.
11. Whatever came out has been beautiful to me.
12. Several pieces of musical notation are extant, but no one today knows exactly how they sounded.

Hackers Test p74

1. 명사절이 완벽한 문장

showed의 목적어 역할을 하는 명사절 찾기
(B)에서 what은 형용사와 결합이 불가능하다. how + 형용사인 (A)번이 정답이다.
(D)의 which도 형용사와 결합하지 못한다.
답 **A**

2. 명사절이 완벽한 문장

전치사 on의 목적어로 절이 나왔으므로 명사절이다. 명사절이 완벽한 문장이므로 명사절 내에서 부사역할을 할 수 있는 접속사가 들어가야 한다. 따라서 부사역할을 하는 how가 들어가 있는 (D)가 답.
답 **D**

3. 명사절이 완벽하지 않은 문장

전치사 of의 목적어로 절이 나왔으므로 명사절이다. 명사절에서 전치사 with의 목적어가 없으므로 완벽하지 않은 문장이다. 따라서 전치사 of와 with의 목적어를 동시에 수행할 수 있는 접속사가 들어가야 하므로 (C)가 답.
B : which가 사용되려면 선행사가 있어야한다.
답 **C**

4. 명사절이 완벽하지 않은 문장

타동사 picture의 목적어로 절이 왔으므로 명사절이다. 이 명사절에서는 주어가 없으므로 완벽하지 않은 문장이다. 따라서 타동사 picture의 목적어와 명사절의 주어역할을 동시에 수행할 수 있는 접속사 what이 들어가야 하므로 (B)가 답.
답 **B**

5. 명사절이 완벽한 문장

be afraid는 명사절을 수반하고 that절 이하는 완벽한 문장이므로 (A)가 답.
답 **A**

6. 명사절이 완벽하지 않은 문장

타동사 resist의 목적어로서 절이 왔으므로 명사절이다. resist는 타동사이기 때문에 목적어가 필요하고 보기 중에서 judge의 경우는 judge A to be의 구조를 필요로 하므로 judge의 목적어도 필요하다. 즉, resist의 목적어가 되기 위한 명사절을 이끄는 접속사 역할과 judge의 목적이 역할 두가지를 동시에 하는 건 선행사를 포함한 what밖에 없다.
답 **B**

7. 명사절이 완벽하지 않은 문장

전치사 of의 목적어로 절이 왔으므로 명사절이다. 명사절에서 타동사 want와 expect의 목적어가 없으므로 명사절은 완벽하지 않은 문장이다. 타동사 want, expect의 목적어가 될 수 있는 접속사가 들어가야 하므로 (B)가 답.
C : which의 선행사가 없다.
답 **B**

8. 명사절이 완벽한 문장

the boundaries ~ drawn까지는 완벽한 문장이므로 부사역할을 할 수 있는 접속사가 들어가야 하므로 (D)가 답.
답 **D**

9. 명사절이 완벽하지 않은 문장

know의 목적어 자리에 온 명사절이 완벽하지 않다. 전치사 like의 목적어가 없으므로, 명사절 접속사는 what.
답 **B**

10. 명사절이 완벽한 문장

타동사 found의 목적어로 절이 왔으므로 명사절이고 명사절은 완벽한 문장이다. 따라서 완벽한 문장을 이끄는 접속사가 들어가야 하므로 (D)가 답.
C : find는 평서문에서 whether절을 이끌 수 없다.
답 **D**

11. 명사절이 완벽한 문장

명사절이 완벽한 문장이므로 (C), (D)번 가능.
문맥상 how보다는 that절 이하의 사실을 '의미한다'는 표현이 맞음
답 **C**

Structure

❹ What / That

Hackers Practice p78

1. That → What
2. 맞음
3. 맞음
4. that → what
5. in that → in what
6. 맞음
7. what → that
8. what → that
9. 맞음
10. what → that
11. That → What

Hackers Test p79

1. what/that 구별문제

A : that이하의 문장이 완벽하므로 맞는 문장이다.
B : what이하의 문장이 완벽하므로 틀림.
C : that이하의 문장이 불완전하므로 틀림.
D : which 앞에 선행사가 없어 틀림.
답 **A**

2. what/that 구별문제

A : that이하의 문장이 완벽하므로 맞는 문장이다.
답 **A**

3. what/that 구별문제

that 이하에서 blank이하에 동사 + 보어가 나왔으므로 blank에는 주어가 들어가야 한다.
주어가 될 수 있는 명사절인 (C)가 답이다.
답 **C**

4. what/that 구별문제

타동사 do의 목적절을 이끌고 동사 will be의 주어 역할을 동시에 수행할 수 있는 접속사가 들어가야 한다.
we expect는 거품절임을 주의해야 한다.
A : that이하는 구성요소가 빠지지않은 완벽한 문장이 되어야 한다. 이 문장에서는 expect가 타동사이기 때문에 완벽한 문장이 되려면 목적어가 필요하다.
답 **C**

5. what/that 구별문제

전치사 of의 목적절을 이끌고 타동사 want의 목적어의 역할을 동시에 수행할 수 있는 접속사가 들어가야 한다.
they wanted + something + (to be) + carved에서 something이 앞으로 나가서 what에 포함되고 to be는 생략된 것이다. 따라서 what they wanted carved가 된 것이다.
B : 전치사의 목적어로서 that절은 절대불가
D : which는 관계대명사로 선행사가 있어야 하는데, 선행사가 없음.
답 **A**

6. what/that 구별문제

전치사 of의 목적절을 이끌고 타동사 consider의 목적어 역할을 동시에 수행할 수 있는 접속사가 들어가야 한다.
동사 consider는 목적어와 목적보어를 갖는 동사이므로 they considered Clinton' s meddling ~은 불완전한 문장이다.
consider A B, consider A as B, consider A to be B모두 A를 B로 여기다, 간주하다의 뜻이다. 이 구조에 what는 A에 대입되고 Clinton' s meddling은 B에 대입되는 것이다.
A : 전치사의 목적어로서 that절은 절대불가.
D : consider의 목적어 역할과 전치사 of의 목적어인 명사절을 이끄는 역할을 동시에 하는 것은 what이다.
답 **D**

7. what/that 구별문제

blank 이하는 claims의 목적절인 명사절이다. 그 명사절은 완벽한 문장이므로 (D)가 답.
benefit은 자동사와, 타동사로 쓰인다.
답 **D**

8. what/that 구별문제

be amazed는 명사절을 수반한다. Greg ~ me는 완전하므로 that, whether, if가 올 수 있으나, 'be amazed'는 whether이나 if를 선택하지 않는다.
in the first place : 우선, 첫 번째는
답 **C**

9. what/that 구별문제

A : which가 주격관계대명사이나 선행사가 없으므로 답이 될 수 없다.
B : what이하의 문장이 완벽하므로 what 이 사용될 수 없다.
C : 동사가 중복되어 있다.
답 **D**

10. what/that 구별문제

A, C : the fact와 a bookworm이 동격이 되어야 하지만 문맥상 같을 수가 없다.
B : what이하의 문장이 완벽하여 what이 올 수 없다.
D : that이후에는 완벽한 문장이 들어가야 한다. 여기에선 that이하의 문장이 완벽하므로 맞는 표현이다.
답 **D**

❺ 부사절 축약

Hackers Practice p83

1. When only in elementary school
2. While an extraordinary pitcher
3. when covered with hides
4. After finishing campaigning in france
5. when out of control
6. although not numerous
7. before hitting his powerful homer
8. while still a senior
9. When still in high school
10. After recognizing the value of the Museum

Hackers Test p85

1. Pattern 3

Since some children are afraid of failure 축약인 (C)가 답이다. be동사 + 형용사의 축약은 be동사를 생략하거나 be동사를 being으로 고친다.

답 **C**

2. Pattern 3

B : 부사절 축약형태로서 원래 문장은 while they searched for a place to settle

C : search의 주체는 the Aztecs이므로 being searched → searching이 되어야 한다.

답 **B**

3. Pattern 1

comma 앞에 분사구문이므로 comma 이하에 주절이 와야 한다. blank에는 주어가 들어가야 한다.

답 **C**

4. Pattern 3

Although Indians were baptized의 축약인 (D)가 답이다.

답 **D**

5. Pattern 4

While the Soviet Union received its sugar~의 축약인 (D)가 답이다. 이 문제에서 For decades는 주절 전체를 수식하므로 이 전치사구는 문장에서 부사구 역할을 한다. 이 문제의 문장구조는 '부사구+주절+부사절축약(분사구문)' 의 구조이다.

답 **D**

6. S + V Rule

주절의 주어, 동사가 실종되어 있음. 주절의 주어는 reading의 주체가 되어야 하므로 (B)가 답

답 **B**

7. Pattern 3

이 문장은 comma뒤의 문장이 주어+동사가 있는 완벽한 문장이므로 부사절이나 분사구문, 혹은 부정사가 와야 한다.

A : 부사절이 온 형태인데 분사구문(when having fallen)으로 바꿔서 쓰던가, 아예 주어, 동사를 제대로 써야 한다.

B : fell into는 동사 과거형이므로 앞에 종속접속사 + 주어가 들어가야 한다.

D : 접속사가 빠져서 성립이 안된다.

답 **C**

8. Pattern 3

부사절 축약문제

While Oprah was still in college의 축약인 (D)가 답이다.

답 **D**

9. Pattern 3

여기서 when으로 시작되는 부사절은 축약된 것이 아니라 debasing the coinage가 동명사구 주어인 형태이다.

답 **D**

10. S + V Rule

분사구문은 'Although Spain was once the leading country' 의 축약이고, 분사구문의 축약된 주어는 주절의 주어와 동일하므로 (D)가 답이다.

답 **D**

11. Pattern 3

'After the chiefs of median's bribes had learned of Muhammad' 이 축약된 현재 분사형이 정답이다.

D : learn이 수동태의 뜻이 아니므로 답이 되려면 learned가 learning이 되어야 한다.

답 **C**

6 형용사절(관계대명사) 축약

Hackers Practice p89

1. which were along the wall
2. who was taking(*or* took) some correspondence courses
3. who was named Adam Gimbel, which was called Gimbel Brothers.
4. who had no cash
5. who were from northern and western Europe
6. who was in remote, undeveloped California
7. that is given to honor merit, service, or achievement.
8. who was in this operation
9. who were dissatisfied with the machine age and with modern ways of life.
10. who are doing(*or* do) hard work in hot climates.

Hackers Test p91

1. Pattern 7

동사 pay의 주체는 the Spanish soldiers가 아니므로 동사는 수동형이 되어야 한다.

A : 동사 paid는 능동이므로 문맥상 적절하지 못함

D : poorly paid앞에 who were가 생략되어 있으므로 수동형.

답 **D**

2. S+V Rule

분사구문의 동사의 주어와 주절의 주어는 같아야 한다. troubled의 주어는 사람이므로 주절의 주어는 사람이어야 한다.

A : Decartes Leaving the country가 주어부임, 앞의 troubled의 주어로 어울리지 않음

답 **C**

3. Pattern 7

A : 의미상 본문에 부합되지 않는다.

B : 거품이 와야 할 자리이므로 동사 + 목적어 구조인 (B)는 틀림.

C : 수동태이므로 뒤에 목적어가 나올 수 없다.

답 **D**

4. **Pattern 3**

comma 이하에 주절이 왔으므로 comma 앞의 절은 부사절이나 분사구문이 되어야 한다.
동사 locate는 주체가 사람이고 객체는 사물이므로 사물이 주어일 경우는 수동형이 되어야 한다.
답 **C**

5. **Pattern 3**

동사 release는 '해방하다, 석방시키다' 의 의미이고 주어 Francis는 문맥상 풀려난 것이므로 blank는 수동분사구문이 되어야 한다.
답 **D**

6. **Pattern 7**

The huge building은 date back의 주체가 되므로 현재분사가 되어야 한다. date back은 자동사로 '거슬러 올라가다' 의 뜻이다.
답 **D**

7. **Pattern 7**

Groundwater, which is found everywhere ~의 축약형인 (C)가 답
답 **C**

8. **Pattern 7**

'which was imported by the Spanish' 의 축약인 (C)가 답이다.
답 **C**

9. **Pattern 7**

'which was confirmed~' 의 축약인 (D)가 답이다.
답 **D**

⑦ 동격

Hackers Practice p94

1. who was Joseph Nicephore Niepce
2. an organ in the throat
3. which is a dilute solution of acetic acid
4. who was the first female dancer
5. cohesion and adhesion
6. who is South Africa' s First black president
7. especially the intricate sculptures
8. the king of Jerusalem
9. a common family of minerals in granite
10. a dense, hot layer of semi-solid rock

Hackers Test p95

1. **Pattern 7**

the United States 와 a land of immigrants는 동격.
C : which 다음에 was가 빠져있다.
답 **B**

2. **Pattern 5**

After Louis' s death는 부사구이고 주어는 the Habsburg Ferdinand of Austria
A : which 다음에 was가 빠져 있다.
B, C :절이 왔으므로 접속사가 들어가야 한다.
D : a narrow corridor앞에 which was가 생략된 동격
답 **D**

3. **Pattern 5**

Christian churches는 claim to의 주체가 되므로 현재분사의 분사구문이 되어야 한다.
답 **C**

4. **Pattern 5**

A : 주어 + 동사의 절이 왔으므로 접속사가 들어가야 한다.
duchy of Milan과 a territory가 동격인 (D)가 정답이다.
답 **D**

5. **Pattern 5**

20,000,000 people과 동격
one of the 최상급 + 복수명사구조
답 **D**

6. **Pattern 7**

주어와 동사사이에 and로 연결되는 동격이 삽입.
C : who 다음에 was가 있어야 한다.
답 **B**

7. **Pattern 7**

주어 + blank + and 주어 + 동사 + 목적어의 구조에서 blank 앞의 주어에 대한 동격이 삽입된 구조이다.
답 **D**

8. **Pattern 7**

C : who를 생략하거나 who was가 되어야 한다.
답 **B**

9. **Pattern 7**

A : 관계대명사 which 다음에 동사가 없다.
C : the Asiento와 a provision이 동격을 이루고 있다.
답 **C**

⑧ 명사 + to 부정사 / that절

Hackers Practice p99

1.to	4.to	7.that	10.to
2.that	5.to	8.to	
3.that	6.to	9.to	

Hackers Test p100

1. **명사 + to 부정사 문제**

opportunity는 to 부정사의 수식을 받는다.
답 **C**

2. 명사 + to 부정사 문제
chance는 to 부정사의 수식을 받는다.
㊐ **B**

3. 명사 + to 부정사 문제
ability는 to 부정사의 수식을 받는다.
㊐ **D**

4. 명사 + that절 문제
idea는 that절의 수식을 받는다.
㊐ **B**

5. 명사 + that절 문제
doubt는 that절의 수식을 받는다.
㊐ **D**

6. 서수 + to 부정사 문제
the first는 서수이므로 to 부정사의 수식을 받는다.
The first (people) to penetrate ~ = The first (people) that penetrated ~
㊐ **D**

7. 명사 + to 부정사 문제
effort는 to 부정사의 수식을 받는다.
㊐ **A**

8. 명사 + to 부정사 문제
need는 to 부정사의 수식을 받는다.
㊐ **C**

9. 명사 + that절 문제
fact는 that절의 수식을 받는다. the fact와 that절은 동격
㊐ **D**

10. 명사 + to 부정사 문제
capacity와 to 부정사는 동격
speak는 자동사일 경우 '이야기하다', '말하다' 의 의미이고, 타동사일 경우 '언어를 말하다(사용하다)' 를 의미한다.
문맥상 자동사이므로 (D)가 답.
㊐ **D**

11. 최상급 + to 부정사문제
the latest는 최상급이므로 to 부정사의 수식을 받는다. 동사 build의 주체는 사람이므로 사물이 주어일 때는 수동형이 되어야 한다.
㊐ **D**

12. 명사 + that절 문제
evidence는 that절의 수식을 받는다.
㊐ **D**

Chapter 2 Mini test p103

1. 접속사 문제 / Pattern 5 [2 – 1과 참조]
'화폐가 없기 때문에 물물교환을 위한 시장이 두개 있었다' 의 내용이므로 for(=becasue)가 있는 (C)가 정답이다. (C)의 주어는 주절의 주어와 다르기 때문에 (B)로 축약될 수 없다.
㊐ **C**

2. 관계대명사 문제 [2 – 2과 참조]
A : who ~의 문장이 완벽하므로 who의 역할이 없음
B : 선행사가 indians이므로 who가 되어야 함.
C : 소유격 관계대명사는 뒤에 명사가 나와야 함
D : 소유격 관계대명사 뒤에 완전한 문장이 왔으므로 D가 답
㊐ **D**

3. Pattern 7 [1 – 2과 참조]
A : is가 생략되거나 동격형태인 which is가 되어야 한다.
B : which가 생략되거나 which is가 되어야 한다.
C : 동격형태이므로 답
D : 절을 이끄는 접속사가 없으므로 틀림
㊐ **C**

4. 부사절 축약문제 / Pattern 7 [2 – 5과 참조]
주어, blank + 전치사구, 부사구 + 동사 + 목적어 + 부사구구조. 따라서 blank + 전치사구는 거품이 되어야 한다.
A, C : 동사 conform의 주체는 Elizabeth이므로 conforming이 되어야 한다.
B : Elizabeth와 the restoration은 동격이 될 수 없으므로 틀림.
D : while she outwardly conformed ~의 축약형태이므로 답
㊐ **D**

5. 동격문제 / Pattern 5 [2 – 7과 참조]
Patagonia와 a region은 동격, between Chile and Argentina는 전치사구
A : a region (which is) shared ~에서 which is가 생략된 형태
B : share의 주체는 region이 아니고 사람이므로 과거분사형이 되어야 한다.
C : 접속사 없이 절이 올 수 없다.
D : 동사인 is가 필요하다.
㊐ **A**

6. S + V Rule [1 – 1과 참조]
부사구, blank, 등위접속사 + 독립절
등위접속사가 있으므로 blank에는 독립절이 들어가야 한다.
A : 주어 + 동사 + 보어이므로 독립절
B : 관계대명사절은 형용사절이므로 제거되면 주어만 있고 동사가 없다.
C : 관계대명사절이므로 독립절이 될 수 없다.
D : that ~ easy는 명사절이므로 독립절이 아니다.
㊐ **A**

7. S + V Rule [1 – 1과 참조]
부사절, blank + 부사구구조이므로 blank에는 주절이 들어가야 한다. 부사절로 시작하면, 주절은 접속사 없이 주어 동사로 시작한다. 따라서 (C)가 답이다.
㊐ **C**

8. 관계대명사 문제 / Pattern 4 [2 – 2과 참조]
A : 주격 관계대명사와 주격대명사가 중복 사용되었다.

B : which + 동사 + 목적어이므로 which는 주격관계대명사의 역할을 수행

C : whom은 동물을 선행사로 가질 수 없고, roamed의 목적어가 남아 있어서 중복이 된다.

D : 전치사 + 관계대명사는 주어가 될 수 없다. 주어가 없으므로 틀림.

답 **B**

9. 관계대명사 문제 / Pattern 5 [2 – 2과 참조]

A : A가 답이 되려면 Muslim Spain과 동격이 와야 하므로 that이 없어야 옳은 표현.

B : 비교급이 사용되면 than이 함께 쓰여야 한다.

C : what은 선행사를 가질 수 없으므로 사용불가

D : which의 선행사는 Muslim Spain이므로 답

답 **D**

10. 관계절 축약문제 / Pattern 7 [2 – 6과 참조]

where ~의 관계부사절에서 주어와 동사사이에 들어갈 수 있는 문형을 찾는 문제

선택지에 분사구문이 있으므로 삽입 될 수 있는 적절한 형태의 분사구문을 찾는다. hold가 타동사 이므로 (B)가 답이다.

답 **B**

11. 관계절 축약문제 / Pattern 7 [2 – 6과 참조]

of the English poets의 of는 최상급의 신호이므로 최상급이 나와야 한다.

답 **D**

12. what/that문제 [2 – 4과 참조]

타동사 redress의 목적어로 절이 왔으므로 명사절이다. 명사절을 이끌 수 있는 (D)가 답이다.

A : consider A B의 형태에서 A에 해당하는 부분이 빠져있으므로 that이 아니라 what이 와야한다.

답 **D**

13. what/that문제 / Pattern 1-A [2 – 4과 참조]

blank는 주어의 자리다. 선택지에 절이 나오므로 명사절이 와야한다. what을 제외한 절이 불완전한 문장인 (B)가 답이다.

답 **B**

14. 명사 + to 부정사/ that절 문제 [2 – 8과 참조]

way는 to 부정사의 수식을 받는다.

답 **A**

15. 명사 + to 부정사/ that절 문제 [2 – 8과 참조]

최상급을 포함한 명사는 to 부정사의 수식을 받는다. 부정사의 형용사적 용법 중에서 '-한(했던) 첫 번째(마지막)사람' 의 의미는 현대 미국식 영어에서 the first / last + (명사) + to 부정사 형태로 표현한다. the + 최상급 + to 부정사, the 서수 + to 부정사와 같은 형태를 숙지해야함.

답 **D**

16. 명사 + to 부정사/ that절 문제 [2 – 8과 참조]

desire는 to 부정사의 수식을 받는다.

답 **C**

17. what/that문제 [2 – 4과 참조]

선택지를 보면 전치사 on의 목적어가 되는 명사절이 와야한다.

A : 명사절이 아닌 관계절이다.

B : 명사절로 답이다. knew의 목적어가 빠졌으므로 불완전한 문장이 되어 what이 쓰인것이다.

C : 명사절이 아닌 관계절이다.

D : 명사절을 이끄는 명사절 접속사가 없다.

답 **B**

❶ 도치

Hackers Practice p113

1. I(Only if is the law changed ~ → Only if the law is changed ~)
2. C
3. I (Not until 1865 when did ~ → Not until 1865 did ~)
4. C
5. C
6. I (No longer these protohorses could slip away ~ → No longer could these protohorses slip away)
7. C
8. C
9. C
10. I (do → does)
11. C
12. C
13. C

Hackers Test p115

1. **부정어가 문장의 앞으로 나온 경우**
부정어가 문두로 나가면 조동사/be동사 도치가 된다.
답 **D**

2. **부정어가 문장의 앞으로 나온 경우**
not until절이 문장의 앞으로 나올 때 주절에서 도치가 된다.
답 **C**

3. **only + 부사구가 문장의 앞으로 나온 경우**
답 **C**

4. **출처 부사구가 문장의 앞으로 나온 경우**
출처 부사구가 문장의 앞으로 나온 경우 동사구 도치가 된다.
from these는 기원 · 출처를 나타내는 부사구로 문두로 이동했다. 원래문장은,
The angiosperms and our present deciduous forests have sprung from these.
답 **A**

5. **보어도치(분사도치)**
a clause that censured the monarchy for imposing slavery upon America was also deleted.에서 분사(보어)가 앞으로 나가면서 도치되었으므로 (D)가 답.
답 **D**

6. **보어도치(분사도치)**
C : 주어가 the land turtles이므로 복수. 따라서 is → are가 되어야 한다.
답 **A**

7. **짝짓기 문제**
not only ~ but also구조
B : of뒤에 명사구가 없으므로 틀림
답 **D**

8. **only + 부사구가 문장의 앞으로 나온 경우**
only + 부사구가 문장의 앞으로 나오면 조동사/be동사 도치가 된다.
(C)는 원상복구 시켰을 때 wives were escaped가 되어 틀린다.
답 **B**

9. **only + 부사구가 문장의 앞으로 나온 경우**
답 **C**

10. **so + 형용사가 문장의 앞으로 나온 경우**
so + 형용사가 문장의 앞으로 나오면 도치가 된다.
원래문장은,
The priests who supervised the work were so successful that over 100 temples were built.
답 **C**

11. **only + 부사구가 문장의 앞으로 나온 경우**
only + 부사구가 문장의 앞으로 나오면 뒤따르는 '주어+동사'가 도치가 된다.
답 **A**

12. **보어도치(분사도치)**
보어(분사)가 문장의 앞으로 나오면 도치가 된다.
원래문장은,
Rooms for the family to meet with friends, cook, eat and store their belongings were surrounding a courtyard.
답 **D**

13. **보어도치**
보어가 문장의 앞으로 나오면 도치가 된다.
원래문장은,
Large baths were close by the citadel buildings, resembling a swimming pool.
D : close를 형용사로 보면 보어가 된다. by citadel buildings는 전치사구 거품이므로 제거, resembling이하는 분사구문으로 거품이니 제외한 후, 주어와 동사를 찾아보면 된다. 보어인 close가 앞으로 도치되어 답은 D가 된다.
답 **D**

14. **장소 부사구가 문장의 앞으로 나온 경우**
A번은 주어가 the imperial palace이므로 단수. 따라서 were → was가 되어야 한다.
답 **B**

15. **as, so, than 도치**
as, so, than이하에 도치가 될 수도 있다. (optional)
A : 동사가 followed를 받고 있으므로 대동사는 did가 되어야 한다.
답 **C**

❷ 비교급

Hackers Practice p121

1. C
2. I (to → than)
3. C
4. C
5. I (least than → less than)
6. I (than → to)
7. I (which we can handle → than we can handle)
8. C
9. C
10. I (as more important as → as important as)
11. I (any other subjects → any other subject)

Hackers Test p122

1. 비교급 어순문제

A : 비교 대상이 없으므로 틀림.

㊐ **D**

2. the 비교급, the 비교급문제

The greater the experience (is), the higher the salary (is)

㊐ **D**

3. 배수비교 문제

배수사 + as + 형용사/부사원급 + as의 어순이 되어야 한다.

㊐ **B**

4. the same ~ as 문제

비교구문은 비교대상(the peoples of North Africa와 the peoples south of the Sahara)이 병치구조를 이루어야 하고 those는 the peoples를 받음.

㊐ **C**

5. as ~ as 문제

blank 뒤에 as가 왔으므로 앞에 원급비교인 as가 있어야 하므로 답은 (D)

㊐ **D**

6. as ~ as possible문제

as ~ as possible = as ~ as one could

as ~ as사이에는 타동사 knock의 목적어가 들어가야 하므로 답은 (C)

as much/many ~as possible로서 '가능한한 많은~'라는 뜻으로 쓰인다. 문제 지문에서 out of the circle은 수식어로 거품이니 제거한다.

㊐ **C**

7. 비교급 강조 문제

than앞에는 비교급이 나와야 하고 비교급강조는 비교급 앞에 much/far를 사용하므로 (C)가 답

㊐ **C**

8. 비교급 형태문제

than앞에는 비교급이 나와야 하므로 (A)가 답.

㊐ **A**

9. 비교급 형태문제

than앞에는 비교급이 나와야 하고 more와 than 사이에는 be동사의 보어 역할을 할 수 있는 형용사(분사)나 명사가 들어가야 한다.

㊐ **C**

10. 비교급 형태문제

비교급 강조는 much/far를 사용하여야 하고 great의 비교급은 1음절이므로 greater가 되어야 하므로 (D)가 답.

㊐ **D**

11. 비교급 형태문제

타동사 carried이하에 명사상당어구가 나와야 한다. much는 greater를 수식하는 비교급강조.

㊐ **D**

12. as .... as문제

under their command는 부사구

비교대상은 the Songs와 the Tangs이고 much territory는 타동사 had의 목적어이다.

㊐ **D**

13. 비교급 형태문제

greater .... than형태이므로 (D)가 답.

㊐ **D**

❸ 최상급

Hackers Practice p127

1. I (violins → violin)
2. C
3. I (worse → worst)
4. I (the more → the most)
5. C
6. I (taller and homelier → the tallest and homeliest)
7. C
8. C
9. I (the stronger and larger → the strongest and largest)
10. I (The more → The most)

Hackers Test p128

1. 최상급 형태문제

the + 최상급 + (명사) + in/of/that

the most abundant of all was salmon에서 주어는 the most abundant이다. 주어가 형용사인 점이 어색하게 보이지만 명사구 the most abundant one에서 one가 생략된 형태이다.

㊐ **D**

2. 최상급 형태문제

the + 최상급형태가 되어야 하고 forthright는 most를 사용하여야 한다.

㊐ **A**

3. **최상급 형태문제**
one of the + 최상급 + 복수명사형태
답 **D**

4. **최상급 형태문제**
one of the + 최상급
답 **C**

5. **최상급 형태문제**
타동사 had의 목적어인 명사를 수식하는 형용사의 최상급문제이다.
of이하는 최상급의 범위를 지정하는 부사구이다.
답 **C**

6. **최상급 형태문제**
소유격과 관사가 동시에 명사를 수식하면 이중 한정이 되어 틀린다.
따라서 소유격에서는 정관사 the가 빠져야 한다.
답 **D**

7. **최상급 형태문제**
주어를 수식하는 형용사의 최상급문제
답 **D**

8. **최상급 형태문제**
the + 최상급 형태 문제
A : 최상급 앞에 the를 안썼으니 틀림
B : active뒤에 대명사 ones이 생략된 형태이나, 도치되기전 문장으로 복원하면 The Labor union was among the most active in establishing free public education이 된다.
답 **B**

9. **최상급 형태문제**
one of the + 최상급 + 복수명사문제이다.
주의할 것은 the도 한정사이고 world's도 한정사이므로 이중한정이라고 생각하기 쉬운 문제이다. 그러나 the는 world를 한정하고, world는 men을 한정하므로 이중한정이 아니므로 문법적으로 맞는 표현이다.
답 **D**

10. **최상급 형태문제**
blank에는 전치사의 목적어로 명사상당어구가 들어가야 하고, 이것을 수식하는 형용사의 최상급문제이다.
답 **D**

11. **최상급 형태문제**
be동사의 보어인 명사를 수식하는 형용사의 최상급 문제
답 **B**

12. **최상급 형태문제**
타동사 made의 목적격 보어인 명사를 수식하는 형용사의 최상급문제
답 **D**

❹ It/There 구문

Hackers Practice p133

1. It is	5. It is	9. There is	13. It was
2. It is	6. There is	10. There are	
3. There are	7. There are	11. It is	
4. There is	8. It is	12. There is	

Hackers Test p134

1. **It/There 문제**
문장의 주어, 동사가 없으므로 주어, 동사가 될 수 있는 것을 찾아야 한다.
A : They가 지시하는 명사가 없으므로 안된다.
B : it가 지시하는 명사가 앞에 없고 뒤에 오는 to 부정사나 that절도 없으므로 it을 사용할 수 없다.
답 **D**

2. **It/There 문제**
부사구, blank + that절 구조
that절 이하에는 완전한 문장이므로 명사절이다. 따라서 명사절을 주어로 받을 수 있는 it가 들어가야 한다.
답 **C**

3. **It/There 문제**
It ~ that 강조구문
답 **D**

4. **It/There 문제**
부사구, blank + 명사구 구조
it가 받을 수 있는 to 부정사나 that절이 없으므로 there 구문이 되어야 한다.
답 **A**

5. **주어 + 동사 + that | blank + 명사구 + 부사구 구조**
뒤에 to부정사가 왔으므로 to부정사를 받는 it가 나와야 한다.
답 **C**

6. **make + 목적어(it) + 목적보어 +가목적어 (to부정사)**
A : it은 the city (of Philadelphia) 를 받은 대명사이며 make의 목적어로 나왔고, one of the world' s first cities는 it의 목적보어이다. 맨뒤의 to 부정사구는 cities를 수식하는 형용사적 용법임. S+V, blank 구문이며 blank에는 분사구문(주어가 같고 능동으로 쓰였으므로 making~)이 올 수 있다.
B : 주어 + 동사이므로 절과 절의 연결에서는 등위접속사가 주어 앞에 나와야 한다.
답 **A**

7. **It/There 문제**
blank + that절 구조
it ~that 구문으로 (D)가 답이다.
C : there was ~ 구문은 뒤의 명사절이 있으므로 나올 수 없다.
D : it was ~ that ~은 강조구문의 형태이다.
답 **D**

8. It/There 문제
blank + 명사 + 부사구 구조
blank에는 주어와 동사가 빠져 있으므로 주어 + 동사가 들어가야 한다.
to 부정사나 that절이 없으므로 there be구문이 되어야 한다.
C : because는 부사절을 이끄는 접속사이므로 뒤에 주절이 따로 나와야 한다.
㉰ **B**

9. It/There 문제
부사구 + blank + 명사구 + 분사구문
to 부정사나 that절이 없으므로 there be구문이 되어야 한다.
㉰ **A**

10. It/There 문제
blank + 명사구 + 부사구 + that + 동사 + 목적어구조
It ~ that 강조구문형태
that 이하를 받는 it가 나와야 한다.
㉰ **D**

❺ make possible 구문

Hackers Practice p138

1. I (have it made possible → have made it possible)
2. I (it 삭제)
3. C
4. I (it 삭제)
5. I (made possible → made it possible)
6. C
7. C
8. I (making more difficult → making it more difficult)
9. C
10. I (made it visible → made visible)

Hackers Test p139

1. make + it +형용사(목적보어) + to 부정사문제
동사 have made의 목적어인 to 부정사가 뒤로 나갈 경우 가목적어 it을 사용하여야 한다.
㉰ **B**

2. make + 목적어 + 형용사(목적보어)문제
it은 가목적어가 아니라 앞에 오는 Home erectus를 받는다.
a bit은 different를 수식한다.
B : made가 3형식동사로 differently의 수식을 받아 '다른 방식으로 만들다' 의 뜻으로 사용되었다. 그러나 이 문장은 '차별화하다' 의 의미로 make~ different가 되어야한다.
㉰ **C**

3. make + it + 형용사(목적보어) + to 부정사문제
동사 have made의 목적어인 to 부정사가 뒤로 나갈 경우 가목적어 it을 사용하여야 한다.
㉰ **C**

4. make + 형용사(목적보어) + 목적어문제
뒤에 오는 명사를 받는 it을 사용할 수 없다.
㉰ **A**

5. make + 형용사(목적보어) + 목적어문제
~ in the air (which is) made visible ~의 구조이고 목적어가 앞으로 나간 형태
which의 선행사는 dust
㉰ **A**

6. make + it + 형용사(목적보어) + to 부정사문제
동사 made의 목적어인 to 부정사가 목적보어 뒤로 나갈 경우 가목적어 it을 사용하여야 한다.
㉰ **C**

7. make + it + 형용사(목적보어) + to 부정사문제
동사 make의 목적어인 to 부정사가 목적보어 뒤로 나갈 경우 가목적어 it을 사용하여야 한다.
㉰ **B**

8. make + it + 형용사(목적보어) + to 부정사문제
동사 have made의 목적어인 to 부정사가 목적보어 뒤로 나갈 경우 가목적어 it을 사용하여야 한다.
for Chicanos는 to부정사의 의미상의 주어
㉰ **A**

9. make + it + 형용사(목적보어) + to 부정사문제
전치사 by이하에 동명사가 오고 동명사의 목적어인 to 부정사가 목적보어 뒤로 나갈 경우 가목적어 it을 사용하여야 한다.
㉰ **D**

10. make + it + 형용사(목적보어) + to 부정사문제
등위접속사 and에 연결되고 blank에는 동사가 없으므로 동사가 들어가야 하고, 동사의 목적어인 to 부정사가 목적보어 뒤로 나갔으므로 가목적어 it을 사용하여야 한다.
㉰ **C**

11. make + it + 형용사(목적보어) + to 부정사문제
comma 뒤는 분사구문이고 동사의 목적어는 to 부정사이고 목적보어 뒤로 나갔으므로 가목적어 it을 사용하여야 한다.
㉰ **D**

12. make + it + 형용사(목적보어) + to 부정사문제
blank에는 동사가 없으므로 동사가 들어가야 하고 동사의 목적어인 to 부정사가 목적보어 뒤로 나갔으므로 가목적어 it을 사용하여야 한다.
㉰ **B**

13. make + it + 형용사(목적보어) + to 부정사문제
동사의 목적어인 to 부정사가 목적보어 뒤로 나갔으므로 가목적어 it을 사용하여야 한다.
㉰ **D**

❻ 동사의 as 선택

Hackers Practice p145

1. C
2. C
3. I (was referred to "a melting pot" → was referred to as " a melting pot")
4. C
5. I (can be defined the ability → can be defined as the ability)
6. C
7. I (is sometimes called as the Jazz Age → is sometimes called the Jazz Age)
8. C

Hackers Test p146

1. define A as B

동사 define은 목적보어로서 as를 사용한다.

㊐ **D**

2. call A B

동사 call은 목적보어로서 as를 사용하지 않는다.

call A B = A is called B~ three-dimensional images, which are called holograms.에서 which are가 생략된 형태인 (C)가 답

㊐ **C**

3. think of A as B

think of A as B = A is thought of as B

㊐ **C**

4. refer to A as B

refer to A as B = A is referred to as B

㊐ **C**

5. consider A (to be/as) B

consider A (to be/as) B = A is considered (to be/as) B

동사 consider의 주체는 사람이므로 blank에는 능동형 동사가 들어가야 한다.

(A), (C)번은 동사가 앞에 who were가 생략된 과거분사이므로 틀림. (B)번은 동사 considered의 주어인 rulers와 them이 같으므로 재귀대명사인 themselves가 되어야 한다.

㊐ **D**

6. identify A as B

identify A as B = A is identified as B

㊐ **A**

7. elect A B

elect A B = A is elected B

㊐ **B**

8. think of A as B

think of A as B = A is thought of as B

thought는 과거분사가 아니라 동사이므로 목적어와 목적보어가 나와야 한다.

㊐ **D**

❼ 병치, 짝짓기

Hackers Practice p150

1. I (and forming a national army → and form a national army)
2. I (Either the Hungarians or are the Slaves → Either the Hungarians or the Slaves)
3. C
4. I (waterways to one community → waterways from one community)
5. C
6. I (but → and)
7. I (built → build)
8. C

Hackers Test p151

1. 병치문제

arrested, shot, sent가 were에 연결되는 구조병치인 (D)가 답

㊐ **D**

2. 병치문제

both A and B 구조

make profits, treat workers는 to 부정사에 연결되는 구조인 (C)가 답

㊐ **C**

3. 병치 및 짝짓기 문제

not only ~ but also 구조

the economic order, religion, government, social stability로 연결되는 품사병치인 (D)가 답

㊐ **D**

4. 병치 및 짝짓기 문제

more ~ than 구조

on growing coffee, on producing의 전치사구로 연결되는 (C)가 답

㊐ **C**

5. 병치구조 문제

A, B, C, and D 구조

to pick up ~, to sell ~, to read ~, to visit ~가 and로 to 부정사에 연결되는 (A)가 답

㊐ **A**

6. 병치 및 짝짓기 문제

either ~ or 구조

in hunting and gathering societies, in an agricultural economy의 부사구가 연결되는 구조 병치인 (D)가 답

㊐ **D**

7. 병치구조 문제

A, B, and C 구조

collecting ~ cutting ~, striking ~이 and로 연결되는 구조병치인 (C)가 답

㊐ **C**

8. 병치 및 짝짓기 문제

not A but B

= B(but/and) not A

= B, not A
답 **D**

9. **주어, 동사 문제**
who ~는 관계절(형용사절)이므로 제거하면 주어, 동사 자리가 비어있으므로 주어, 동사가 들어가는 (C)가 답.
답 **C**

10. **병치구조 문제**
A, B, and C 구조
speak, publish, worship이 to부정사에 연결되는 (D)가 답
답 **D**

11. **병치구조 문제**
A, B, and C 구조
Railroads were built, coal mines were opened, iron and steel mills were put이 주어 + be + 과거분사의 형태로 연결되는 구조병치문제
답 **C**

Chapter 3 Mini test p154

1. **It/There 문제 [3 – 4과 참조]**
blank + that + 동사 + 목적어, 등위접속사 + 독립절구조 접속사가 하나 있으므로 컴마 앞에는 동사가 두 개가 들어가야 한다.
A : that절이 관계절이므로 that절 앞에는 완전한 문장이 나와야 한다.
B : that ~는 관계대명사절이므로 제거되면 what ~ trapping은 주어가 되므로 동사가 없다.
C : that ~를 제거하면 주어만 있고 동사가 없다.
D : It ~ that 강조구문
답 **D**

2. **It/There문제 [3 – 4과 참조]**
to recover ~의 주어구가 뒤로 나가면서 가주어 it을 사용
D : 수동태이므로 목적어가 나올 수 없다.
답 **C**

3. **도치문제 [3 – 1과 참조]**
Not until 부사절이 오는 경우는 주절에서 조동사 도치가 일어난다.
답 **A**

4. **비교급 형태문제 [3 – 2과 참조]**
비교대상은 Ernest와 Martin
D : that이 지시하는 바가 없으므로 틀림
답 **A**

5. **Only 부사절 도치문제 [3 – 1과 참조]**
only when절 이후 주절의 조동사 도치
at two of three years of age의 양쪽 comma는 부사절 + 콤마 + 주절에서의 comma가 아니라 삽입구 양쪽에 삽입되는 comma로써, 부사절과 주절을 경계하는 comma가 아니므로 도치되는 것을 막지 않는다.
답 **D**

6. **It/There문제 [3 – 4과 참조]**
there 구문에서의 주어는 disadvantages이므로 복수동사 are가 쓰임.
답 **C**

7. **make possible문제 [3 – 5과 참조]**
to 부정사가 make의 목적어이므로 to 부정사를 it으로 받는다. 문장내에서 does는 강조의 역할을 한다.
답 **D**

8. **동사구 도치문제 [3 – 1과 참조]**
출처부사구가 앞으로 나갈 때는 조동사가 아니라 동사구 도치가 된다. 따라서 (A)는 답이 될 수 없다.
답 **D**

9. **비교급 문제 [3 – 2과 참조]**
much는 비교급 앞에서 비교급을 강조한다.
답 **C**

10. **최상급 문제 [3 – 3과 참조]**
최상급 앞에는 예외적인 경우를 제외하고는 the가 들어가야 한다.
답 **B**

11. **make possible문제 [3 – 5과 참조]**
make의 목적어가 to 부정사이고 목적보어 뒤로 나갔으므로 가목적어 it을 사용하여야 한다.
D : 목적보어로 부사는 사용할 수 없다.
답 **B**

12. **병치문제 [3 – 7과 참조]**
A, B, and C 형태의 구조병치
A, B, C는 절
답 **D**

13. **make possible문제 [3 – 5과 참조]**
to 부정사가 make의 목적어이므로 to 부정사를 it으로 받는다. 주어는 To pollute, 목적어는 to contaminate이고 dash이하는 to contaminate를 부연설명하고 있다.
답 **D**

14. **주어 + 목적어 + 보어문제 [3 – 6과 참조]**
consider + 목적어 + (to be) + 보어의 구조
B : 만약 as가 오려면 to be자리에 대신 들어가야 한다.
답 **A**

15. **주어 + 목적어 + 보어문제 [3 – 6과 참조]**
call A B = A is called B
답 **B**

16. **병치문제 [3 – 7과 참조]**
A, B, and C 구조
to congregate ~, to construct ~, to govern ~의 형태로 연결되는 구조병치이다.
답 **D**

17. **도치문제 [3 – 1과 참조]**
문장의 보어가 앞으로 나갈 때 도치가 된다.
답 **C**

18. **such as/as such문제 [written 4 – 4참조]**
such 명사 as = such as 명사, as such는 문미에 사용한다.
답 **D**

19. **no/not 문제 [written 5 – 1참조]**
no는 형용사로서 명사를 수식하므로 (D)가 답
답 **D**

Written Expression

Chapter 1. 동사구

❶ 주어와의 수 일치

Hackers Practice p165

1. is
2. was
3. exists
4. are
5. was
6. were
7. were
8. has
9. become
10. help
11. were

Hckers Test p166

1. 주어, 동사 수 일치 문제
Many가 복수를 나타내는 형용사이므로 복수명사가 되어야 하고 동사도 복수가 되어야 한다
답 **B (was → were)**

2. 관계대명사의 선행사와 관계절의 동사와의 수 일치 문제
which의 선행사는 conflict이므로 동사는 단수로 수일치가 되어야 한다.
답 **B (which are → which is)**

3. 주어, 동사 수 일치 문제
주어가 단수 one이므로 단수동사 is를 사용한다.
C : between A and B 의 상관접속사
답 **B (were → is)**

4. 주어, 동사 수 일치 문제
주어는 student, 동사는 hold이므로 주어 동사의 수 불일치.
out of : ~중에서(전치사구)
crossing → which crossed 의 축약형(동사 cross의 주어는 the ships)
답 **B (hold → holds)**

5. 주어, 동사 수 일치 문제
Every 단수명사 + 단수동사구조
that의 선행사는 holiday이므로 동사도 단수동사가 되어야 한다.
dance = dancing (불가산명사이므로 단수형태)
sports, dancing, processions는 병치구조
답 **A (celebrate → celebrates)**

6. 주어, 동사 수 일치 문제
A number of + 복수명사 + 복수동사
The number of + 복수명사 + 단수동사
D : 군도앞에 정관사 사용
답 **A (have now → has now)**

7. 주어, 동사 수 일치 문제
주어는 The migration 이므로 단수동사
of 이하는 부사구 거품
other + 복수명사, the other + 단, 복수 모두 가능
답 **B (were → was)**

8. 관계대명사의 선행사와 관계절의 동사와의 수 일치 문제
'a group of + 복수명사' 이므로, 관계절의 동사는 복수동사여야 한다.
답 **B (regulates → regulate)**

9. 주어, 동사 수 일치 문제
another + 단수명사 + 단수동사
contributing to → which contributed to의 축약형
답 **C (were → was)**

10. 주어, 동사 수 일치 문제
학명은 형태는 복수일지라도 단수취급함.
directly는 동사 affects를 수식하므로 부사가 됨
the other는 앞의 one과 호응(one - the other의 용법)
that절 이하의 what은 동사 happens와 affects의 주어 역할을 하고 있음.
답 **A (have → has)**

11. 주어, 동사 수 일치 문제
시간, 거리, 중량, 가격은 단수취급한다.
동사 appear는 자동사로서 목적어를 필요로 하지 않는다.
답 **A (were → was)**

12. 관계대명사의 선행사와 관계절의 동사와의 수 일치 문제
that의 선행사는 everything이므로 단수로 수일치 되어야 함
답 **C (are important → is important)**

❷ 동사의 시제 일치

Hackers Practice p171

1. became
2. was / occurred
3. was
4. has been
5. say
(had better + 동사의 원형)
6. decide
7. be
8. came
9. achieved
10. give up

Hackers Test p172

1. **과거표시 부사구와의 시제일치**
In the past 30 years : 부사구
시제에서 'in + past + 시간' 은
'과거부터 지금까지' 의 의미이므로
시제는 현재완료가 와야한다.
답 **A (appeared → have appeared)**

2. **proposal 동사문제**
주장, 명령, 제안, 희망, 요청 등의 동사가 오면 종속절의 시제는 원형동사가 온다.
답 **B (is → be)**

3. **과거표시 부사구와의 시제일치**
과거를 나타내는 부사구가 오면 동사는 과거로 시제일치가 되어야 한다.
who = and he
답 **A (is improved → was improved)**

4. **since + 과거시점과 현재완료의 시제일치**
since + 과거시점은 과거시점에서 지금까지의 의미이므로 현재완료시제와 호응하여야 한다.
답 **B (clustered → have clustered)**

5. **과거표시 부사구와 동사의 시제일치문제**
과거 표시 부사구가 왔으므로 동사는 과거를 사용한다.
답 **B (send → sent)**

6. **주절의 시제와 종속절의 시제 선후관계 파악문제**
주절의 동사 was suspended와 종속절의 동사 fell back을 비교하면 종속절의 시제가 원인사건시제이고 주절의 시제가 결과사건시제이므로 시차가 발생한다. 그러므로 종속절의 시제는 주절의 시제보다 한 시제 앞선 시제가 되어야 함
between A and B : 상관접속사
that절 이하는 완전한 문장이고 the news와 동격을 이룸
답 **D (has fallen back → had fallen back)**

7. **과거표시 부사구와 동사의 시제일치문제**
during + 과거의 특정기간은 과거시제와 호응
답 **C (have been → were)**

8. **과거표시 부사구와 동사의 시제일치문제**
during + 과거의 특정기간은 과거시제와 호응
주어는 the growth이고 of이하는 부사구 거품
답 **C (is → was)**

9. **proposal동사 문제**
주장, 희망, 제안, 명령, 요구 등의 동사는 종속절에 동사원형이 와야한다.
답 **C (were treated → be treated)**

10. **since와 현재완료의 시제일치 문제**
since와 현재완료를 짝짓는다.
proven은 sites를 수식하고 number은 동사이다.
답 **C (worked → have worked)**

11. **부사구와 동사의 시제일치 문제**
by 1900이 과거인 1900년 시점까지 완료를 나타내므로 과거완료가 되어야 한다.
답 **B (has reached → had reached)**

12. **부사구와 동사의 시제일치 문제**
until + 과거시점은 대과거에서부터 과거까지의 시간(계속)을 나타내므로 과거완료시제와 일치되어야 한다.
for는 등위접속사
답 **B (has → had)**

❸ 동사의 형태 · 선택 문제

Hackers Practice p176

1. learn	6. be enhanced
2. get	7. become
3. free	8. be sacrificed
4. laid	9. laid
5. raised	10. raised

Hackers Test p177

1. **동사와 분사(형용사) 구별문제**
문장에 동사가 두개 이므로 문맥상 gave를 분사형태로 만든다.
동사 gave의 주체는 the camera이고 대상은 information 이므로 gave는 과거분사형이 되어야 한다.
답 **B (gave → given)**

2. **to 부정사의 형태문제**
to 부정사의 형태문제로 원형동사가 되어야 함
답 **C (taken → take)**

3. **전치사의 목적어 형태문제**
전치사 다음에 동사가 나오고 목적어가 오면 동사는 동명사로서 V+ing형태를 취한다.
during은 과거의 특정기간의 처음부터 끝까지의 의미로 사용된다.
답 **A (allocated → allocating)**

4. **to 부정사의 형태문제**
조건절과 주절의 구조로서 미래시제이다. 다만, 조건절의 시제가 현재시제인 것은 시간, 조건 부사절에서는 현재시제가 미래시제를, 현재완료시제가 미래완료시제를 대체하기 때문이다.
답 **C (having → have)**

5. **전치사의 목적어 형태문제**
전치사의 목적어는 명사상당어구가 되어야 한다.
답 **D (burn → being burned)**

6. **자동사와 타동사 구별문제**
수동태가 될 수 있는 것은 타동사(lay - laid - laid)
답 **C (lay → laid)**

7. **조동사 + 원형동사 문제**
조동사가 오면 원형동사가 와야 한다.
several + 복수명사
land는 양을 나타내는 the amount of의 수식을 받으므로 단수가 되어야 한다.
답 **C (is → be)**

8. **자동사와 타동사 구별문제**
자동사는 목적어를 취하지 않으므로 수동태로 만들 수 없다. 그러므로 여기에서는 타동사가 되어야 한다.
rise - rose - risen (자동사)
raise - raised - raised (타동사)
㉢ **C (risen → raised)**

9. **전치사의 목적어 형태문제**
전치사의 목적어는 명사상당어구.
'V + ing' 동명사로 만들어 줘야 한다.
㉢ **C (for introduce → for introducing)**

10. **조동사 + 원형동사 문제**
조동사와 본동사 사이에 부사가 삽입되어도 본동사는 원형이 되어야 한다.
the country는 know의 주체가 아니라 대상이므로 수동태로 사용되었다.
㉢ **B (known → be known)**

❹ 태

Hackers Practice p181

1. was introduced
2. been replaced
3. wrote
4. were used
5. is constructed
6. are referred to as
7. are issued
8. carved
9. were held up
10. made

Hackers Test p182

1. **능동 · 수동 구별문제**
on application of ~는 전치사구 거품. 타동사 remove(추방하다)의 목적어가 없으므로 수동태가 되어야 한다.
㉢ **B (remove → be removed)**

2. **동사 consider의 수동태 문제**
consider A (to be)B = A is considered (to be) B : A를 B로 여기다. 주어가 사람이 아니고 사물이므로 5형식의 수동문형임
따라서 수동태라 하더라도 보어가 나와야 한다.
주어는 communication and the consequent integration이므로 복수 동사
㉢ **B (were considering → were considered)**

3. **능동 · 수동 구별 문제**
aid가 타동사 임에도 뒤에 목적어가 없으므로 수동형의 축약인 과거분사를 사용하여야 한다.
㉢ **B (aiding → aided)**

4. **동사 consider의 수동태 문제**
타동사 consider의 목적어가 없으므로 수동태가 되어야 한다.
㉢ **C (considered → are considered)**

5. **동사 call의 수동태 문제**
동사 call은 call A B의 형태를 갖지만, call A as B의 형태를 갖지 않는다.
㉢ **B (as a → a)**

6. **동사 regard의 태에 관한 문제**
regard A as B = A is regarded as B
neither ~ nor ~는 상관접속사. but은 전치사
㉢ **B (regarded → regarded as)**

7. **자동사는 수동태가 될 수 없음**
자동사는 목적어를 갖지 않으므로 수동형이 될 수 없다.
㉢ **D (was come → came)**

8. **수동태는 목적어를 가질 수 없음**
welcome뒤에 any diminution이라는 목적어가 오므로 welcome은 능동태가 되어야 한다.
㉢ **A (was not welcome → did not welcome)**

9. **능동 · 수동 구별 문제**
타동사 expand의 목적어가 나오므로 능동태가 맞는 표현.
their가 지시하는 것은 Wealthy Romans
joining은 전치사 by에 연결되는 병치구조
㉢ **A (were expanded → expanded)**

10. **능동 · 수동 구별 문제**
병명 decimate 사람 : 병이 사람을 죽이다. decimate의 주체는 병명이고 대상은 사람
that절 이하의 주어가 사람이므로 동사는 수동태가 되어야 함
㉢ **C (had decimated → was decimated)**

11. **능동 · 수동 구별 문제**
동사 humiliate는 타동사이므로 목적어를 필요. by 이하의 부사구가 왔으므로 수동태가 되어야 한다.
㉢ **C (publically humiliated → been publically humiliated)**

12. **능동 · 수동 구별 문제**
타동사 cultivate의 목적어가 없으므로 수동태가 되어야 한다.
㉢ **B (has cultivated → has been cultivated)**

❺ 분사

Hackers Practice p187

1. bearing
2. holding
3. divided
4. computerized
5. called
6. formed
7. cut
8. Living
9. surrounded
10. set

Hackers Test p188

1. **능동 · 수동 구별문제**
   동사 depict는 '~을 묘사하다' 라는 타동사이고 주체는 사람
   The integral connection between vassal and serf depicted가 성립하므로 과거분사가 되어야 한다.
   The integral connection between vassal and serf depicted = The integral connection between vassal and serf which was depicted
   답 **B (depicting → depicted)**

2. **능동 · 수동 구별문제**
   동사 unify의 주체는 사람
   A kingdom is unified가 성립하므로 과거분사가 되어야 한다.
   as, so, than이하에 주어, 동사가 도치될 수도 있음 (option)
   답 **A (unifying kingdom → unified kingdom)**

3. **능동 · 수동 구별문제**
   who were interested의 축약인 interested가 맞는다.
   답 **C (interesting → interested)**

4. **집합명사 문제**
   cattle은 bull, bullock, cow의 총칭으로 부정관사나 복수형 불가, 무조건 복수취급해야 한다.
   답 **B (cattles → cattle)**

5. **동사와 분사의 구별문제**
   that절 이하에 동사가 두 개. were held를 분사로 만든다.
   답 **C (were held → held)**

6. **동사와 분사의 구별문제**
   replaced뒤에 목적어가 있기 때문에 과거분사가 아니고 동사. 따라서 were made를 분사형으로 고쳐야 한다.
   답 **A (were made of → made of)**

7. **동사와 분사의 구별문제**
   동사 violate의 주체는 사람. 목적어가 나와 있으므로 과거분사가 아니라 현재분사형이 되어야 한다.
   답 **A (violated → violating 또는 who violated)**

8. **능동 · 수동 구별문제**
   be interested in이 되어야 한다.
   답 **D (interesting → interested)**

9. **능동 · 수동 구별문제**
   by fleas가 있으므로 수동태를 사용한다.
   flea : 벼룩
   답 **B (carrying → carried)**

10. **능동 · 수동 구별문제**
    victimizing의 목적어가 없으므로 수동의 의미의 과거분사를 사용한다.
    답 **C (victimizing → victimized)**

❻ 동명사와 to부정사

Hackers Practice p193

1. to be / being
2. to live
3. to work
4. to choose
5. looking
6. to judge
7. to rehire
8. to be
9. shipbuilding
10. to share

Hackers Test p194

1. **quit + ~ing 문제**
   what은 동사 tell의 직접 목적어와 동사 hear의 목적어 역할을 동시에 수행
   답 **C (to bother → bothering)**

2. **형용사/부사 선택 문제**
   feel의 보어로 형용사가 오므로 comfortable이 사용되어야 한다.
   답 **A (more comfortably → more comfortable)**

3. **be able to V 문제**
   행성중에서 지구, 달, 태양은 정관사
   no one = none은 단수
   답 **B (explain → to explain)**

4. **동명사/to부정사 문제**
   revising이 수식하는 명사는 the Continental Congress가 아니라 the delegates이므로 수식어의 불일치가 발생. 따라서 목적을 나타내는 to부정사가 되어야 한다.
   답 **C (revising → to revise)**

5. **동명사/to부정사 문제**
   allow A to B.
   답 **D (attending → to attend)**

6. **encourage + 목적어 + to V 문제**
   establish, enforce는 to부정사로 연결되는 병치구조
   답 **B (establishing → to establish)**

7. **fail to V문제**
   fail to V = cannot V, do not V : ~하지 못하다
   답 **D (gaining → to gain)**

8. **be willing to V 문제**
   답 **B (limiting → to limit)**

9. cause + 목적어 + to V 문제
free peasants : 자유 소작농
off their farms는 전치사구
threw free peasants off their farms : 자유 소작농들을 그들의 농장 밖으로 내쫓다
causing은 분사구문의 부대상황으로 연속동작
causing them to wander ~ = and caused them to wander ~
㉠ **D (wandered → to wander)**

10. allow + 목적어 + to V문제
㉠ **C (killing → to kill)**

Chapter 1 Mini test p196

1. 주어, 동사 수일치 문제 [1 – 1과 참조]
when은 시간을 나타내는 접속사이므로 주어 + be 동사가 생략되어 있다. 주어는 주절의 주어인 much of the cotton과 일치하므로 단수. 동사도 또한 단수. when not in use는 삽입된 부사절이 축약된 것이다.
㉠ **C (are → is)**

2. 자동사, 타동사 구별문제 [1 – 3과 참조]
take는 타동사 구문이므로 목적어를 수반해야 한다. 그러나 as ~는 부사구이므로 목적어가 없다. 따라서 수동태가 되어야 한다.
㉠ **A (taking as → taken as)**

3. 주어, 동사 수 일치 문제 [1 – 1과 참조]
a number of + 복수명사 + 복수동사
㉠ **B (improvement → improvements)**

4. 동사의 시제일치문제 [1 – 2과 참조]
in 1954는 과거표시 부사구이므로 동사의 시제는 과거가 되어야 한다.
㉠ **A (comes → came)**

5. 주어, 동사 수 일치 문제 [1 – 1과 참조]
주어는 Thousands of Cubans이므로 복수
㉠ **A (has fled → have fled)**

6. 동사의 형태문제 [1 – 3과 참조]
조동사 + 동사원형의 형태
found : 설립하다(타동사)
C → That ~ century는 주어이고 단수
㉠ **A (could founded → could be founded)**

7. 주어, 동사 수 일치 문제 [1 – 1과 참조]
most of + 복수명사 + 복수동사
㉠ **A (was located → were located)**

8. 분사문제 [1 – 5과 참조]
동사 causing은 타동사이므로 목적어가 있어야 한다. 목적어가 없으므로 과거분사형이 되어야 한다.
㉠ **B (causing → caused)**

9. 주어, 동사 수 일치 문제 [1 – 1과 참조]
party politics는 단수취급
㉠ **A (were → was)**

10. 동사의 형태문제 [1 – 3과 참조]
전치사 + 동명사
㉠ **D (obtain → obtaining)**

11. 분사문제 [1 – 5과 참조]
one other + 단수명사, every other + 단수명사
brought의 주체는 European men and women이므로 bringing이 되어야 한다.
㉠ **D (brought → bringing)**

12. 주어, 동사 시제일치문제 [1 – 2과 참조]
주장, 희망, 제안, 명령, 요청 등의 동사들은 미래에 일어날 행위를 가정하는 것이므로 가정법 시제를 사용하고 should를 생략한 원형동사만을 쓴다.
㉠ **B (are → be)**

13. 주어, 동사 수 일치 문제 [1 – 1과 참조]
관계대명사 that의 선행사는 skills이므로 복수
㉠ **C (helps → help)**

14. 명사 수 일치 문제 [2 – 1과 참조]
several은 복수의 의미를 갖는 형용사이므로 복수명사와 수 일치 되어야 한다.
㉠ **B (town → towns)**

15. 동사 + 목적어 + to부정사 문제 [1 – 6과 참조]
encourage + 목적어 + to V
㉠ **C (offering → to offer)**

❶ 명사

Hackers Practice p205

1. C
2. I (episode → episodes)
3. I (go → goes)
4. I (kind → kinds)
5. I (pairs → pair)
6. I (were → was)
7. I (hat → hats)
8. I (electrician → electricity)
9. I (man → men)
10. C
11. C
12. I (priest → priests)

Hackers Test p207

1. 형용사와 명사의 수 일치 문제
few, many, several, various 등과 복수를 지칭하는 형용사는 복수명사와 호응
정 **B (direction → directions)**

2. 명사의 의미 선택 문제
authorization : 인증, 허가, 위임 authority : 권위, 권력
both A and B : 상관접속사
정 **D (authorization with men → authority with men)**

3. 인간 vs 추상문제
poet : 시인 poetry : 시 prose : 산문
부사 certainly는 문장 전체를 수식
Certainly one of ~ = It is certain that one of ~ 에서 it is ~ that이 생략되면서 부사가 됨
the day, one's day : 전성기시대
정 **D (poet → poetry)**

4. 명사 수일치 문제
kind(type) of + 단수명사, kinds(types) of + 복수명사
뒤의 절의 시제가 현재완료인 것은 over millennia 즉, 과거 시점부터 지금까지의 의미이므로 현재완료와 호응이 되어야 하기 때문이다.
정 **D (kind of → kinds of)**

5. 주어와 동사 수 일치 문제
주어는 American dictionary이므로 단수명사
동사도 단수로 수 일치가 되어야 한다.
the lawyer and lexicographer : 의미 병치
정 **B (were compiled → was compiled)**

6. 인간 vs 추상 문제
criminal : 범죄자, crime : 범죄, crime rate : 범죄율
be based on : ~에 기초(근거)를 두다
정 **B (criminal rate → crime rate)**

7. 명사 어순문제
복합명사가 나올 경우 어순을 의심할 것
population growth : 인구성장
encourage + 목적어 + to V
eastward는 부사로서 동사 move를 수식
정 **A (growth population → population growth)**

8. hundreds of + 복수명사 문제
hundreds of, a couple of, a number of, a group of, a sequence of, a majority of, a range of, a series of, an array of, a swarm of, a variety of, a host of등은 복수명사와 호응하여야 함
aide : 조수, 부관
A(사물) be headed by B(사람) : B는 A를 지휘하다
정 **A (aide → aides)**

9. 인간 vs 추상 문제
architecture : 건축, architect : 건축가
정 **A (architecture → architect)**

10. various + 복수명사문제
research는 무관사
연구하다, 조사하다일 경우는 do research
복수형 국명앞에 정관사 the가 들어가야 한다.
정 **A (foundation → foundations)**

11. every + 단수명사 문제
each, every 뒤에는 단수명사
정 **B (every farmers → every farmer)**

12. 인간 vs 추상문제
athletics : 운동경기 athlete : 운동가
attributed는 found와 병치
정 **B (nude athletics → nude athletes)**

13. numerous + 복수명사 문제
self-appointed : 자칭의
정 **A (self-appointed general → self-appointed generals)**

14. 인간 vs 추상문제
neighbor : 이웃사람 neighborhood : 마을
many of에서 전치사 of의 목적격인 whom이 되어야 함
call A B = A is called B
A is called as B는 잘못된 표현
정 **C (neighbor → neighborhood)**

15. kinds of + 복수명사 문제
kind(type) of + 단수명사, kinds(types) of + 복수명사
정 **B(material → materials)**

❷ 부정관사

Hackers Practice p212

1. a	6. a
2. a	7. a
3. an	8. x
4. a	9. an
5. a	10. a

Hackers Test p213

1. a/an 문제
a는 자음으로 발음되는 명사 앞에 an은 모음으로 발음되는 명사 앞에 옴
for가 comma 뒤에서는 because의 의미가 됨
㉠ **B (a → an)**

2. naked noun문제
a height of / a weight of
명사는 특별한 경우를 제외하고 관사없이 사용불가
falls : 폭포
falls가 고유명사와 결합하면 단수취급하고 이외의 경우는 복수취급함
㉠ **D (height --> a height)**

3 a/x 문제
불가산명사에는 부정관사 사용불가
in proportion to(as) : ~에 비례하여
the same A as B : B와 동등한(같은) A
㉠ **C (a proportion → proportion)**

4. a/an 문제
unique[ju:ni:k]의 /ju/는 자음이므로 a가 되어야 함
a group of + 복수명사
㉠ **C (an → a)**

5. 주어, 동사 수 일치 문제
주어는 the importance이므로 단수
of Spanish discoveries는 부사구 거품
㉠ **A (were → was)**

6. a/an 문제
single의 /s/는 자음이므로 a가 되어야 한다.
a single의 형태는 가능함 ex) a single case
all + 가산명사 + 복수동사, all + 물질 · 추상명사 + 단수동사
㉠ **B (an → a)**

7. 주어, 동사 수 일치 문제
동사가 복수이므로 주어도 복수가 되어야 한다.
㉠ **A (Archaeological investigation → Archaeological investigations)**

8. a/an 문제
French는 자음이므로 a가 되어야 한다.
㉠ **A (An → A)**

9. the/x 문제
학명은 무관사 geography : 지리학
sparked by 앞에는 which is가 생략됨.
동사 spark의 주어는 the Renaissance fascination, 목적어는 curiosity
㉠ **C (the geography → geography)**

10 a/an 문제
average는 모음이므로 an이 되어야 한다.
grow tall : 키가 커지다
㉠ **A (a → an)**

11. a/the 문제
단위를 나타낼 때에는 a가 되어야 한다. hour는 h가 묵음이므로 모음
주어는 ships이고 with이하는 부사구 거품
square sails (which were) unfurled
㉠ **D (the hour → an hour)**

❸ 정관사

Hackers Practice p218

1. x	6. x
2. The	7. The
3. the	8. the
4. x	9. the
5. the, the	10. x
	11. the

Hackers Test p219

1. the/x 문제
지구, 달, 태양은 정관사 the가 들어감. named 앞에는 who was가 생략되어 있다.
㉠ **D (moon → the moon)**

2. the/x 문제
학명은 무관사 ecology : 생태학
interested in 앞에는 which are가 생략되어 있다.
㉠ **D (the ecology → ecology)**

3. a/the 문제
연대 앞에는 정관사
antipollution device : 환경오염 방지장치
㉠ **A (a → the)**

4. 세기 앞에는 정관사
주어는 cultivation이므로 단수
of 이하는 부사구 거품
㉠ **A (20th century → the 20th century)**

5. Naked Noun문제

명사에 관사가 없으므로 관사가 들어가거나 복수형이 되어야 한다.
The materials (주어) that are ~ study (관계대명사절, 형용사절) include (동사) ~
ⓓ **D (human being → human beings)**

6. the + 형용사 = 복수보통명사

전치사 for이하는 the farmers와 병치구조를 이뤄야 한다.
the unemployed = unemployed people
ⓓ **D (unemployed → the unemployed)**

7. 강 이름 앞에는 정관사

it = the Yellow River
ⓓ **A (Yellow River → the Yellow River)**

8. 시간/사물의 부위 앞에 정관사

ⓓ **B (on surface → on the surface)**

9. 관계대명사절 문제

주격 관계대명사 다음에 동사가 들어가야 한다.
Thomas Malthus와 an English economist는 동격
ⓓ **A (who an → who was an 또는 an)**

10. 형용사, 부사 선택문제

be in need of : ~을 필요로 하다, ~이 필요하다
in need of가 전치사구이므로 desperate는 부사형이 되어야 한다.
deadly는 "치명적인" 이란 의미의 형용사
called a deadly disease diphtheria(5형식) = a deadly disease is called diphtheria
in Nome, Alaska, : 주 이름 뒤에는 comma가 와야 함 (삽입구문의 comma가 아님)
ⓓ **B (desperate → desperately)**

11. 최상급 앞에 정관사 문제

most : 대부분의
the most : 가장 큰, 최대의
ⓓ **A (most promising → the most promising)**

12. the/x 문제

at the beginning : 처음부터
operate는 자, 타동사 모두 쓰임
ⓓ **A (beginning → the beginning)**

❹ 대명사

Hackers Practice p224

1. I (them → themselves)
2. C
3. I (themselves → them)
4. I (his → its)
5. C
6. I (her → its)
7. C
8. I (his → their)
9. C
10. I (their → his)
11. C
12. I (it → itself)

Hackers Test p225

1. 주어 반복문제

The classic Neanderthals 과 they가 중복되므로 they를 생략해야 한다.
a number of + 복수명사
ⓓ **A (who they → who)**

2. 재귀대명사 문제

them = Jazz trumpeters and saxophonists이므로 목적어는 재귀대명사가 되어야 한다.
depart from ~ : 빗나가다, 벗어나다
ⓓ **D (them → themselves)**

3. 대명사 소유격 문제

전치사 + 대명사 + 명사구조에서 대명사는 소유격이 되어야 한다.
end up ~ing : 결국 ~하게 되다
ⓓ **C (him → his)**

4. 선행사와 성 일치 문제

Joseph Nicephore Niepce, his camera등에서 남자임을 알 수 있다.
dip : 담그다, 적시다
camera obscura : 어둠상자, 암실
ⓓ **C (she → he)**

5. 대명사 수 일치 문제

their = Each Pueblo community이므로 단수 소유격이 되어야 한다.
ⓓ **B (their → its)**

6. 대명사 수 일치 문제

Many = himself이므로 선택문제 발생
동사가 복수이므로 주어도 복수
따라서 재귀대명사도 복수로 수 일치가 되어야 한다.
ⓓ **C (himself → themselves)**

7. 대명사 성 일치 문제

Cesar Chavez 를 받는 대명사는 단수가 되어야 한다.
부사 particularly는 형용사 well-known을 수식
ⓓ **B (their → his 또는 her)**

8. 재귀대명사 문제

himself가 지시하는 것은 the job market이므로 itself가 되어야 한다.
ⓓ **D (himself → itself)**

9. 재귀대명사 문제

주어 The Indians = them(목적어)이므로 them은 재귀대명사가 되어야 한다.
ⓓ **C (them → themselves)**

10. 대명사 수 일치 문제

their가 가리키는 것은 the United States이므로 단수가 되어야 한다.
ⓓ **C (their place → its place)**

11. **주어 반복 문제**
관계대명사 who의 선행사인 the generals와 they가 중복되었으므로 they를 생략하여야 한다.
C (who they → who)

12. **대명사 수 일치 문제**
their가 가리키는 것은 Greece이므로 단수가 되어야 한다.
pass through : (위험을) 겪다, 경험하다
B (their golden age → its golden age)

Chapter 2 Mini test p227

1. 명사 수일치 문제 [2 – 1과 참조]
few + 복수가산명사이므로 observers가 되어야 한다.
A (observer → observers)

2. Naked Noun문제 [2 – 2과 참조]
party에 관사가 없으므로 관사가 들어가야 한다.
iconodule : 성상숭배자
B (party → a party)

3. 명사 수 일치 문제 [2 – 1과 참조]
a series of + 복수명사
A (hammer → hammers)

4. 명사 수 일치 문제 [2 – 1과 참조]
between + 복수명사
B (tooth → teeth)

5. a/an문제 [2 – 2과 참조]
unique/ju:ni:k/에서 /ju/는 반자음이므로 a가 되어야 한다.
A (an → a)

6. the/x 문제 [2 – 3과 참조]
지구, 달, 태양을 제외한 모든 행성들은 무관사
B (the → 생략)

7. 명사 수 일치 문제 [2 – 1과 참조]
a variety of + 복수명사
C (tribe → tribes)

8. the/x 문제 [2 – 3과 참조]
buildings, factories, workers등과 병치를 이루기 위해 machinery도 무관사 사용.
B (the → 생략)

9. 대명사 수 일치 문제 [2 – 4과 참조]
their가 가리키는 것이 Every nation이므로 단수
A (their → its)

10. 명사 수 일치 문제 [2 – 1과 참조]
관사가 a이므로 명사는 단수로 수 일치가 되어야 한다.
A (engineers → engineer)

11. the/x 문제 [2 – 3과 참조]
영국사람들을 의미할 때는 the English가 되어야 한다.
A (English → the English)

12. 대명사 수 일치문제 [2 –4 참조]
their가 지시하는 것은 the body이므로 단수가 되어야 한다.
C (their → its)

13. 인간 vs 추상문제 [2 – 1 참조]
infancy와 병치를 이루기 위해서는 childhood가 되어야 한다.
D (child → childhood)

14. 명사 수 일치 문제 [2 – 1 참조]
are가 복수이므로 주어도 복수로 수 일치가 되어야 한다.
B (building → buildings)

15. 명사 수 일치 문제 [2 – 1 참조]
a는 단수명사와 수 일치가 되어야 한다.
D (kinds → kind)

Chapter 3. 수식어구

❶ 형용사와 부사

Hackers Practice p234

1. C
2. I (chiefly → chief)
3. C
4. I (regular → regularly)
5. C
6. I (comfortable → comfortably)
7. C
8. I (to 생략)
9. I (narrow → narrowly)
10. I (important → importantly)

Hackers Test p235

1. **형용사, 부사 선택 문제**
조동사와 be동사 사이에는 부사가 되어야 한다.
Ⓔ **B (probable → probably)**

2. **주어, 동사 수 일치 문제**
that ~ others까지는 주어 the chief characteristic을 수식하는 관계대명사절(형용사절)
주어가 단수이므로 동사도 단수가 되어야 한다.
the large measure of self-government (which) it(=the corporate colony) enjoyed.
it 앞에 목적격 관계대명사 which가 생략되어 있다.
Ⓔ **B (were → was)**

3. **주어, 동사 수 일치 문제**
In atherosclerosis(동맥경화증) : 부사구
composed 앞에는 which is가 생략되어 있다.
주어는 small patches이므로 복수
Ⓔ **C (forms → form)**

4. **현재분사, 과거분사 혼동문제**
동사 hide의 주체는 사람이므로 명사 explosives를 수식하기 위해서는 과거분사형이 되어야 함
locating explosives ~ and helping ships ~ : 병치구조
help + 목적어 + to부정사(또는 원형부정사) : help의 목적보어로 to부정사와 원형부정사 모두 가능
Ⓔ **C (hiding → hidden)**

5. **형용사, 부사 선택문제**
형용사 actual은 뒤에 부정관사 a가 있으므로 명사 fruit를 수식하지 못함
Tomatoes와 a fruit는 동격
동사 begin은 목적어로 동명사나 to부정사 모두 가능
Ⓔ **A (actual → actually)**

6. **many + 복수 가산명사, much + 단수 불가산명사 문제**
treaties는 복수이므로 many로 수식이 되어야 함
Ⓔ **C (much → many)**

7. **형용사, 부사 선택문제**
eager는 뒤의 형용사 absorbed를 수식하므로 부사가 되어야 함
Ⓔ **B (eager → eagerly)**

8. **형용사, 부사 선택문제**
fabulous는 형용사 rich를 수식하므로 부사가 되어야 함
fabulous : 거짓말같은, 엄청난
Ⓔ **A (fabulous → fabulously)**

9. **부사 어순 문제**
almost는 수식하는 모든 부사의 앞에 위치한다.
almost completely : 거의 완전히
be indifferent to : 무관심한
Ⓔ **C (completely almost → almost completely)**

10. **형용사, 부사 선택문제**
a way of life (which was) remarkably suited to ~
suited는 형용사(분사)이므로 remarkable은 부사가 되어야 함
their = The Indians
living in ~ = who lived in ~
nature : 자연, the nature : 성격
Ⓔ **B (remarkable suited → remarkably suited)**

11. **형용사, 부사 선택문제**
careful이 명사 garden을 수식하지 않고 형용사(분사) tended를 수식하고 있으므로 부사가 되어야 한다.
Ⓔ **A (careful → carefully)**

12. **부사 + 전치사 문제**
immediately after, long before, long after, 20minutes after등과 같이 전치사 앞에 부사가 올 수 있다.
Ⓔ **B (after immediately → immediately after)**

❷ 전치사

Hackers Practice p239

1. I (referred as → referred to as)
2. I (go to abroad → go abroad)
3. I (arrived my office → arrived at my office)
4. I (consists → consists of)
5. I (called as a lyre → called a lyre)
6. I (Due as → Due to)
7. I (Addition → In addition)
8. I (proud → proud of)
9. I (responsibility → responsibility for)
10. I (dependent → dependent on)
11. C
12. C

Hackers Test p241

1. 전치사 실종문제
   regard A as B = A is regarded as B
   be used to V ~ : ~하는데 사용되다
   답 **C (regarded → regarded as)**

2. 전치사 선택문제
   a native of = native to : 출생의, 태생의, 원산의
   native 앞에 관사가 없으므로 native to가 되어야 함
   a means of ~ : ~의 수단
   who was ~는 의문사절
   답 **D (native of → native to)**

3. 전치사 선택문제
   the reason that 절 = the reason for 구
   be due to : ~ 때문에
   답 **B (reason as → reason for)**

4. 전치사 실종문제
   describe A as B = A is described as B
   답 **D (described → described as)**

5. 전치사 실종 문제
   consist of = be made up of : ~으로 구성되다
   wearing은 앞에 which were가 생략되었음
   답 **A (consisted → consisted of)**

6. 전치사 실종문제
   focus on : 초점을 맞추다
   several + 복수명사
   답 **B (focused → focused on)**

7. 전치사 + 명사문제
   전치사 다음에는 명사상당어구가 와야 한다.
   주어는 the policy, 동사는 is called
   economic : 경제의
   economical : 검소한
   economics : 경제학
   interfere with : 방해하다
   laissez-faire : 자유방임주의
   답 **A (economic → economics)**

8. 전치사 실종문제
   in accordance with : ~과 일치하여
   other + 복수명사
   their = many other leaders and sects
   답 **C (accordance → accordance with)**

9. 전치사 실종문제
   in addition : 게다가 interfere with : 방해하다
   답 **D (interfere → interfere with)**

10. 전치사 선택문제
    separate A from B
    답 **C (to → from)**

11. 전치사 선택문제
    the effect of A on B : B에 영향을 미치는 A의 효과
    주어는 the effect, 동사는 demonstrates
    답 **A (to → on)**

12. 현재분사와 과거분사의 혼동문제
    동사 contain은 사물이 주체이므로 현재분사형이 되어야 한다.
    답 **B (contained → containing)**

13. 전치사 선택문제
    in + 년도
    과거 시제표시 부사구는 과거 동사와 호응
    답 **A (On → In)**

❸ 관계대명사

Hackers Practice p246

1. I (who → which)
2. I (which locates → which it locates)
3. C
4. I (that enable → which enable)
5. C
6. I (in which live → in which we live)
7. I (that was → that were)
8. I (which → who)
9. I (who → which)
10. I (who → which)

Hackers Test p247

1. who/which 선택문제
   who의 선행사는 exocrine이므로 which가 되어야 한다. their = glands
   답 **B (who is → which is)**

2. 원상복구 문제
   they are related to shrimp or lobster. = shrimp or lobster, to which they are related.
   crustacean : 갑각류 동물, shrimp : 작은 새우, lobster : 바닷가재
   답 **D (in which → to which)**

3. 전치사 선택문제
   be capable of + ~ing
   답 **C (to fire → of firing)**

4. who/which 선택문제
   who의 선행사는 long houses이므로 which가 되어야 한다.
   called 앞에는 which were가 생략됨
   답 **D (who → which)**

5. who/which 선택문제
   which의 선행사가 many of us이므로 사람
   go back : 되돌아가다
   답 **A (which → who)**

6. **주어반복 문제**
who는 주격 관계대명사이므로 they와 중복
㉢ **D (they → 생략)**

7. **비교급 than 문제**
than 앞에는 비교급이 나와야 한다.
puzzling features = features which are puzzling
on the whole : 대체로
㉢ **C (most complicated → more complicated)**

8. **many + 복수명사 문제**
in + 연도, 장소 + where, many + 복수명사
㉢ **D (project → projects)**

9. **who/which 선택문제**
Language has been one of the chief problems of the Puerto Ricans과 English is foreign to the Puerto Ricans. 두 문장을 하나로 합치면,
Language has been one of the chief problems of the Puerto Ricans to whom English is foreign.
be foreign to : 낯선, 생소한
㉢ **D (to which → to whom)**

10. **동사변화 형태 문제**
hold는 타동사이다. hold - held - held
타동사뒤에 목적어가 없으므로 수동형인 be+과거분사가 되어야 한다. discuss는 타동사이므로 뒤에 바로 목적어가 온다.
㉢ **A (to be hold → to be held)**

11. **관계대명사와 관계부사의 혼동문제**
which의 선행사인 the estates와 they는 문맥상 같지 않으므로 주어반복문제가 아니다. which 이하는 완전한 문장이므로 관계부사절이 되어야 한다.
장소 + where
㉢ **C (which → where 또는 in which)**

12. **every + 단수명사 문제**
every는 단수명사와 호응
call A B = A is called B
called 앞에는 which were가 생략되어 있다.
㉢ **A (towns → town)**

13. **원상복구 문제**
뒷 문장이 완전하므로 관계부사 or 전치사 + 관계대명사가 나타난다.
Andalusia was the major channel.
Western Europe obtained products from Asia and Africa through the channel.
→ Andalusia was the major channel through which western Europe obtained products from Asia and Africa.
㉢ **B (which → through which)**

14. **목적어 반복문제**
목적격 관계대명사 whom이 있음에도 목적어 them이 반복되었다.
㉢ **D (them → 삭제)**

❹ 접속사

Hackers Practice p252

1. I (during → while)
2. C
3. I (due to → because)
4. C
5. I (Because → Although)
6. C
7. I (in spite of → although)
8. I (Despite of → Despite)
9. C
10. I (because → because of)
11. C

Hackers Test p253

1. **전치사/접속사 문제**
regardless는 이하에 구가 나왔으므로 전치사가 되어야 한다.
A:century는 Louisiana를 수식하는 수식명사이므로 the의 사용여부는 수식받는 명사인 Louisiana에 의해 결정되고, Louisiana는 주이름이므로 the를 사용하지 않는다.
be used to V ~ : ~ 하는 데 사용되다
be(get) used to ~ing : ~ 하는데 익숙하다
used to V : 과거의 규칙적인 습관
㉢ **C (regardless → regardless of)**

2. **since(because) + 절, because of + 구**
접속사 since이하에 구가 왔으므로 전치사가 되어야 한다.
appear as ~ : ~로서 나타나다
접속사 when 이하에서는 부사절 축약에 의해 they are가 생략되었다.
㉢ **A (Since → Because of)**

3. **because + 절, because of + 구**
because of 이하에 절이 왔으므로 접속사가 되어야 한다.
㉢ **C (because of → because)**

4. **관계대명사 격 문제**
관계대명사 whom이하에 동사+목적어가 왔으므로 주격이 되어야 한다.
㉢ **C (whom → who)**

5. **관계부사 문제**
장소 + where , 시간 + when
during his twenties를 선행사로 갖는 when이 와야한다.
㉢ **D (which → when)**

6. **형용사, 부사 선택 문제**
형용사 essential 뒤에 관사 a가 나와 위치상 명사를 수식할 수 없다. 따라서 동사 have를 수식하는 부사가 되어야 한다.
㉢ **D (essential → essentially)**

7. **전치사/접속사 문제**
while + 절, during + 구
접속사 while 이하에 구가 왔으므로 전치사가 되어야 한다.
thousands of : 수 천명의
㉡ **A (While → During)**

8. **전치사/접속사 문제**
although + 절, in spite of + 구
접속사 although 이하에 구가 왔으므로 전치사가 되어야 한다.
㉡ **A (Although → In spite of)**

9. **동명사/to 부정사 문제**
tend to : ~ 하는 경향이 있다
whereas는 접속사로서 절이 온다.
㉡ **A (being → to be)**

10. **접속부사 선택문제**
문맥상 부사절은 양보의 의미가 되어야 하므로 although가 되어야 한다.
cloister : 수도원 hardly ever : 거의 ~하지 않다
㉡ **A (Because → Although)**

11. **부사와 어순 문제**
before long = soon의 의미로 부사임
㉡ **D (before long → long before)**

12. **전치사/접속사 문제**
although는 접속사이므로 구가 올 수 없다.
㉡ **A (Although → Despite)**

Chapter 3 Mini test p255

1. **형용사/부사 어순문제 [3 – 1과 참조]**
형용사 + 부사 + 명사 → 부사 + 형용사 + 명사의 어순
㉡ **D (trading lively → lively trading)**

2. **전치사 선택 문제 [3 – 2과 참조]**
challenge to ~ : ~에 대한 도전
㉡ **B (at → to)**

3. **형용사/부사 문제 [3 – 1과 참조]**
friendly는 형용사이므로 명사인 territory를 수식할 수 있다.(ly가 붙는 형용사 주의문제)
a million은 복수이므로 복수명사와 같이 사용된다.
㉡ **B (soldier → soldiers)**

4. **전치사 선택문제 [3 – 2과 참조]**
become a major influence on ~ : ~에 주요 영향을 주다.
twentieth century Europe art는 복합명사이고 정관사 the를 사용하지 않는 것은 주체가 art이기 때문이다.
A → 부사는 명사를 제외한 모든 것을 수식할 수 있다.
㉡ **C (with → on)**

5. **관계부사 문제 [3 – 3과 참조]**
장소 + where, 시간 + when
선행사가 Burma(장소)이므로 where이 되어야 한다.
㉡ **B (when → where)**

6. **전치사 사족문제 [3 – 2과 참조]**
westward는 부사이므로 부사 앞에 전치사가 들어갈 수 없다.
㉡ **B (to westward → westward)**

7. **전치사 실종문제 [3 – 2과 참조]**
in charge of ~ : ~을 맡고 있는
㉡ **A (in charge → in charge of)**

8. **접속사/전치사 구별문제 [3 – 4과 참조]**
Despite는 전치사이므로 절과 함께 사용할 수 없다.
㉡ **A (Despite → Although)**

9. **관계대명사 문제 [3 – 3과 참조]**
목적격 관계대명사인 whom과 them이 중복된 표현이므로 them을 생략해야 한다.
㉡ **C (of them → of)**

10. **전치사 선택문제 [3 – 2과 참조]**
on + 월, 일, 연도, in + 월, 연도 , in + 연도
㉡ **A (At → On)**

11. **관계부사 문제 [3 – 3과 참조]**
when + 시간, where + 장소
선행사는 the empire (장소)이므로 where가 되어야 한다.
㉡ **C (when → where)**

12. **전치사 선택문제 [3 – 2과 참조]**
be familiar with ~ : ~을 잘 아는
㉡ **C (at → with)**

13. **전치사/접속사 선택문제 [3 – 4과 참조]**
while은 접속사이므로 구와 함께 사용할 수 없다.
㉡ **D (while → during)**

14. **형용사/부사 선택문제 [3 – 1과 참조]**
satisfied는 형용사(분사)이므로 형용사를 수식하는 부사가 되어야 한다.
㉡ **B (complete → completely)**

15. **형용사/부사 선택문제 [3 – 1과 참조]**
advancement는 명사이므로 명사를 수식하는 형용사가 되어야 한다.
㉡ **D (socially → social)**

❶ 병치

Hackers Practice p260

1. C
2. C
3. I (to wait → waiting)
4. I (frustrate → frustration)
5. C
6. I (to take → taking)
7. I (biweek → biweekly)
8. I (farming → for farming)
9. C
10. I (devouring → devoured)

Hackers Test p261

1. 구조병치 문제

collecting~, caring ~, and expanding ~은 전치사 by의 목적어로 연결되는 구조병치

답 **D (to expand → expanding)**

2. 구조병치 문제

what will be~, what can be ~, and what we would ~는 전치사 of의 목적어로 연결되는 구조병치

답 **D (and which → and what)**

3. 품사병치 문제

동사 attack을 수식하는 swiftly, quietly, and accurately의 부사로 연결되는 품사병치

답 **D (accuracy → accurately)**

4. 구조병치 문제

had made ~, had written ~, and had accrued~로 연결되는 구조

답 **A (wrote → had written)**

5. 품사병치 문제

전치사 + 명사상당어구이므로 red, green, and blue와 명사로 병치가 되어야 한다. bluish는 형용사

The zircon과 a semiprecious stone은 동격

답 **D (bluish → blue)**

6. 구조병치 문제

are made ~, (are) formed ~, and (are) fired ~로 연결되는 구조병치

답 **B (form → formed)**

7. 의미병치 문제

a humorist and lecturer로 연결되는 병치구조

roamed ~, settled down~, and lectured로 연결되는 병치구조로 오인하지 않기 바람

답 **D (lecturing → lecturer)**

8. 구조병치 문제

rounding up ~, branding ~, and repairing ~으로 연결되는 구조병치

답 **D (repaired → repairing)**

9. 의미병치 문제

teaching, nursing, and office work로 연결되는 의미병치

nurse : 간호사 nursing : 간호

to는 전치사이므로 명사상당어구가 나와야 함

답 **D (nurse → nursing)**

10. 구조병치 문제

hunting, fishing, riding ~, or giving ~으로 연결되는 구조병치

spend + 시간 + (in) + ~ing, spend + 돈 + (on) + ~ing

답 **D (to ride → riding)**

❷ 짝짓기

Hackers Practice p265

1. both
2. to
3. neither
4. whether
5. not only
6. such as, from
7. too
8. such as
9. and
10. as

Hackers Test p266

1. both ... and

both A and B : A와 B 모두

later는 late의 비교급이고 형용사, 부사 형태가 같다.

답 **D (or → and)**

2. both ... and

that they ... and that the harm ...은 when 절 이하에 타동사 believe의 목적절로 연결되는 구조병치

답 **D (either → both)**

3. not only .... but also

not only A but also B : A뿐만 아니라 B 역시

답 **D (and → but)**

4. as well as

A as well as B : B뿐만 아니라 A역시

as well은 문미에 사용되어 '또한'의 의미

sales potential : 잠재 수요중 기업이 얻는 점유율

답 **C (as well → as well as)**

5. 비교급 + than
정 **D (as → than)**

6. whether .... or
whether A or B
정 **D (and → or)**

7. not only ... but also
proximity : 근접, 접근, ample : 큰, 충분한 여유가 있는
정 **C (only → not only)**

8. such ... as
as 이하는 rent, food bills, and the mortgage가 병치 구조를 이루고 있다.
정 **C (to → as)**

9. 병치구조 문제
not only A but also B에서 A, B는 병치구조를 이루고 있어야 한다.
not only 이하가 to 부정사를 이루고 있으므로 but also이하에도 to 부정사가 와야 한다.
정 **C (also breaking → also to break)**

10. such as
예를 들때는 'such as + 명사' 혹은 'such + 명사 + as' 를 사용한다.
정 **A (as such → such as)**

③ 비교급과 최상급

Hackers Practice p271

1. the most small → the smallest
2. the famousest → the most famous
3. that → than
4. than higher → higher than
5. than → as
6. the greater → the greatest
7. the old → the oldest
8. as faster than → as fast as / faster than
9. as cleverer as → as clever as
10. the more → the most
11. lesser → less
12. the most → the more

Hackers Test p273

1. 최상급 형태 문제
most도 최상급이고, easiest도 최상급이므로 중복표현
involve ~ing : ~을 필요로 하다, 수반하다, ~을 필연적으로 수반하다
정 **A (most easiest → easiest)**

2. 비교급 · 최상급 선택 문제
the 최상급 + in/of/that절
정 **B (fewer → fewest)**

3. 비교급 형태 문제
more도 비교급이고 taller도 비교급이므로 중복표현
at least : 적어도, 최소한
정 **D (more taller → taller)**

4. 비교급 · 최상급 형태 문제
one of the 최상급 복수명사구조에서 최상급의 병치
Certainly one of the most intelligent ~ = It is certain that one of the most intelligent ~
her day : 그녀의 전성시대, 한창 때
정 **B (better educated → best educated)**

5. 비교급 짝짓기 문제
비교급 greater와 than이 호응하여야 함
비교대상은 from northern과 from the Old South이므로 뒤의 비교대상 앞에 than이 들어가야 한다.
정 **D (that → than)**

6. 형용사 선택 문제
period는 기간이므로 longer가 되어야 한다.
정 **A (higher → longer)**

7. 비교급 형태 문제
비교급 .... than 형태가 되어야 함
ironclad ships : 철갑선
wooden counterparts = wooden ships
정 **B (than more often → more often than)**

8. 형용사 · 부사 선택문제
부사 comfortably는 명사 houses를 수식하므로 형용사가 되어야 한다.
정 **A (comfortably → comfortable)**

9. 비교급 형태 문제
비교급 .... than any other 단수명사의 형태가 되어야 한다.
이 유형은 형태는 비교급이고 의미는 최상급
any animal이라 하지 않고 any other animal이라고 하는 것은 any속에 당나귀도 포함되므로 당나귀를 빼고 비교해야 하므로 any other animal이 되어야 한다.
get about : 여행하다, 여기저기 돌아다니다
정 **C (animals → animal)**

10. farther/further 문제
farther는 거리에 사용되고 further는 거리, 정도에 사용
to enhance : 향상시키기 위하여(부사구 목적)
as : ~로서(지격)
정 **A (farther → further)**

11. 비교급 짝짓기 문제
more dependent와 상응하는 것은 than이다.
much는 비교급 강조
정 **D (as → than)**

❹ So That / Such That구문

Hackers Practice p277

1. so	4. so	7. so	10. such
2. so	5. so	8. as such	
3. such	6. such as	9. so	

Hackers Test p278

1. so 형용사/부사 that 문제
   답 **C (too mysterious → so mysterious)**

2. 명사 수 일치 문제
   a는 단수명사와 수 일치가 되어야 한다.
   human, human being은 복수형이 가능
   mankind, humankind, humanity는 복수형 불가
   답 **C (sources → source)**

3. such + 형용사 + 명사 + that 문제
   답 **C (so → such)**

4. 비교급 형태 문제
   big은 1음절이므로 비교급은 bigger가 되어야 한다.
   used앞에는 which were가 생략되어 있다.
   답 **C (more big → bigger)**

5. so + 형용사 + that 문제
   답 **C (too → so)**

6. so + 수량 형용사 + that 문제
   답 **B (such → so)**

7. so + 형용사 + that 문제
   about the misery of the poor는 부사구
   답 **A (such → so)**

8. such as/as such 문제
   such as + 명사, as such는 문미에 사용
   succeed in : 성공하다 various + 복수명사
   답 **C (as such → such as)**

9. 동사 형태 문제
   become - became - become
   현재완료 : have(has) + p · p
   답 **B (became → become)**

10. so + 형용사 + that 문제
    Manchuria : 만주
    답 **A (very → so)**

11. such ... as 문제
    답 **C (with → as)**

12. so ... that 문제
    so + 형용사/부사 + that
    답 **C (such → so)**

Chapter 4 Mini test p280

1. 비교급 형태문제 [4 – 3과 참조]
   as ~ as사이에 비교급이 들어갈 수 없다.
   답 **C (more → many)**

2. 병치문제 [4 – 1과 참조]
   동사의 병치구조문제로서 caused가 과거동사이므로 benefit도 과거동사가 되어야 한다.
   significantly는 부사로서 동사 benefited를 수식
   답 **B (benefit → benefited)**

3. 짝짓기 문제 [4 – 2과 참조]
   A as well as B : B 뿐만 아니라 A도
   as well은 문미에 사용하여 '게다가', '또한', '더욱이' 의 의미를 갖는다.
   답 **D (as well → as well as)**

4. 짝짓기 문제 [4 – 2과 참조]
   too ... to ~ : 너무 ... 해서 ~할 수 없다.
   but not the war = but it could not win the war
   답 **D (very → too)**

5. 최상급 형태문제 [4 – 3과 참조]
   비교급 앞에 the가 왔으므로 최상급이 되어야 한다.
   답 **B (longer → longest)**

6. 전치사 선택문제 [3 – 2과 참조]
   답 **C (to → until)**

7. such as 문제 [4 – 2과 참조]
   such as + 명사 = such + 명사 + as
   답 **C (so → such)**

8. so ~ that 문제 [4 – 4과 참조]
   답 **A (very → so)**

9. so ~ that 문제 [4 – 4과 참조]
   so는 부사로서 형용사를 수식하고,
   such는 형용사로서 명사를 수식한다.
   답 **B (such → so)**

10. 짝짓기 문제 [4 – 2과 참조]
    not only ... but (also).
    답 **B (and → but)**

11. 비교급 선택문제 [4 – 3과 참조]
    farther : 거리에 사용, further : 거리, 정도에 사용
    답 **A (farther → further)**

12. so that / such that 선택문제 [4 – 4과 참조]
    so + 수량형용사 + 명사 + that문제로 수량형용사가 올 경우 명사가 온다 하더라도 so가 들어가야 한다.
    답 **B (such → so)**

13. 비교급 강조표현 문제 [4 – 3과 참조]
    far는 비교급인 more expensive를 강조하므로 앞에서 수식하여야 한다.
    답 **B (more far → far more)**

14. 병치문제 [4 – 1과 참조]
    make~, estimate~, manage~로 연결되는 구조 병치
    답 **D (managing → manage)**

15. 병치문제 [4 – 1과 참조]
    surrounding~, living ~, trapping ~, raising ~으로 연결되는 구조 병치
    답 **D (raise → raising)**

❶ 단어선택A

Hackers Practice p288

1. around
2. somewhat
3. before
4. round
5. percent
6. double
7. no, not
8. no
9. near
10. enable

Hackers Test p289

1. near/nearly 문제
near는 전치사로서 '가까운' 의 의미이고, nearly는 부사로서 '거의=almost' 의 의미
답 **A (near → nearly)**

2. ago/before 문제
ago : 현재를 기준으로 이전
before : 과거의 어느 시점을 기준으로 이전
before entering은 before they enter가 부사절 축약된 것임
5000 years ago : 부사구
답 **C (before → ago)**

3. able/enable 문제
able은 형용사이고 enable은 동사
enable은 주어가 사물이어야 함
for = because
cuneiform : 설형문자
답 **A (enable → able)**

4. near/nearly 문제
near가 형용사 60,000,000을 수식하기 위해서는 부사가 되어야 함
demographer : 인구 통계학자
답 **B (near → nearly)**

5. percent/percentage 문제
percent는 복수형 불가이고 숫자와 함께 사용
percentage는 숫자와 함께 사용하지 않음
답 **B (percentage → percent)**

6. twice/double 문제
twice는 부사이고, double은 형용사와 동사로 사용
enquire after = inquire after : 문병하다
답 **A (double → twice)**

7. some/somewhat 문제
some은 형용사, somewhat은 부사
형용사 serious는 2형식 동사 become의 보어
동사 vanish는 자동사, 타동사 모두 사용
답 **C (somewhat → some)**

8. after/afterwards 문제
after는 전치사, 접속사, 형용사, 부사로 사용
afterwards는 부사로 사용
답 **B (afterwards → after)**

9. percent/percentage 문제
percent는 복수형 불가이고 숫자와 함께 사용
동사 require의 주체는 사람이므로 deposits와 required사이에는 which were가 생략되어 있다.
주어는 increase, 동사는 would reduce
답 **B (percent → percentage)**

10. no/none 문제
no는 형용사, none = no one이므로 대명사
because이하의 주어는 the number이고, 동사는 was로서 단수 수 일치
답 **A (No → None)**

11. some/somewhere문제
somewhere between A and B
답 **C (some → somewhere)**

12. soonest/earliest 문제
soonest는 현재나 어떤 시점을 기준으로 곧, 즉시의 의미이고, earliest는 시간적 의미에서 가장 초기에는 의미
Despite ~ research : 부사구
주어는 many unanswered questions, 동사는 remain
답 **C (soonest → earliest)**

❷ 단어선택B

Hackers Practice p293

1. Almost, almost
2. Unlike
3. Like
4. like
5. making
6. most
7. Almost
8. Most
9. made
10. made

Hackers Test p294

1. most/almost 문제
양을 나타내는 형용사 fifty앞에는 almost가 온다.
a section of the city (which was) called "Over the Rhine" (by them)
= They called a section of the city "Over the Rhine" (5형식)
답 **B (most → almost)**

2. do/make 문제
-tion/-sion은 make와 같이 사용
Two days ~ again은 부사구

Two days앞에 전치사가 없는 것은 Two days가 전치사 없이도 부사역할을 하는 것으로서 이것을 부사적 대격이라고 한다.
㉠ **B (did → made)**

3. do/make 문제
job을 나타내는 명사는 do와 같이 사용
㉠ **C (made → done)**

4. most/almost 문제
almost all : 거의 모든
all은 양을 나타내는 형용사이므로 almost로 수식
㉠ **B (most → almost)**

5. do/make 문제
make an effort : 노력하다, until recently : 최근까지
despite + 구
until은 전치사와 접속사로 쓰이고 부사도 올 수 있다.
㉠ **B (done → made)**

6. like/unlike 문제
not likely는 부사이므로 뒤에 목적어가 올 수 없다. 따라서 전치사가 되어야 한다. 주어는 the technology, 동사는 developed. that = the technology
㉠ **A (Not likely → Unlike)**

7. most/almost 문제
half는 양을 나타내는 형용사이므로 almost로 수식
주어는 half of the students이고 of이하와 수 일치
㉠ **A (Most → Almost)**

8. do/make 문제
do work
of + 추상명사 = 형용사
of much interest = very interesting
㉠ **C (made → did)**

9. do/make 문제
do(cause) damage to ~ : ~에게 손해를 입히다, ~을 파괴하다
under control : 통제하에 있는
the Philippines : 필리핀 (복수형-나라이름 앞에는 정관사)
㉠ **C (made → done)**

10. like/alike 문제
alike는 서술적 용법의 형용사이므로 명사를 수식하거나 목적어를 취할 수 없다.
㉠ **B (alike → like)**

11. do/make 문제
do work
주어는 A good ~ make, 동사는 involves
㉠ **B (make → do)**

❸ Other와 관련된 표현

Hackers Practice p298

1. The other
2. other
3. others
4. other
5. another
6. others/others
7. other
8. other
9. other
10. other

Hackers Test p299

1. other + 복수명사 문제
another는 단수명사와 호응
the handicapped = handicapped people 신체 장애자들
㉠ **D (another → other)**

2. other + 복수명사 문제
be used as ~ : ~로서 사용되다
㉠ **D (subject → subjects)**

3. others 문제
other + 복수명사 = others
others는 복수이므로 복수로 수 일치가 되어야 함
㉠ **B (is → are)**

4. other + 복수명사 문제
㉠ **B (another → other)**

5. other + 복수명사 문제
but = except
㉠ **A (animal → animals)**

6. another + 단수명사 + 단수동사 문제
such A as B : B와 같은 A
㉠ **C (establish → establishes)**

7. another + 단수명사 문제
㉠ **C (other → another)**

8. other + 복수명사 문제
㉠ **C (another → other)**

9. others 문제
other는 대명사로 사용될 수 없다. 불특정 대명사인 others를 사용한다. 동사 continue는 to부정사나 동명사 모두를 목적어로 취할 수 있다.
㉠ **D (other → others)**

10. another + 단수명사 문제
㉠ **A (other → another)**

11. another + 단수명사 문제
be indebted to ~ : ~에게 빚지고 있는, 은혜를 입고 있는
poem : 시 (개별적 의미), poetry : 시(집합적 의미)
㉠ **A (writers → writer)**

12. than any other + 단수명사 문제
than any other은 복수명사를 취할 수 없다.
㉠ **D (violins → violin)**

❹ 어순

Hackers Practice p303

1. C
2. I (marvelous place)
3. I (long miles → miles long)
4. C
5. I (years old)
6. I (France' s position)
7. I (in which)
8. I (previously unexplored)
9. I (almost always)
10. C

Hackers Test p304

1. 어순 문제
   형용사는 특수한 경우를 제외하고는 명사 앞에서 수식
   답 **B (group ethnic → ethnic group)**
2. 부사 + 전치사/접속사 문제
   동사 decide는 to 부정사를 목적어로 취한다.
   답 **B (after soon → soon after)**
3. number + 형용사 + 단위 문제
   답 **B (7 wide feet → 7 feet wide)**
4. almost + 부사/형용사문제
   drape over ~ : ~에 예쁘게 걸치다
   답 **D (impossible almost → almost impossible)**
5. 어순문제
   how + 동사 + 주어 → how + 주어 + 동사
   답 **B (could be used gunpowder → gunpowder could be used)**
6. 부사 + 전치사/접속사 문제
   답 **C (after long → long after)**
7. 부사 + 형용사 문제
   부사가 형용사를 수식할 때, 대부분 형용사 앞에서 수식한다.
   답 **B (rural predominantly → predominantly rural)**
8. 부사 + 형용사 문제
   the possibility와 that절은 동격
   답 **A (conscious extremely → extremely conscious)**
9. 형용사 (분사)+ 명사 문제
   go into exile : 망명하다, 추방이 되다
   답 **A (forces armed → armed forces)**
10. 전치사 + 관계대명사 문제
    human beings = humans
    답 **C (whom from → from whom)**

❺ Enough의 어순

Hackers Practice p308

1. heavy enough
2. no longer enough
3. Quickly enough
4. solid enough
5. well enough
6. enough money/money enough
7. lucky enough
8. hardly enough
9. tough enough to
10. well enough to

Hackers Test p309

1. 형용사/부사 + enough 문제
   in that : ~ 라는 점에 있어서
   in that은 in the fact that에서 the fact가 생략된 것.
   wield : 권력을 휘두르다, 지배하다
   답 **C (enough significant → significant enough)**
2. such as/as such문제
   several + 복수명사
   답 **B (as such → such as)**
3. to 부정사 문제
   enough to의 to는 전치사가 아니고 부정시의 to이므로 원형동사가 온다.
   답 **D (allowing → allow)**
4. 형용사 / 부사 + enough 문제
   답 **C (enough far → far enough)**
5. 형용사/부사 문제
   형용사 general 이하에 수식할 수 있는 명사가 없으므로 부사가 되어야 한다.
   부사는 명사를 수식하지 못한다.
   답 **A (general → generally)**
6. 형용사/부사 + enough문제
   more than은 부사이므로 enough앞에서 수식하여야 한다.
   until은 전치사와 접속사로 사용될 수 있고 뒤에 부사가 올 수 있다.
   답 **C (enough more than → more than enough)**
7. 병치문제
   form, create, produce가 to부정사에 연결되는 구조병치.
   부사 seemingly는 형용사 natural을 수식
   which는 주격관계대명사
   답 **D (producing → produce)**
8. 형용사/부사 + enough문제
   답 **A (enough long → long enough)**
9. 형용사/부사 + enough문제
   fast는 동사 increase를 수식하므로 부사
   fast는 형용사, 부사 동형
   답 **D (enough fast → fast enough)**

10. 형용사 + enough + 명사 문제
답 **C (enough large → large enough)**

11. the/x 문제
at night : 밤중에, at nights : 밤마다
답 **D (the night → night)**

12. every + 단수명사
every 다음에는 단수명사가 온다.
답 **B (rulers → ruler)**

Chapter 5 Mini test p311

1. 단어선택문제 [5 – 1과 참조]
nearly : 거의(=almost)
near : 가까운, 근처의
답 **D (nearly → near)**

2. 어순문제 [5 – 3과 참조]
형용사 + 부사 + 명사 → 부사 + 형용사 + 명사의 어순이 되어야 한다.
답 **A (Few relatively → Relatively few)**

3. 어순문제 [5 – 3과 참조]
had + p.p
답 **B (earned had → had earned)**

4. the other문제 [5 – 2과 참조]
the other뒤에는 단수명사나 복수명사가 올 수 있다. 그러나 others가 대명사이므로 the others뒤에는 명사가 올 수 없다.
답 **B (others → other)**

5. able/enable문제 [5 – 2과 참조]
able은 형용사, enable은 동사이고 사물을 주어로 받는다.
enable + 목적어 + to 부정사
답 **B (abled → enabled)**

6. other + 복수명사 문제 [5 – 3과 참조]
fail to V : cannot, do not = ~할 수 없다
fail in ~ing : ~에 실패하다
답 **D (churchman → churchmen)**

7. 동명사/to부정사 문제 [1 – 6과 참조]
동사 threaten은 to부정사를 목적어로 취한다.
답 **C (dragging → to drag)**

8. do/make 문제 [5 – 2과 참조]
job을 나타내는 명사는 do를 사용한다.
답 **B (making → doing)**

9. no/not/none 선택문제 [5 – 1과 참조]
뒤에 명사가 있으므로 no가 되어야 한다.
답 **C (not → no)**

10. 어순문제 [5 – 3과 참조]
형용사 + 부사 + 명사 → 부사 + 형용사 + 명사의 어순이 되어야 한다.
답 **C (invented newly → newly invented)**

11. enough to V 문제 [5– 4과 참조]
답 **C (keeping → keep)**

12. 형용사/부사 + enough 문제 [5 – 4과 참조]
ward off : 격퇴하다
D → people은 단수, 복수 동형이므로 another의 수식을 받을 수 있다.
답 **C (enough powerful → powerful enough)**

13. like/unlike/alike 문제 [5 – 2과 참조]
alike는 서술적 용법의 형용사이고, like/unlike는 전치사이다
답 **A (Alike → Unlike)**

14. 어순문제 [5 – 3과 참조]
형용사 + 부사 + 명사 → 부사 + 형용사 + 명사의 어순이 되어야 한다.
답 **A (unknown preciously → preciously unknown)**

15. other + 복수명사 문제 [5 – 2과 참조]
답 **A (bare bone → bare bones)**

인덱스

INDEX